all recipes™ tried & true

favorites
top 300 recipes

all recipes™   tried & true

favorites

top 300 recipes

Published by Allrecipes.com, Inc.
524 Dexter Ave. N., Seattle, WA 98109
(206) 292-3990

For distribution information, contact Allrecipes.

Printed in U.S.A.
Second Printing June 2002

Library of Congress Cataloging-in-Publication data is on file with
the publisher.

10 9 8 7 6 5 4 3 2 1

ISBN 0-9711-7230-7

EDITOR: Tim Hunt
SENIOR RECIPE EDITOR: Syd Carter
SENIOR FOOD EDITOR: Jennifer Anderson
SENIOR PRODUCTION MANAGER: Liz Rogers
RECIPE EDITORS: Emily Brune, Britt Swearingen, Richard Kozel
CREATIVE DIRECTION: Yann Oehl
DESIGN: Jeff Cummings
ILLUSTRATION: Richard Ruiz

Cover photograph copyright 2002, The Reuben Group

Recipe shown on cover: *Romantic Chicken with Artichokes and
Mushrooms* (134) and *Oven Roasted Red Potatoes* (198)

dedication

This book is dedicated to those who strive
every day to please their loved ones at the
dinner table; to those who experiment,
create, and refine new recipes; and to those
who preserve the traditional recipes
handed down to them by their parents
and grandparents.

acknowledgments

The book you are holding is a community cookbook: the recipes within come from the community of cooks who gather online at Allrecipes.com. It is the members of this community, first and foremost, whom we would like to thank — anyone who has shared, reviewed, requested, or tried an Allrecipes recipe. The success of the Allrecipes community resides in your experience, enthusiasm, and generosity.

In addition, a huge debt of thanks is owed to the staff of Allrecipes — the people who have dedicated themselves to building a helpful, supportive environment for our community.

We'd also like to thank all the members of the Allrecipes team who have devoted themselves to making this cookbook a reality. This was truly a team effort, and we couldn't have done it without any of these dedicated people: the visionaries who began Allrecipes and remain at the stove as we cook our way into the future; those who conceived of this book; those who researched everything involved in learning how to translate a fantastic online recipe website to the beautiful cookbook you are holding in your hands; each person who lovingly and carefully selected and edited each recipe; and the talented individuals who designed each page and filled out the book with delicious prose and enticing art.

table of contents

introduction

It's easy to glance at someone's cookbook collection and tell right away which are the most useful and best-loved volumes on the shelf. While some cookbooks, opened once a year, manage to stay in pristine condition for decades, others gradually become dog-eared and tattered, the pages gently stuck together with bits of cookie dough or stained with droplets of flying olive oil. We hope this book is destined to become one of those beloved, worn-out books — one you'll turn to every single night of the week for quick dinners, tempting treats, and special occasions galore.

what is allrecipes?

Allrecipes.com is the leading recipe and meal-planning website on the Internet, and the most successful community cookbook ever published: more than ten million people have come to the website for recipes, and tens of thousands of recipes have been submitted, published, and reviewed.

For as long as people have had fire, cooks have been sharing recipes with each other and passing them down from generation to generation. Over the last century and a half, cookbooks with recipes contributed by communities of people (community cookbooks) have been an important part of our culture. These cookbooks have become a chronicle of the way people really eat and how they really cook. Good community cookbooks are distinct from traditional authored cookbooks. They are not professional recommendations of how we "ought" to eat or what dishes we "should" like, but instead are compendiums of what we do eat and what recipes we love enough to share.

Allrecipes is proud to be a community cookbook with a 21st century difference: our community is worldwide. The website allows anyone to instantaneously find recipes as well as share their own favorites, and our collection of tens of thousands of "real world" recipes grows every day. The combined creative genius and generosity of thousands of cooks who have shared their latest creations and their oldest family recipes have gone into making Allrecipes what it is — a warm and friendly place where you know you can always find the recipe you were looking for and bushels of others you didn't know you needed until you saw them. Behind the recipes is a team you've come to know as The Staff at Allrecipes, folks who combine a passion for cooking with an absolute dedication to building a community of people helping each other to feed their families.

With the contributions of our worldwide community and the dedication of our staff, we've created a dynamic place where you can find a thousand inventive dinner solutions, a recipe for cookies just like the ones your grandma used to make, an array of appetizers, a decadent cake recipe for that special birthday party, and everything you need to know to cook your first or your fiftieth holiday dinner. Allrecipes is that and so much more, all there for you at the click of a mouse.

so, why a cookbook?

Using a website to get your recipes has lots of advantages over using a traditional cookbook. The recipe collection at Allrecipes gets bigger every day, and with our easy search features you know you can always find exactly what you want. We've written hundreds of articles full of cooking tips and techniques, as well as party and holiday planning ideas. All of our recipes can be automatically scaled to make just the number of servings you need and every person who tries a recipe has the opportunity to rate and review it — sharing their opinion with the rest of the community. We think Allrecipes.com is the greatest thing to hit the kitchen since running water, but there are times when a good old-fashioned cookbook comes in handy, too.

For starters, most of you share your computers with the whole family, and you can't always shove your loved ones aside when you need to get a recipe. It can also be challenging to keep track of piles of printed pages as your collection of Allrecipes favorites grows. Maybe you even know some people without computers who would love to, at last, have access to some of these wonderful recipes. And the best reason of all to have a cookbook: we've saved you hours of browsing and printing by picking out 300 of our all-time highest rated recipes! Every recipe in this book has won repeated standing ovations from the people who have tried it, creative cooks and picky eaters alike. Even better than a traditional cookbook (where the recipes are tested once or twice), each of the recipes you'll find on the following pages has been tested dozens, if not hundreds, of times — not by culinary professionals in specially equipped test kitchens, but in the home kitchens of people just like you.

Look forward to a whole series of Allrecipes cookbooks as more people share, rate, and review more recipes every day. For as long as people continue to cook, we'll have continuing collections of new favorites and old classics to share with you. After you try these recipes, come rate them on Allrecipes.com to tell everyone what you think. While you're there, try some new recipes and rate them — you'll be casting your votes for cookbooks to come.

Welcome to our first cookbook: *Allrecipes Tried and True Favorites*. We think you're going to love it.

Happy Cooking,

The Staff at Allrecipes

recipe tips

variations on a theme

You may wonder why we have more than one recipe for some items, such as banana bread or lasagna or chocolate chip cookies. Don't worry — these are far from being duplicate recipes! Some dishes are so popular that our community members share multiple variations of them. In fact, when you visit Allrecipes.com, you'll find that we have dozens of variations on many of your favorite recipes. As we post new versions of a recipe, we'll add a Roman numeral to the title to distinguish it (for example, the "London Broil II" recipe which appears in this book). There are many different ways to approach even the old standards, and in this book you can enjoy your next batch of banana bread with the rich tang of sour cream, with a double dose of chocolate, or, if you're a purist, just a whole lot of sweet, ripe bananas! Come see us at Allrecipes.com to explore new variations on all your old favorites.

about the recipes

Half the fun of an Allrecipes recipe is the story behind it — each of our recipes has comments submitted by the contributor to help explain how the recipe came about, what it's like, or how they use it. As the editors of the Allrecipes cookbooks (both online and in print), the staff works hard to preserve the character of the contributed recipe, but also strives to ensure consistency, accuracy, and completeness in the published version and throughout the collection.

all in the timing

At the top right corner of every recipe in the book, you'll find "Preparation," "Cooking," and "Total" times. These times are approximate! Depending on how fast you chop vegetables, how hot your oven is, your altitude, local humidity, sun spot activity, and any number of other factors — you may find that it takes less or more time than what we've estimated. The "Total" times will tell you, on average, how much time the recipe takes from start to finish. With some recipes, this will be longer than the "Preparation" time plus the "Cooking" time. These are recipes that contain intermediate steps that aren't prepping or cooking, such as waiting — for the bread to rise, for the meat to marinate, for the beans to soak, or for the salad to chill. Refer to the "Total" time to know roughly how long you need between opening the book and serving the finished dish to an appreciative crowd.

need help? we're here for you!

Need more information about an unfamiliar ingredient or cooking term, general cooking information, or difficult techniques? We've got a whole section of Allrecipes.com dedicated to giving you all the help you need. In our "Cooking Basics" section, you can search for thousands of kitchen terms, follow photo-filled step-by-step tutorials to learn important cooking skills, and browse or search hundreds of articles that will help you decide what to make and teach you how to make it. You can access the "Cooking Basics" section at Allrecipes.

http://allrecipes.com/cb/

beyond the book

Each of the recipes in this book can be accessed online on Allrecipes.com. The online versions have some handy, whiz-bang features we didn't manage to squeeze into this book. If you'd like to adjust the number of servings for a recipe, view detailed nutritional information, convert the measurements to metric, or email a copy to a friend, it's all just a click away! We've created a special place on Allrecipes.com where you can find any recipe in this book simply by entering its page number. Check it out!

http://allrecipes.com/tnt/favorites/page.asp

your two cents

Once you try a recipe in this book, you can tell the rest of the world all about it! First, locate the recipe on Allrecipes.com (see above). Next, click on the link that says "Add to Recipe Box" (below the recipe's description). Then, follow the instructions to set up a FREE recipe box of your own. Once you've added the recipe to your box, you can rate it on a scale of 1 to 5 stars and share your comments with the millions of other people who use the site. Come tell us what you think!

tried and true

If you'd like to find out more about this book, the recipes, and other Allrecipes "tried and true" cookbooks, join us online at **http://allrecipes.com/tnt/** or send us an email at **tnt@allrecipes.com**.

appetizers & dips

Time to get the party started! There's nothing like a few well-chosen appetizers for setting the mood, quieting rumbling tummies, and spreading good cheer. A tray of these nibbles, munchies, and dips will be equally at home at children's birthday parties, potlucks, or cocktail parties. These appetizers have been known to disappear before the cook even gets a taste — better make a double batch!

Creamy Dill Cucumber Toasties

Submitted by: **Dianne McKenzie**

Makes: 1½ cups

Preparation: 15 minutes

Total: 15 minutes

"I got this recipe years ago from a friend of a friend. I love it and make it all the time for parties. It looks great on the platter, and it is super easy! Everyone loves it!"

INGREDIENTS

1 (8 ounce) package cream cheese, softened

1 (.7 ounce) package dry Italian-style salad dressing mix

½ cup mayonnaise

1 French baguette, cut into ½ inch thick circles

1 cucumber, sliced

2 teaspoons dried dill weed

DIRECTIONS

1. In a medium bowl, mix together cream cheese, dressing mix and mayonnaise.

2. Spread a thin layer of the cream cheese mixture on a slice of bread, and top with a slice of cucumber. Sprinkle with dill. Repeat with remaining ingredients.

Garden Veggie Pizza Squares

Submitted by: **Meghan Brand**

Makes: 48 squares

Preparation: 5 minutes

Cooking: 15 minutes

Total: 1 hour 30 minutes

"This is a must make appetizer for every event in my house. I received it from a friend years ago and everyone loves it. Great for Christmas parties."

INGREDIENTS

1 (8 ounce) package refrigerated crescent rolls

1 (8 ounce) package cream cheese, softened

1 (1 ounce) package Ranch-style dressing mix

2 carrots, finely chopped

½ cup chopped red bell peppers

½ cup chopped green bell pepper

½ cup fresh broccoli, chopped

½ cup chopped green onions

DIRECTIONS

1. Preheat oven to 375°F (190°C).

2. Roll out crescent rolls onto a large non-stick baking sheet. Stretch and flatten to form a single rectangular shape on the baking sheet. Bake 11 to 13 minutes in the preheated oven, or until golden brown. Allow to cool.

3. Place cream cheese in a medium bowl. Mix cream cheese with ½ of the ranch dressing mix. Adjust the amount of dressing mix to taste. Spread the mixture over the cooled crust. Arrange carrots, red bell pepper, broccoli and green onions on top. Chill in the refrigerator approximately 1 hour. Cut into bite-size squares to serve.

Mouth-Watering Stuffed Mushrooms

Submitted by: **Angie Zayac**

Makes: 12 large mushrooms

Preparation: 25 minutes

Cooking: 20 minutes

Total: 45 minutes

"These delicious mushrooms taste just like restaurant-style stuffed mushrooms and are my guy's absolute favorite."

INGREDIENTS

12 whole fresh mushrooms

1 tablespoon vegetable oil

1 tablespoon minced garlic

1 (8 ounce) package cream cheese, softened

¼ cup grated Parmesan cheese

¼ teaspoon ground black pepper

¼ teaspoon onion powder

¼ teaspoon ground cayenne pepper

DIRECTIONS

1. Preheat oven to 350°F (175°C). Spray a baking sheet with cooking spray. Clean mushrooms with a damp paper towel. Carefully break off stems. Chop stems extremely fine, discarding tough end of stems.

2. Heat oil in a large skillet over medium heat. Add garlic and chopped mushroom stems to the skillet. Fry until any moisture has disappeared, taking care not to burn garlic. Set aside to cool.

3. When garlic and mushroom mixture is no longer hot, stir in cream cheese, Parmesan cheese, black pepper, onion powder and cayenne pepper. Mixture should be very thick. Using a little spoon, fill each mushroom cap with a generous amount of stuffing. Arrange the mushroom caps on prepared cookie sheet.

4. Bake for 20 minutes in the preheated oven, or until the mushrooms are piping hot and liquid starts to form under caps.

Mexican Cream Cheese Rollups

Submitted by: **Kathy Jenkins**

Makes: 8 to 10 servings

Preparation: 5 minutes

Total: 1 hour 5 minutes

"Got this one from my best friend's mom. They are so delicious, nobody believes how easy they are."

INGREDIENTS

1 (8 ounce) package cream cheese, softened

1/3 cup mayonnaise

2/3 cup pitted green olives, chopped

1 (2.25 ounce) can black olives, chopped

6 green onions, chopped

8 (10 inch) flour tortillas

1/2 cup salsa

DIRECTIONS

1. In a medium bowl, mix together cream cheese, mayonnaise, green olives, black olives and green onions.

2. Spread cream cheese mixture in a thin layer onto each tortilla. Roll up tortillas. Chill about 1 hour, or until the filling is firm.

3. Slice chilled rollups into 1 inch pieces. Serve with salsa for dipping.

Bacon And Tomato Cups

Submitted by: **Kelli**

Makes: 15 servings

Preparation: 10 minutes

Cooking: 12 minutes

Total: 30 minutes

"Little buttermilk biscuit cups are baked with a savory mixture of bacon and tomato inside."

INGREDIENTS

8 slices bacon

1 tomato, chopped

1/2 onion, chopped

3 ounces shredded Swiss cheese

1/2 cup mayonnaise

1 teaspoon dried basil

1 (16 ounce) can refrigerated buttermilk biscuit dough

DIRECTIONS

1. Preheat oven to 375°F (190°C). Lightly grease a mini muffin pan.

2. In a skillet over medium heat, cook bacon until evenly brown. Drain on paper towels. Crumble bacon into a medium mixing bowl, and mix with tomato, onion, Swiss cheese, mayonnaise and basil.

3. Separate biscuits into halves horizontally. Place each half into cups of the prepared mini muffin pan. Fill each biscuit half with the bacon mixture.

4. Bake for 10 to 12 minutes in the preheated oven , or until golden brown.

Asian Beef Skewers

Submitted by: **Vivian Chu**

Makes: 3 servings

Preparation: 30 minutes

Cooking: 15 minutes

Total: 2 hours 50 minutes

"Ginger flavored beef skewers are excellent as an appetizer as well as an entree."

INGREDIENTS

3 tablespoons hoisin sauce

3 tablespoons sherry

1/4 cup soy sauce

1 teaspoon barbeque sauce

2 green onions, chopped

2 cloves garlic, minced

1 tablespoon minced fresh ginger root

1 1/2 pounds flank steak

DIRECTIONS

1. In a small bowl, mix together hoisin sauce, sherry, soy sauce, barbeque sauce, green onions, garlic and ginger.

2. Cut flank steak across grain on a diagonal, yielding thin, 2 inch wide slices. Place slices in a 1 gallon, resealable plastic bag. Pour hoisin sauce mixture over slices, and mix well. Refrigerate 2 hours, or overnight.

3. Preheat an outdoor grill for high heat.

4. Thread steak on skewers. Grill 3 minutes per side, or to desired doneness.

Chicken and Broccoli Braid

Submitted by: **Kelly Grimes**

Makes: 6 servings

Preparation: 20 minutes

Cooking: 28 minutes

Total: 48 minutes

"Beautiful braided crescent roll with chicken and broccoli."

INGREDIENTS

2 cups diced, cooked chicken meat

1 cup fresh broccoli, chopped

1/2 cup red bell pepper, chopped

1 clove crushed garlic

1 cup shredded Cheddar cheese

1/2 cup mayonnaise

2 teaspoons dried dill weed

1/4 teaspoon salt

2 tablespoons slivered almonds

1/4 cup diced onion

2 (8 ounce) packages refrigerated crescent rolls

1 egg white, beaten

DIRECTIONS

1. Preheat oven to 375°F (190°F).

2. In a large bowl, toss together chicken, broccoli, red bell pepper, garlic, Cheddar cheese, mayonnaise, dill weed, salt, almonds and onion.

3. Unroll crescent roll dough, and arrange flat on a medium baking sheet. Pinch together perforations to form a single sheet of dough. Using a knife or scissors, cut 1 inch wide strips in towards the center, starting on the long sides. There should be a solid strip about 3 inches wide down the center, with the cut strips forming a fringe down each side. Spread the chicken mixture along the center strip. Fold the side strips over chicken mixture, alternating strips from each side. Pinch or twist to seal.

4. Brush braided dough with the egg white. Bake in the preheated oven 25 to 28 minutes, or until golden brown.

Pico de Gallo Chicken Quesadillas

Submitted by: **Tony Cortez**

Makes: 2 servings

Preparation: 25 minutes

Cooking: 30 minutes

Total: 55 minutes

"Flour tortillas filled with chicken breast, onions, peppers, pico de gallo and Monterey Jack cheese."

INGREDIENTS

1 tomato, diced

1/2 onion, finely chopped

1 lime, juiced

1 tablespoon chopped fresh cilantro

1/2 jalapeno pepper, seeded and minced

salt and pepper to taste

1 tablespoon olive oil

1 skinless, boneless chicken breast halves - cut into strips

1/4 onion, thinly sliced

1/2 green bell pepper, thinly sliced

1 clove garlic, minced

2 (12 inch) flour tortillas

2 ounces shredded Monterey Jack cheese

salt and pepper to taste

1 (8 ounce) container sour cream

DIRECTIONS

1. In a small bowl, combine the tomato, chopped onion, lime juice, cilantro, jalapeno, salt and pepper. Set the pico de gallo aside.

2. In a large skillet, heat 1/2 tablespoon olive oil. Add the chicken breast meat, and sauté until cooked through and juices run clear. Remove chicken from skillet, and set aside.

3. Put the remaining 1/2 tablespoon of olive oil in the hot skillet and sauté the sliced onion and green pepper until tender. Stir in the minced garlic, and sauté until the aroma is strong. Finally, mix in half of the pico de gallo and the previously sautéed chicken breast meat. Set this mixture aside; keep warm.

4. In a heavy skillet, heat one flour tortilla. Spread 1/2 of the shredded cheese on the tortilla, and top with the chicken mixture. Sprinkle remaining cheese over the chicken, and top with the remaining tortilla. Flip, and cook on the opposite side. Remove quesadilla from skillet, and cut into quarters. Serve with sour cream and remaining pico de gallo.

Sinless Mississippi Sin

Submitted by: **Kat Wood**

Makes: 10 servings

Preparation: 25 minutes

Cooking: 40 minutes

Total: 1 hour 5 minutes

"The 'sinful' version of this recipe was served at my Bridal Shower, and now the recipe is the favorite appetizer of everyone I know! It's delicious, easy, healthier than the original, and a hit at any party!"

INGREDIENTS

1 (8 ounce) package Neufchatel cheese

1½ cups shredded white Cheddar cheese

2 cups fat free sour cream

1 (4 ounce) can green chile peppers

1 teaspoon Worcestershire sauce

1 clove garlic, crushed

1 bunch green onions, chopped

1 (6.5 ounce) jar marinated artichoke hearts, drained and chopped

salt and pepper to taste

1 (1 pound) loaf round sourdough bread

1 cup chopped tomatoes

DIRECTIONS

1. Preheat oven to 375°F (190°C).

2. In a medium bowl, beat the Neufchatel cheese until soft. Stir in Cheddar cheese, sour cream, green chiles, Worcestershire sauce, garlic, green onions, artichoke hearts, salt and pepper.

3. Slice the top off the bread, and hollow the bread out. Spoon cheese and artichoke mixture into the bread bowl. Replace the top of the bread, and wrap entire bread bowl in aluminum foil.

4. Bake for 40 minutes in the preheated oven. Remove from oven, and stir in tomatoes. Serve hot.

Hot Artichoke Spinach Dip

Submitted by: **Sherrie D.**

Makes: 4 cups

Preparation: 20 minutes

Cooking: 25 minutes

Total: 45 minutes

"This is a warm delicious dip...but it's very rich! Serve warm with tortilla chips. Garnish with extra sour cream and salsa if you like."

INGREDIENTS

1 (14 ounce) can artichoke hearts, drained

⅓ cup grated Romano cheese

¼ cup grated Parmesan cheese

½ teaspoon minced garlic

1 cup shredded mozzarella cheese

1 (10 ounce) package frozen chopped spinach, thawed and drained

⅓ cup heavy cream

½ cup sour cream

DIRECTIONS

1. Preheat oven to 350°F (175°C). Grease a 9x13 inch baking dish.

2. In a blender or food processor, place artichoke hearts, Romano cheese, Parmesan cheese and garlic . Pulse until chopped, but not ground. Set aside.

3. In a medium bowl, mix together mozzarella cheese, spinach, heavy cream and sour cream. Stir in artichoke mixture. Spoon into prepared baking dish.

4. Bake in the preheated oven for 20 to 25 minutes, or until cheese is melted and bubbly.

BLT Dip

Submitted by: **Kathy Walstrom**

Makes: 3 cups dip

Preparation: 2 minutes

Cooking: 10 minutes

Total: 22 minutes

"This dip is a hit whether you serve it at a block party or a formal dinner party! It really tastes like a BLT. You can cut the fat down if you want to use low-fat or fat free ingredients. Serve with crackers or chips."

INGREDIENTS

1 pound bacon

1 cup mayonnaise

1 cup sour cream

1 tomato - peeled, seeded and diced

DIRECTIONS

1. Place bacon in a large, deep skillet. Cook over medium high heat until evenly brown. Drain on paper towels.

2. In a medium bowl, combine mayonnaise and sour cream. Crumble bacon into the sour cream and mayonnaise mixture. Mix in tomatoes just before serving.

Crab Dip

Submitted by: **Laurie O'Grady**

Makes: 16 servings

Preparation: 15 minutes

Cooking: 30 minutes

Total: 45 minutes

"Hot crab dip served in a bread bowl. Perfect for parties!"

INGREDIENTS

11 ounces cream cheese, softened

1 small onion, finely chopped

5 tablespoons mayonnaise

2 (6 ounce) cans crabmeat, drained and flaked

1/8 teaspoon garlic powder

salt and pepper to taste

1 (1 pound) loaf round, crusty Italian bread

DIRECTIONS

1. Preheat oven to 350°F (175°C).

2. In a medium bowl, combine the cream cheese, onion, mayonnaise, crabmeat, garlic powder, salt and pepper. Spread mixture into a 1 quart baking dish.

3. Bake for 20 minutes in the preheated oven. While the dip is baking, cut a circle in the top of the bread, and scoop out the inside to create a bread bowl. Tear the removed bread into pieces for dipping.

4. Remove baked crab dip from the oven, and stir well. Spoon the mixture into the hollowed out loaf. Place bread bowl and chunks of bread on a medium baking sheet, and bake for an additional 10 minutes. Serve hot.

Easy Guacamole

Submitted by: **Denise Goodman**

Makes: 2 cups

Preparation: 10 minutes

Total: 40 minutes

"Simply a quick recipe for tasty guacamole! Great with tortilla chips or as a topping for Mexican foods!"

INGREDIENTS

2 avocados

1 small onion, finely chopped

1 clove garlic, minced

1 ripe tomato, chopped

1 lime, juiced

salt and pepper to taste

DIRECTIONS

1. Peel and mash avocados in a medium serving bowl. Stir in onion, garlic, tomato, lime juice, salt and pepper. Season with remaining lime juice and salt and pepper to taste. Chill for half an hour to blend flavors.

Spicy Bean Salsa

Submitted by: **Susan Navarrete**

Makes: 4 cups

Preparation: 10 minutes

Total: 8 hours 10 minutes

"Serve with tortilla chips. Very addicting!"

INGREDIENTS

1 (15 ounce) can black-eyed peas

1 (15 ounce) can black beans, rinsed and drained

1 (15 ounce) can whole kernel corn, drained

1/2 cup chopped onion

1/2 cup chopped green bell pepper

1 (4 ounce) can diced jalapeno peppers

1 (14.5 ounce) can diced tomatoes, drained

1 cup Italian-style salad dressing

1/2 teaspoon garlic salt

DIRECTIONS

1. In a medium bowl, combine black-eyed peas, black beans, corn, onion, green bell pepper, jalapeno peppers and tomatoes. Season with Italian-style salad dressing and garlic salt; mix well. Cover, and refrigerate overnight to blend flavors.

Hummus III

Submitted by: **Rhoda McIntosh**

Makes: 2 cups

Preparation: 10 minutes

Total: 10 minutes

"Hummus is a pureed garbanzo bean dip with Middle Eastern origins. Serve with pita and an assortment of fresh vegetables. This is the secret combination straight from a Boston restaurant. Tahini, or sesame seed paste, can be found in health food stores, gourmet shops and even many grocery stores."

INGREDIENTS

2 cups canned garbanzo beans, drained

1/3 cup tahini

1/4 cup lemon juice

1 teaspoon salt

2 cloves garlic, halved

1 tablespoon olive oil

1 pinch paprika

1 teaspoon minced fresh parsley

DIRECTIONS

1. Place the garbanzo beans, tahini, lemon juice, salt and garlic in a blender or food processor. Blend until smooth. Transfer mixture to a serving bowl.

2. Drizzle olive oil over the garbanzo bean mixture. Sprinkle with paprika and parsley.

soups & salads

If you've come to think of salads as merely a pile of greens that stands between you and the main course, open your eyes to the marvelous things people are doing with produce these days! While you're here, try these heart-warming soup recipes that no cook should be without. Once you sample these dishes, your salad forks and soup spoons may become the most popular utensils in the drawer.

Caesar Salad Supreme

Submitted by: **Karen Weir**

Makes: 6 servings

Preparation: 20 minutes

Cooking: 15 minutes

Total: 35 minutes

"A wonderful, rich, anchovy dressing makes this salad a meal. Serve with crusty Italian Bread."

INGREDIENTS

6 cloves garlic, peeled

3/4 cup mayonnaise

5 anchovy fillets, rinsed

6 tablespoons grated Parmesan cheese

1 tablespoon lemon juice

1 teaspoon Worcestershire sauce

1 teaspoon prepared Dijon-style mustard

salt to taste

ground black pepper to taste

1/4 cup olive oil

4 cups day-old bread, cubed

1 head romaine lettuce - rinsed, dried and torn into bite-size pieces

DIRECTIONS

1. Mince 3 cloves of the garlic, and combine in a small bowl with mayonnaise, anchovies, 2 tablespoons of the Parmesan cheese, Worcestershire sauce, mustard and lemon juice. Season to taste with salt and black pepper. Refrigerate until ready to use.

2. In a large sauté pan, heat oil over medium heat. Cut the remaining 3 cloves of garlic into quarters, and add to hot oil. Cook and stir until brown, and then remove garlic from pan. Add bread cubes to the hot oil. Cook, turning frequently, until lightly browned. Remove bread cubes from oil, and season with salt and pepper to taste.

3. Place lettuce in a large bowl. Toss with dressing, remaining Parmesan cheese, and croutons.

BLT Salad

Submitted by: **D. L. Mooney**

Makes: 6 servings

Preparation: 15 minutes

Cooking: 10 minutes

Total: 25 minutes

"This recipe is reminiscent of the classic BLT or bacon, lettuce, and tomato sandwich. It's a great summertime salad!"

INGREDIENTS

1 pound bacon

¾ cup mayonnaise

¼ cup milk

1 teaspoon garlic powder

⅛ teaspoon ground black pepper

salt to taste

1 head romaine lettuce - rinsed, dried and shredded

2 large tomatoes, chopped

2 cups seasoned croutons

DIRECTIONS

1. Place bacon in a large, deep skillet. Cook over medium high heat, turning frequently, until evenly browned. Drain, crumble and set aside.

2. In a blender or food processor, combine mayonnaise, milk, garlic powder and black pepper. Blend until smooth. Season the dressing with salt.

3. Combine lettuce, tomatoes, bacon and croutons in a large salad bowl. Toss with dressing, and serve immediately.

Mandarin Almond Salad

Submitted by: **Bonnie A. Deger**

Makes: 8 servings

Preparation: 20 minutes

Cooking: 10 minutes

Total: 40 minutes

"A wonderful medley of flavors and textures!"

INGREDIENTS

1 head romaine lettuce - rinsed, dried and chopped

2 (11 ounce) cans mandarin oranges, drained

6 green onions, thinly sliced

2 tablespoons white sugar

1/2 cup sliced almonds

1/4 cup red wine vinegar

1/2 cup olive oil

1 tablespoon white sugar

1/8 teaspoon crushed red pepper flakes

ground black pepper to taste

DIRECTIONS

1. In a large bowl, combine the romaine lettuce, oranges and green onions.

2. Heat 2 tablespoons sugar with the almonds in saucepan over medium heat. Cook and stir while sugar starts to melt and coat almonds. Stir constantly until almonds are light brown. Turn onto a plate, and cool for 10 minutes.

3. Combine red wine vinegar, olive oil, one tablespoon sugar, red pepper flakes and black pepper in a jar with a tight fitting lid. Shake vigorously until sugar is dissolved.

4. Before serving, toss lettuce with salad dressing until coated. Transfer to a decorative serving bowl, and sprinkle with sugared almonds.

Jamie's Cranberry Spinach Salad

Submitted by: Jamie Hensley

Makes: 12 servings

Preparation: 10 minutes

Cooking: 10 minutes

Total: 20 minutes

"Everyone I have made this for RAVES about it! It's different and so easy to make!"

INGREDIENTS

1 tablespoon butter

³/₄ cup blanched and slivered almonds

1 pound spinach, rinsed and torn into bite-size pieces

1 cup dried cranberries

2 tablespoons toasted sesame seeds

1 tablespoon poppy seeds

¹/₂ cup white sugar

2 teaspoons minced onion

¹/₄ teaspoon paprika

¹/₄ cup white wine vinegar

¹/₄ cup cider vinegar

¹/₂ cup vegetable oil

DIRECTIONS

1. In a medium saucepan, melt butter over medium heat. Cook and stir almonds in butter until lightly toasted. Remove from heat, and let cool.

2. In a large bowl, toss the spinach with the toasted almonds and cranberries.

3. In a medium bowl, whisk together the sesame seeds, poppy seeds, sugar, onion, paprika, white wine vinegar, cider vinegar and vegetable oil. Toss with spinach just before serving.

Strawberry Spinach Salad

Submitted by: **Andrea McInnis**

Makes: 4 servings

Preparation: 10 minutes

Total: 1 hour 10 minutes

"Someone brought this salad to a pot luck dinner and I had to have the recipe. I have made it many, many times since then and I have been asked for the recipe every time I bring it somewhere. It is also a great way to get kids to eat spinach!"

INGREDIENTS

2 tablespoons sesame seeds

1 tablespoon poppy seeds

1/2 cup white sugar

1/2 cup olive oil

1/4 cup distilled white vinegar

1/4 teaspoon paprika

1/4 teaspoon Worcestershire sauce

1 tablespoon minced onion

10 ounces fresh spinach - rinsed, dried and torn into bite-size pieces

1 quart strawberries - cleaned, hulled and sliced

1/4 cup blanched and slivered almonds

DIRECTIONS

1. In a medium bowl, whisk together the sesame seeds, poppy seeds, sugar, olive oil, vinegar, paprika, Worcestershire sauce and onion. Cover, and chill for one hour.

2. In a large bowl, combine the spinach, strawberries and almonds. Pour dressing over salad, and toss. Refrigerate 10 to 15 minutes before serving.

Ramen Coleslaw

Submitted by: **Mary**

Makes: 4 servings

Preparation: 15 minutes

Cooking: 10 minutes

Total: 25 minutes

"This is nothing like the mayonnaise based coleslaws that most people think of."

INGREDIENTS

2 tablespoons vegetable oil

3 tablespoons white wine vinegar

2 tablespoons white sugar

1 (3 ounce) package chicken flavored ramen noodles, crushed, seasoning packet reserved

1/2 teaspoon salt

1/2 teaspoon ground black pepper

2 tablespoons sesame seeds

1/4 cup sliced almonds

1/2 medium head cabbage, shredded

5 green onions, chopped

DIRECTIONS

1. Preheat oven to 350°F (175°C).

2. In a medium bowl, whisk together the oil, vinegar, sugar, ramen noodle spice mix, salt and pepper to create a dressing.

3. Place sesame seeds and almonds in a single layer on a medium baking sheet. Bake in the preheated oven 10 minutes, or until lightly brown.

4. In a large salad bowl, combine the cabbage, green onions and crushed ramen noodles. Pour dressing over the cabbage, and toss to coat evenly. Top with toasted sesame seeds and almonds.

Alyson's Broccoli Salad

Submitted by: **Eleanor Johnson**

Makes: 6 servings

Preparation: 15 minutes

Cooking: 15 minutes

Total: 30 minutes

"Confirmed broccoli haters have changed their minds after tasting this salad. It is great for potlucks or buffet meals. Make a day or so before you wish to serve to meld the ingredients. I have used sugar substitutes for the white sugar and also used nonfat or low-fat mayonnaise and it still tastes great!"

INGREDIENTS

10 slices bacon

1 head fresh broccoli, cut into bite size pieces

¼ cup red onion, chopped

½ cup raisins

3 tablespoons white wine vinegar

2 tablespoons white sugar

1 cup mayonnaise

1 cup sunflower seeds

DIRECTIONS

1. Place bacon in a large, deep skillet. Cook over medium high heat until evenly brown. Drain, crumble and set aside.

2. In a medium bowl, combine the broccoli, onion and raisins. In a small bowl, whisk together the vinegar, sugar and mayonnaise. Pour over broccoli mixture, and toss until well mixed. Refrigerate for at least two hours.

3. Before serving, toss salad with crumbled bacon and sunflower seeds.

Bodacious Broccoli Salad

Submitted by: **Cassandra Kennedy**

Makes: 12 servings

Preparation: 15 minutes

Cooking: 15 minutes

Total: 30 minutes

"This recipe is requested at every family gathering. Let it be your next dish that they crave! I like this dish to be prepared at least two hours before serving. Be sure to have copies of the recipe on hand, as everyone will ask for it!"

INGREDIENTS

8 slices bacon

2 heads fresh broccoli, chopped

1 1/2 cups shredded sharp Cheddar cheese

1/2 large red onion, chopped

1/4 cup red wine vinegar

1/8 cup white sugar

2 teaspoons ground black pepper

1 teaspoon salt

2/3 cup mayonnaise

1 teaspoon fresh lemon juice

DIRECTIONS

1. Place bacon in a large, deep skillet. Cook over medium high heat until evenly brown. Drain, and crumble.

2. In a large bowl, combine broccoli, cheese, bacon and onion.

3. Prepare the dressing in a small bowl by whisking together the red wine vinegar, sugar, pepper, salt, mayonnaise and lemon juice. Combine dressing with salad. Cover, and refrigerate until ready to serve.

Potato Salad

Submitted by: **Ellen Rainey**

Makes: 12 servings

Preparation: 15 minutes

Cooking: 30 minutes

Total: 3 hours 45 minutes

"I have been working very hard since I married to come up with a perfect potato salad. This is it - a sweet, creamy recipe made with red potatoes. Very tasty. You can substitute sweet pickle relish for the sweet pickle cubes."

INGREDIENTS

5 pounds red potatoes, diced

4 eggs

4 stalks celery, chopped

1 green bell pepper, chopped

1 (16 ounce) jar sweet pickles, cubed

3/4 tablespoon prepared mustard

3/4 cup mayonnaise

1 onion, finely chopped

1 teaspoon white sugar

salt and pepper to taste

DIRECTIONS

1. Bring a large pot of salted water to a boil. Add potatoes, and cook until tender but still firm, about 15 minutes. Drain, and transfer to a large bowl.

2. Place eggs in a medium saucepan, and cover completely with cold water. Bring water to a boil. Cover, remove from heat, and let eggs stand in hot water for 10 to 12 minutes. Remove from hot water, and peel under cold, running water. Chop, and set aside.

3. Stir the eggs, celery, green bell pepper, sweet pickle cubes, prepared mustard, mayonnaise, onion and white sugar into the potatoes. Season to taste with salt and pepper. Cover, and chill in the refrigerator for at least 3 hours before serving.

Antipasto Pasta Salad

Submitted by: **Dayna**

Makes: 12 servings

Preparation: 20 minutes

Cooking: 15 minutes

Total: 1 hour 35 minutes

"A delicious pasta, meat and cheese combination with a homemade dressing. It serves a crowd and is great for a picnic."

INGREDIENTS

1 pound seashell pasta

¼ pound Genoa salami, chopped

¼ pound pepperoni sausage, chopped

½ pound Asiago cheese, diced

1 (6 ounce) can black olives, drained and chopped

1 red bell pepper, diced

1 green bell pepper, chopped

3 tomatoes, chopped

1 (.7 ounce) package dry Italian-style salad dressing mix

¾ cup extra virgin olive oil

¼ cup balsamic vinegar

2 tablespoons dried oregano

1 tablespoon dried parsley

1 tablespoon grated Parmesan cheese

salt and ground black pepper to taste

DIRECTIONS

1. Cook the pasta in a large pot of salted boiling water until al dente. Drain, and cool under cold water.

2. In a large bowl, combine the pasta, salami, pepperoni, Asiago cheese, black olives, red bell pepper, green bell pepper and tomatoes. Stir in the envelope of dressing mix. Cover, and refrigerate for at least one hour.

3. To prepare the dressing, whisk together the olive oil, balsamic vinegar, oregano, parsley, Parmesan cheese, salt and pepper. Just before serving, pour dressing over the salad, and mix well.

Broccoli and Tortellini Salad

Submitted by: **Judy McNamara**

Makes: 12 servings

Preparation: 10 minutes

Cooking: 20 minutes

Total: 30 minutes

"Crisp, fresh broccoli and cheese tortellini with a creamy dressing are the basis of this salad. Raisins, sunflower seeds and red onion dress it up. This recipe is most requested at potlucks."

INGREDIENTS

6 slices bacon

20 ounces fresh cheese-filled tortellini

½ cup mayonnaise

½ cup white sugar

2 teaspoons cider vinegar

3 heads fresh broccoli, cut into florets

1 cup raisins

1 cup sunflower seeds

1 red onion, finely chopped

DIRECTIONS

1. Place bacon in a large, deep skillet. Cook over medium high heat until evenly brown. Drain, crumble and set aside.

2. Bring a large pot of lightly salted water to a boil. Cook tortellini in boiling water for 8 to 10 minutes or until al dente. Drain, and rinse under cold water.

3. In a small bowl, mix together mayonnaise, sugar and vinegar to make the dressing.

4. In a large bowl, combine broccoli, tortellini, bacon, raisins, sunflower seeds and red onion. Pour dressing over salad, and toss.

Best Chicken Pasta Salad

Submitted by: **Gail Wagner**

Makes: 8 servings

Preparation: 15 minutes

Cooking: 35 minutes

Total: 3 hours

"This wonderful chicken and pasta salad is perfect for any ladies' luncheon, yet hearty enough for bigger supper appetites."

INGREDIENTS

2 boneless, skinless chicken breast halves

¾ cup steak sauce

1 (12 ounce) package fusilli pasta

2 cubes chicken bouillon

1 Vidalia onion, diced

2 avocados - peeled, pitted and diced

1 cup halved cherry tomatoes

1 cup Ranch-style salad dressing

DIRECTIONS

1. Preheat an outdoor grill for high heat. Place breasts into a glass baking dish and marinate in steak sauce for 15 to 60 minutes.

2. Grill chicken until no longer pink and the juices run clear. Remove from grill, and chop into bite-size pieces.

3. To a large pot of boiling water, add bouillon cubes and pasta. Cook pasta until al dente. Drain, and rinse under cold water.

4. In a large bowl, combine chicken, pasta, onion, avocados and tomatoes. Mix in salad dressing, cover, and refrigerate until chilled.

Judy's Strawberry Pretzel Salad

Submitted by: **Tom Quinlin**

Makes: 8 servings

Preparation: 15 minutes

Cooking: 10 minutes

Total: 2 hours

"This three layer salad includes a pretzel crust, cream cheese center, and strawberry top."

INGREDIENTS

1½ cups crushed pretzels

4½ tablespoons white sugar

¾ cup butter, melted

1 cup white sugar

2 (8 ounce) packages cream cheese

1 (8 ounce) container frozen whipped topping, thawed

1 (6 ounce) package strawberry flavored gelatin

2 cups boiling water

1 (16 ounce) package frozen strawberries

DIRECTIONS

1. Preheat oven to 350°F (175°C). Mix together the pretzels, 4½ tablespoons sugar and melted butter. Press into the bottom of a 9x13 inch pan. Bake for 10 minutes, or lightly toasted. Set aside to cool completely.

2. In a medium bowl, beat the sugar and cream cheese until smooth. Fold in whipped topping. Spread evenly over the cooled crust. Refrigerate until set, about 30 minutes.

3. In a medium bowl, stir together the gelatin mix and boiling water. Mix in frozen strawberries, and stir until thawed. Pour over cream cheese mixture in pan. Refrigerate until completely chilled, at least 1 hour.

Grandma's Chicken Noodle Soup

Submitted by: **Corwynn Darkholme**

Makes: 8 servings

Preparation: 20 minutes

Cooking: 25 minutes

Total: 45 minutes

"This is a recipe that was given to me by my grandmother. It is a very savory and tasty soup and I believe that all will like it. If you would like to add even more flavor, try using smoked chicken!!"

INGREDIENTS

2½ cups wide egg noodles

1 teaspoon vegetable oil

12 cups chicken broth

1½ tablespoons salt

1 teaspoon poultry seasoning

1 cup chopped celery

1 cup chopped onion

⅓ cup cornstarch

¼ cup water

3 cups diced, cooked chicken meat

DIRECTIONS

1. Bring a large pot of lightly salted water to a boil. Add egg noodles and oil, and boil for 8 minutes, or until tender. Drain. Rinse under cool running water.

2. In a large saucepan or Dutch oven, combine broth, salt, and poultry seasoning. Bring to a boil. Stir in celery and onion. Reduce heat, cover, and simmer 15 minutes.

3. In a small bowl, mix cornstarch and water together until cornstarch is completely dissolved. Gradually add to soup, stirring constantly. Stir in noodles and chicken, and heat through.

Cream of Chicken with Wild Rice Soup

Submitted by: **Thomas**

Makes: 8 servings

Preparation: 20 minutes

Cooking: 1 hour 55 minutes

Total: 2 hours 15 minutes

"This makes a lovely chicken and wild rice soup."

INGREDIENTS

1⅓ cups wild rice

1 (3 pound) whole chicken, cut into pieces

7 cups water

1 cup chopped celery

1 cup chopped onion

2 tablespoons vegetable oil

1 cup sliced fresh mushrooms

2 tablespoons chicken bouillon granules

¾ teaspoon ground white pepper

½ teaspoon salt

½ cup margarine

¾ cup all-purpose flour

4 cups milk

¾ cup white wine

DIRECTIONS

1. Cook the wild rice according to package directions, but remove from heat about 15 minutes before it's done. Drain the excess liquid, and set aside.

2. In a stock pot over high heat, combine the chicken and the water. Bring to a boil, and then reduce heat to low. Simmer for 40 minutes, or until chicken is cooked and tender. Remove chicken from the pot, and allow it to cool. Strain the broth from the pot, and reserve for later. When chicken is cool, remove the meat from the bones, cut into bite size pieces, and reserve. Discard the fat and the bones.

3. In the same stock pot over medium heat, sauté the celery and onion in the oil for 5 minutes. Add the mushrooms, and cover. Cook for 5 to 10 minutes, stirring occasionally, until everything is tender. Return the broth to the stock pot, and add the partially cooked wild rice. Stir in the bouillon, white pepper and salt; simmer, uncovered, for 15 minutes.

4. Meanwhile, melt margarine in a medium saucepan over medium heat. Stir in the flour until smooth. Whisk in the milk, and continue cooking until mixture is bubbly and thick. Add some of the broth mixture to the milk mixture, continuing to stir, then stir all of the milk mixture into the broth mixture.

5. Mix in the reserved chicken meat and the white wine. Allow this to heat through for about 15 minutes.

Cheese and Broccoli Chicken Soup

Submitted by: **Rebecca Miller**

Makes: 5 servings

Preparation: 10 minutes

Cooking: 1 hour

Total: 1 hour 10 minutes

"Talk about comfort food!"

INGREDIENTS

½ cup butter

1 cup all-purpose flour

11 cups water

3 cubes chicken bouillon

2 pounds boneless chicken breasts, cut into bite-sized pieces

2 heads fresh broccoli, cut into florets

1½ teaspoons salt

1 teaspoon ground black pepper

1 cup light cream

3 cups shredded Cheddar cheese

DIRECTIONS

1. In a 5-quart pot, melt butter over medium heat. Mix in flour, stirring constantly until a thick paste forms. Remove from pot, and set aside.

2. In same pot, combine water, bouillon cubes, chicken, broccoli, salt and pepper. Bring to boil over high heat. Reduce heat to medium low, and simmer for 45 minutes.

3. Stir in the flour mixture a little bit at a time until soup thickens. Simmer 5 minutes. Reduce heat, and stir in cream. Mix in cheese 1 cup at a time, and stir until melted.

Chicken Tortilla Soup

Submitted by: **Star Pooley**

Makes: 4 servings

Preparation: 20 minutes

Cooking: 20 minutes

Total: 40 minutes

"This soup is quick to make, flavorful, and filling! Serve with warm corn bread or tortillas. This also freezes well. Garnish with chopped fresh avocado, Monterey Jack cheese, crushed tortilla chips or green onion!"

INGREDIENTS

1 onion, chopped

3 cloves garlic, minced

1 tablespoon olive oil

2 teaspoons chili powder

1 teaspoon dried oregano

1 (28 ounce) can crushed tomatoes

1 (10.5 ounce) can chicken broth

1¼ cups water

1 cup whole corn kernels, cooked

1 cup white hominy

1 (4 ounce) can chopped green chile peppers

1 (15 ounce) can black beans, rinsed and drained

¼ cup chopped fresh cilantro

2 boneless chicken breast halves, cooked and cut into bite-sized pieces

crushed tortilla chips

sliced avocado

shredded Monterey Jack cheese

chopped green onion

DIRECTIONS

1. In a medium stock pot, heat oil over medium heat. Sauté onion and garlic in oil until soft. Stir in chili powder, oregano, tomatoes, broth and water. Bring to a boil, and simmer for 5 to 10 minutes.

2. Stir in corn, hominy, chiles, beans, cilantro and chicken. Simmer for 10 minutes.

3. Ladle soup into individual serving bowls and top with crushed tortilla chips, avocado slices, cheese and chopped green onion.

Classic Minestrone

Submitted by: **Michelle Chen**

Makes: 4 servings

Preparation: 15 minutes

Cooking: 1 hour

Total: 1 hour 15 minutes

"This famous Italian soup has been much imitated around the world with very different results. The homemade version is a delicious revelation and is also extremely healthy, as it has pasta, beans and fresh vegetables. Try to make the minestrone a day early and refrigerate as this improves the flavors. Serve with grated Parmesan cheese and chopped fresh parsley."

INGREDIENTS

3 tablespoons olive oil

1 leek, sliced

2 carrots, chopped

1 zucchini, thinly sliced

4 ounces green beans, cut into 1 inch pieces

2 stalks celery, thinly sliced

1½ quarts vegetable stock

1 pound tomatoes, chopped

1 tablespoon chopped fresh thyme

1 (15 ounce) can cannellini beans, with liquid

¼ cup elbow macaroni

salt and ground black pepper to taste

DIRECTIONS

1. Heat olive oil in a large saucepan, over medium heat. Add leek, carrots, zucchini, green beans and celery. Cover, and reduce heat to low. Cook for 15 minutes, shaking the pan occasionally.

2. Stir in the stock, tomatoes and thyme. Bring to a boil, then replace the lid, and reduce heat to low; simmer gently for 30 minutes.

3. Stir in the cannellini beans with liquid and pasta. Simmer for an additional 10 minutes, or until pasta is al dente. Season with salt and pepper to taste before serving.

Italian Sausage Soup

Submitted by: **Karen Marshall**

"A hearty winter favorite."

Makes: 6 servings

Preparation: 10 minutes

Cooking: 40 minutes

Total: 50 minutes

INGREDIENTS

1 pound Italian sausage

1 clove garlic, minced

2 (14 ounce) cans beef broth

1 (14.5 ounce) can Italian-style stewed tomatoes

1 cup sliced carrots

1 (14.5 ounce) can great northern beans, undrained

2 small zucchini, cubed

2 cups spinach - packed, rinsed and torn

¼ teaspoon ground black pepper

¼ teaspoon salt

DIRECTIONS

1. In a stockpot or Dutch oven, brown sausage with garlic. Stir in broth, tomatoes and carrots, and season with salt and pepper. Reduce heat, cover, and simmer 15 minutes.

2. Stir in beans with liquid and zucchini. Cover, and simmer another 15 minutes, or until zucchini is tender.

3. Remove from heat, and add spinach. Replace lid allowing the heat from the soup to cook the spinach leaves. Soup is ready to serve after 5 minutes.

Italian Vegetable Soup

Submitted by: **Jackie**

Makes: 8 servings

Preparation: 20 minutes

Cooking: 50 minutes

Total: 1 hour 10 minutes

"Makes a lot and is very, very good."

INGREDIENTS

1 pound ground beef

1 cup chopped onion

1 cup chopped celery

1 cup chopped carrots

2 cloves garlic, minced

1 (14.5 ounce) can peeled and diced tomatoes

1 (15 ounce) can tomato sauce

2 (19 ounce) cans kidney beans, drained and rinsed

2 cups water

5 teaspoons beef bouillon granules

1 tablespoon dried parsley

1/2 teaspoon dried oregano

1/2 teaspoon dried basil

2 cups chopped cabbage

1 (15.25 ounce) can whole kernel corn

1 (15 ounce) can green beans

1 cup macaroni

DIRECTIONS

1. Place ground beef in a large soup pot. Cook over medium heat until evenly browned. Drain excess fat. Stir in onion, celery, carrots, garlic, chopped tomatoes, tomato sauce, beans, water and bouillon. Season with parsley, oregano and basil. Simmer for 20 minutes.

2. Stir in cabbage, corn, green beans and pasta. Bring to a boil, then reduce heat. Simmer until vegetables are tender and pasta is al dente. Add more water if needed.

Italian Wedding Soup

Submitted by: **Star Pooley**

Makes: 4 servings

Preparation: 20 minutes

Cooking: 30 minutes

Total: 50 minutes

"Coming from Rhode Island, a very ethnic state, this soup was traditionally served at Italian weddings. Serve with grated Parmesan cheese."

INGREDIENTS

½ pound extra-lean ground beef

1 egg, lightly beaten

2 tablespoons dry bread crumbs

1 tablespoon grated Parmesan cheese

½ teaspoon dried basil

½ teaspoon onion powder

5¾ cups chicken broth

2 cups thinly sliced escarole

1 cup uncooked orzo pasta

⅓ cup finely chopped carrot

DIRECTIONS

1. In medium bowl, combine meat, egg, bread crumbs, cheese, basil and onion powder; shape into ¾ inch balls.

2. In large saucepan, heat broth to boiling; stir in escarole, orzo pasta, chopped carrot and meatballs. Return to boil, then reduce heat to medium. Cook at slow boil for 10 minutes, or until pasta is al dente. Stir frequently to prevent sticking.

Slow Cooker Taco Soup

Submitted by: **Janeen**

Makes: 8 servings

Preparation: 10 minutes

Cooking: 8 hours

Total: 8 hours 10 minutes

"This is a quick, throw together slow cooker soup with a Mexican flair. Teenagers love it. Serve topped with corn chips, shredded Cheddar cheese and a dollop of sour cream. Make sure you adjust the amount of chile peppers if you're sensitive about spicy foods."

INGREDIENTS

1 pound ground beef

1 onion, chopped

1 (16 ounce) can chili beans, with liquid

1 (15 ounce) can kidney beans with liquid

1 (15 ounce) can whole kernel corn, with liquid

1 (8 ounce) can tomato sauce

2 cups water

2 (14.5 ounce) cans peeled and diced tomatoes

1 (4 ounce) can diced green chile peppers

1 (1.25 ounce) package taco seasoning mix

DIRECTIONS

1. In a medium skillet, cook the ground beef until browned over medium heat. Drain, and set aside.

2. Place the ground beef, onion, chili beans, kidney beans, corn, tomato sauce, water, diced tomatoes, green chile peppers and taco seasoning mix in a slow cooker. Mix to blend, and cook on Low setting for 8 hours.

Absolutely Ultimate Potato Soup

Submitted by: **Karena H. Denton**

Makes: 8 servings

Preparation: 10 minutes

Cooking: 30 minutes

Total: 40 minutes

"I have made this for many whom have given it the title. This takes a bit of effort but is well worth it. Please note: for those who do not wish to use bacon, substitute 1/4 cup melted butter for the bacon grease and continue with the recipe. (I generally serve this soup as a special treat as it is not recommended for people counting calories.)"

INGREDIENTS

1 pound bacon, chopped

2 stalks celery, diced

1 onion, chopped

3 cloves garlic, minced

8 potatoes, peeled and cubed

4 cups chicken broth

3 tablespoons margarine

¼ cup all-purpose flour

1 cup heavy cream

1 teaspoon dried tarragon

3 teaspoons chopped fresh cilantro

salt and pepper to taste

DIRECTIONS

1. In a Dutch oven, cook the bacon over medium heat until done. Remove bacon from pan, and set aside. Drain off all but ¼ cup of the bacon grease.

2. In the bacon grease remaining in the pan, sauté the celery and onion until onion begins to turn clear. Add the garlic, and continue cooking for 1 to 2 minutes. Add the cubed potatoes, and toss to coat. Sauté for 3 to 4 minutes. Return the bacon to the pan, and add enough chicken stock to just cover the potatoes. Cover, and simmer until potatoes are tender.

3. In a separate pan, melt the margarine over medium heat. Whisk in the flour. Cook stirring constantly, for 1 to 2 minutes. Whisk in the heavy cream, tarragon and cilantro. Bring the cream mixture to a boil, and cook, stirring constantly, until thickened. Stir the cream mixture into the potato mixture. Puree about ½ the soup, and return to the pan. Adjust seasonings to taste.

Baked Potato Soup

Submitted by: **Sherry Haupt**

Makes: 6 servings

Preparation: 15 minutes

Cooking: 25 minutes

Total: 40 minutes

"Thick and creamy. Uses leftover baked potatoes."

INGREDIENTS

2/3 cup margarine

2/3 cup all-purpose flour

7 cups milk

4 potatoes - baked, cooled, peeled and cubed

4 green onions, chopped

12 slices bacon

1¼ cups shredded Cheddar cheese

1 cup sour cream

1 teaspoon salt

1 teaspoon ground black pepper

DIRECTIONS

1. Place bacon in a large, deep skillet. Cook over medium heat until browned. Drain, crumble, and set aside.

2. In a stock pot or Dutch oven, melt the margarine over medium heat. Whisk in flour, until smooth. Gradually stir in milk, whisking constantly until thickened. Stir in potatoes and onions. Bring to a boil, stirring frequently.

3. Reduce heat, and simmer 10 minutes. Mix in bacon, cheese, sour cream, salt, and pepper. Continue cooking, stirring frequently, until cheese is melted.

Butternut Squash Soup

Submitted by: **Mary**

Makes: 6 servings

Preparation: 25 minutes

Cooking: 35 minutes

Total: 1 hour

"Delicious and very easy to make. You can use 3 to 4 cups of chicken broth instead of the water and bouillon cubes. Also works well with half as much cream cheese if you don't want it too rich."

INGREDIENTS

6 tablespoons chopped onion

4 tablespoons margarine

6 cups peeled and cubed butternut squash

3 cups water

4 cubes chicken bouillon

1/2 teaspoon dried marjoram

1/4 teaspoon ground black pepper

1/8 teaspoon ground cayenne pepper

2 (8 ounce) packages cream cheese

DIRECTIONS

1. In a large saucepan, sauté onions in margarine until tender. Add squash, water, bouillon, marjoram, black pepper and cayenne pepper. Bring to boil; cook 20 minutes, or until squash is tender.

2. Puree squash and cream cheese in a blender or food processor in batches until smooth. Return to saucepan, and heat through. Do not allow to boil.

Hungarian Mushroom Soup

Submitted by: **Cathy T**

Makes: 6 servings

Preparation: 15 minutes

Cooking: 35 minutes

Total: 50 minutes

"My family loves soup and this is one of their favorites. It has lots of flavor and is fairly quick to make. It's primarily a mushroom soup but derives a lot of its flavor from other ingredients."

INGREDIENTS

4 tablespoons unsalted butter

2 cups chopped onions

1 pound fresh mushrooms, sliced

2 teaspoons dried dill weed

1 tablespoon paprika

1 tablespoon soy sauce

2 cups chicken broth

1 cup milk

3 tablespoons all-purpose flour

1 teaspoon salt

ground black pepper to taste

2 teaspoons lemon juice

1/4 cup chopped fresh parsley

1/2 cup sour cream

DIRECTIONS

1. Melt the butter in a large pot over medium heat. Sauté the onions in the butter for 5 minutes. Add the mushrooms and sauté for 5 more minutes. Stir in the dill, paprika, soy sauce and broth. Reduce heat to low, cover, and simmer for 15 minutes.

2. In a separate small bowl, whisk the milk and flour together. Pour this into the soup and stir well to blend. Cover and simmer for 15 more minutes, stirring occasionally.

3. Finally, stir in the salt, ground black pepper, lemon juice, parsley and sour cream. Mix together and allow to heat through over low heat, about 3 to 5 minutes. Do not boil. Serve immediately.

Broccoli Cheese Soup

Submitted by: **Karin Christian**

Makes: 12 servings

Preparation: 5 minutes

Cooking: 35 minutes

Total: 40 minutes

"This is a great, very flavorful soup. Good for serving at luncheons or special gatherings with a quiche. To make this soup a little fancier, add 1 cup sliced mushrooms and 1 cup white wine, and sauté along with the onions."

INGREDIENTS

1 onion, chopped

½ cup butter

1 (16 ounce) package frozen chopped broccoli

4 (14.5 ounce) cans chicken broth

1 (1 pound) loaf processed cheese food, cubed

2 cups milk

1 tablespoon garlic powder

⅔ cup cornstarch

1 cup water

DIRECTIONS

1. In a stockpot, melt butter over medium heat. Cook onion in butter until softened. Stir in broccoli, and cover with chicken broth. Simmer until broccoli is tender, 10 to 15 minutes.

2. Reduce heat, and stir in cheese cubes until melted. Mix in milk and garlic powder.

3. In a small bowl, stir cornstarch into water until dissolved. Mix into soup; cook and stir until thick.

Chili

Submitted by: **Robert J. Arsenault**

Makes: 8 servings

Preparation: 20 minutes

Cooking: 2 hours

Total: 2 hours 20 minutes

"Thick and spicy chili. Coffee and beer give this chili a unique and dynamite flavor. Garnish with shredded cheese and diced chile peppers."

INGREDIENTS

2 tablespoons vegetable oil

2 onions, chopped

3 cloves garlic, minced

1 pound ground beef

3/4 pound beef sirloin, cubed

1 (14.5 ounce) can peeled and diced tomatoes with juice

1 (12 fluid ounce) can or bottle dark beer

1 cup strong brewed coffee

2 (6 ounce) cans tomato paste

1 (14 ounce) can beef broth

1/2 cup packed brown sugar

3 1/2 tablespoons chili powder

1 tablespoon ground cumin

1 teaspoon unsweetened cocoa powder

1 teaspoon dried oregano

1 teaspoon ground cayenne pepper

1 teaspoon ground coriander

1 teaspoon salt

4 (15 ounce) cans kidney beans

4 fresh hot chile peppers, seeded and chopped

DIRECTIONS

1. Heat oil in a large saucepan over medium heat. Cook onions, garlic, ground beef and cubed sirloin in oil for 10 minutes, or until the meat is well browned and the onions are tender.

2. Mix in the diced tomatoes with juice, dark beer, coffee, tomato paste and beef broth. Season with chili powder, cumin, cocoa powder, oregano, cayenne pepper, coriander and salt. Stir in 2 cans of the beans and hot chile peppers. Reduce heat to low, and simmer for 1 1/2 hours.

3. Stir in the 2 remaining cans of beans, and simmer for another 30 minutes.

White Chili

Submitted by: **Dierdre Dee**

Makes: 4 servings

Preparation: 10 minutes

Cooking: 20 minutes

Total: 30 minutes

"Serve with corn bread and salad. If you cube the chicken ahead of time, make corn bread muffins while preparing the chili and use a bagged salad mix from the produce department, this is a very fast meal to put together."

INGREDIENTS

1 tablespoon olive oil

1 pound skinless, boneless chicken breast halves - cubed

1 onion, chopped

1¼ cups chicken broth

1 (4 ounce) can diced green chiles

1 teaspoon garlic powder

1 teaspoon ground cumin

½ teaspoon dried oregano

½ teaspoon dried cilantro

⅛ teaspoon cayenne pepper

1 (15 ounce) can cannellini beans, drained and rinsed

2 green onions, chopped

2 ounces shredded Monterey Jack cheese

DIRECTIONS

1. Heat oil in a large saucepan over medium high heat. Cook chicken and onion in oil for 4 to 5 minutes, or until onion is tender.

2. Stir in the chicken broth, green chiles, garlic powder, cumin, oregano, cilantro and cayenne pepper. Reduce heat, and simmer for 15 minutes.

3. Stir in the beans, and simmer for 5 more minutes, or until chicken is no longer pink and juices run clear. Garnish with green onion and shredded cheese, and serve immediately.

African Chicken Stew

Submitted by: **Leah Shaw**

Makes: 6 servings

Preparation: 10 minutes

Cooking: 35 minutes

Total: 45 minutes

"This delicious stew is inspired by my friend from Sierra Leone, West Africa, who cooks often for her family. Many ingredients can be modified. This is kind of a 'whatever is handy now' recipe. You can use a whole roasting chicken cut into bite-sized pieces, or just breasts and thighs if you prefer. Other suggested additions are turnips, carrots and celery. This looks great served over white rice with a garnish of fresh chopped cilantro, parsley or unsalted peanuts."

INGREDIENTS

1 tablespoon olive oil

1 (3 pound) roasting chicken, deboned and cut into bite size pieces

2 cloves garlic, crushed

1 onion, chopped

1 large potato, diced

1 teaspoon ground cumin

1 teaspoon ground coriander seed

1 teaspoon ground black pepper

1 teaspoon crushed red pepper flakes

1 teaspoon salt

1 cup water

3/4 cup unsalted natural-style peanut butter

1 (15 ounce) can garbanzo beans, drained and rinsed

DIRECTIONS

1. In a large skillet with a tight-fitting lid, heat oil over medium high heat. Add chicken, and brown quickly. Remove chicken from pan. Reduce heat to medium low, and add garlic, onion and potato to the pan; sauté for 2 to 3 minutes. Season with cumin, coriander, black pepper, red pepper and salt. Do not let garlic brown.

2. Mix in water and browned chicken, and any accumulated juices. Place lid on skillet and simmer, stirring occasionally, for 10 to 15 minutes.

3. Remove lid, and stir in the peanut butter and garbanzo beans. Make sure the peanut butter is blended in. Replace lid to simmer for 10 more minutes, or until chicken is cooked through and potatoes are tender. Remove from heat, adjust seasoning, and serve.

Oven Beef Stew

Submitted by: **Karen Pitschneider**

Makes: 8 servings

Preparation: 15 minutes

Cooking: 4 hours

Total: 4 hours 15 minutes

"A stew that is easy to put together and fills your kitchen with a mouth watering aroma. Doubling the recipe makes for an easy company dinner."

INGREDIENTS

1 pound beef stew meat, cut into 1 inch cubes

2 cups cubed potatoes

2 cups chopped carrots

1 (10.75 ounce) can condensed cream of
mushroom soup

1 (10.5 ounce) can condensed French onion soup

1³/4 cups water

1 cup frozen green peas

DIRECTIONS

1. Preheat oven to 250°F (120°C).

2. In a 2 to 3 quart casserole dish, combine the stew meat, potatoes, carrots, mushroom soup, French onion soup and water. Mix together well.

3. Bake, uncovered, for 4 to 5 hours, stirring occasionally. Mix in the peas 15 minutes before serving.

pasta

· ·

Cooked just so — tender but chewy — pasta is something you can really sink your teeth into. While some see pasta as merely a vehicle for tomato sauce, with the right recipe, it's a versatile foundation for the perfect meal. Try an American spin on a traditional Italian dish or take a flight of fancy with your noodles, borrowing flavors from Greece, Mexico, or even Cajun country. Sauce it and toss it — dinner's ready!

Angel Chicken Pasta

Submitted by: **Marian Collins**

Makes: 6 servings

Preparation: 30 minutes

Cooking: 1 hour

Total: 1 hour 30 minutes

"A delicious, easy company dish - the flavors are wonderful. A favorite with my family. I usually double the recipe so we can have leftovers."

INGREDIENTS

6 skinless, boneless chicken breast halves

¼ cup butter

1 (.7 ounce) package dry Italian-style salad dressing mix

½ cup white wine

1 (10.75 ounce) can condensed golden mushroom soup

4 ounces cream cheese with chives

1 pound angel hair pasta

DIRECTIONS

1. Preheat oven to 325°F (165°C).

2. In a large saucepan, melt butter over low heat. Stir in the package of dressing mix. Blend in wine and golden mushroom soup. Mix in cream cheese, and stir until smooth. Heat through, but do not boil. Arrange chicken breasts in a single layer in a 9x13 inch baking dish. Pour sauce over.

3. Bake for 60 minutes in the preheated oven. Twenty minutes before the chicken is done, bring a large pot of lightly salted water to a rolling boil. Cook pasta until al dente, about 5 minutes. Drain. Serve chicken and sauce over pasta.

Basil Chicken over Angel Hair

Submitted by: **Wendy Mercadante**

"A tasty chicken and pasta dish."

Makes: 4 servings

Preparation: 15 minutes

Cooking: 20 minutes

Total: 35 minutes

INGREDIENTS

1 (8 ounce) package angel hair pasta

2 teaspoons olive oil

1/2 cup finely chopped onion

1 clove garlic, chopped

2 1/2 cups chopped tomatoes

2 cups cooked and cubed boneless chicken breast

1/4 cup chopped fresh basil

1/2 teaspoon salt

1/8 teaspoon hot pepper sauce

1/4 cup Parmesan cheese

DIRECTIONS

1. In a large pot of salted boiling water, cook angel hair pasta until it is al dente, about 8 to 10 minutes. Drain, and set aside.

2. In a large skillet, heat oil over medium-high heat. Sauté the onions and garlic. Stir in the tomatoes, chicken, basil, salt and hot pepper sauce. Reduce heat to medium, and cover skillet. Simmer for about 5 minutes, stirring frequently, until mixture is hot and tomatoes are soft.

3. Toss sauce with hot cooked angel hair pasta to coat. Serve with Parmesan cheese.

Cajun Chicken Pasta

Submitted by: **Tammy Schill**

Makes: 2 servings

Preparation: 15 minutes

Cooking: 15 minutes

Total: 30 minutes

"Try this when you are feeling daring and want to mix things up a bit! A Southern inspired recipe that is sure to add a little fun to your dinner table. Try serving it with corn bread."

INGREDIENTS

4 ounces linguine pasta

2 boneless, skinless chicken breast halves, sliced into thin strips

2 teaspoons Cajun seasoning

2 tablespoons butter

1 green bell pepper, chopped

1/2 red bell pepper, chopped

4 fresh mushrooms, sliced

1 green onion, minced

1 1/2 cups heavy cream

1/4 teaspoon dried basil

1/4 teaspoon lemon pepper

1/4 teaspoon salt

1/8 teaspoon garlic powder

1/8 teaspoon ground black pepper

2 tablespoons grated Parmesan cheese

DIRECTIONS

1. Bring a large pot of lightly salted water to a boil. Add linguini pasta, and cook for 8 to 10 minutes, or until al dente; drain.

2. Meanwhile, place chicken and Cajun seasoning in a bowl, and toss to coat.

3. In a large skillet over medium heat, sauté chicken in butter until no longer pink and juices run clear, about 5 to 7 minutes. Add green and red bell peppers, sliced mushrooms and green onions; cook for 2 to 3 minutes. Reduce heat, and stir in heavy cream. Season the sauce with basil, lemon pepper, salt, garlic powder and ground black pepper, and heat through.

4. In a large bowl, toss linguini with sauce. Sprinkle with grated Parmesan cheese.

Greek Chicken Pasta

Submitted by: **Lalena**

Makes: 6 servings

Preparation: 15 minutes

Cooking: 15 minutes

Total: 30 minutes

"This pasta dish incorporates some of the flavors of Greece. It makes a wonderfully complete and satisfying meal. For extra flavor, toss in a few kalamata olives."

INGREDIENTS

1 pound uncooked pasta

1 tablespoon olive oil

2 cloves garlic, crushed

1/2 cup chopped red onion

1 pound skinless, boneless chicken breasts - cut into bite size pieces

1 (14 ounce) can marinated artichoke hearts, drained and chopped

1 large tomato, chopped

1/2 cup crumbled feta cheese

3 tablespoons chopped fresh parsley

2 tablespoons lemon juice

2 teaspoons dried oregano

salt and pepper to taste

2 lemons, wedged, for garnish

DIRECTIONS

1. Bring a large pot of lightly salted water to a boil. Cook pasta in boiling water for 8 to 10 minutes, or until al dente; drain.

2. Meanwhile, heat olive oil in a large skillet over medium-high heat. Add garlic and onion, and sauté for 2 minutes. Stir in the chicken. Cook, stirring occasionally, until chicken is no longer pink and the juices run clear, about 5 to 6 minutes.

3. Reduce heat to medium-low, and add the artichoke hearts, tomato, feta cheese, parsley, lemon juice, oregano and cooked pasta. Stir until heated through, about 2 to 3 minutes. Remove from heat, season to taste with salt and pepper, and garnish with lemon wedges.

Creamy Pesto Shrimp

Submitted by: **Loretta Buffa**

Makes: 6 servings

Preparation: 15 minutes

Cooking: 15 minutes

Total: 30 minutes

"One of our family's favorites, it's also great when made with crab meat instead of the shrimp."

INGREDIENTS

1 pound linguine pasta

½ cup butter

2 cups heavy cream

½ teaspoon ground black pepper

1 cup grated Parmesan cheese

⅓ cup pesto

1 pound large shrimp, peeled and deveined

DIRECTIONS

1. Bring a large pot of lightly salted water to a boil. Add linguine pasta, and cook for 8 to 10 minutes, or until al dente; drain.

2. In a large skillet, melt the butter over medium heat. Stir in cream, and season with pepper. Cook 6 to 8 minutes, stirring constantly.

3. Stir Parmesan cheese into cream sauce, stirring until thoroughly mixed. Blend in the pesto, and cook for 3 to 5 minutes, until thickened.

4. Stir in the shrimp, and cook until they turn pink, about 5 minutes. Serve over the hot linguine.

Angel Hair Pasta with Shrimp and Basil

Submitted by: **Pat Lowe**

Makes: 4 servings

Preparation: 5 minutes

Cooking: 35 minutes

Total: 40 minutes

"If you like the ingredients in the name, you'll love the dish. Freshly grated Parmesan cheese makes it complete."

INGREDIENTS

¼ cup light olive oil

1 (8 ounce) package angel hair pasta

1 teaspoon chopped garlic

1 pound large shrimp - peeled and deveined

2 (28 ounce) cans Italian-style diced tomatoes, drained

½ cup dry white wine

¼ cup chopped parsley

3 tablespoons chopped fresh basil

3 tablespoons grated Parmesan cheese

DIRECTIONS

1. Add 1 tablespoon olive oil to a large pot of lightly salted water, and bring to a boil. Add pasta, and cook until al dente; drain. To keep pasta from sticking together, rinse it quickly with cold water.

2. Heat remaining olive oil in a 10 inch skillet. Cook garlic over medium heat, stirring constantly until the garlic is tender, about 1 minute. Do not let the garlic burn. Add shrimp, and continue stirring until pink, about 3 to 5 minutes. Remove shrimp from the skillet, and set aside.

3. Stir tomatoes, wine, parsley and basil into the skillet. Continue cooking, stirring occasionally, until liquid is reduced by half, 8 to 12 minutes. Return shrimp to the skillet, and continue cooking until the shrimp are heated through, about 2 to 3 minutes. Serve the shrimp mixture over the pasta. Top with Parmesan cheese.

Shrimp Linguine Alfredo

Submitted by: **Tina**

Makes: 4 servings

Preparation: 10 minutes

Cooking: 25 minutes

Total: 35 minutes

"Elegant but simple, fast and very impressive!"

INGREDIENTS

1 (12 ounce) package linguine pasta

¼ cup butter, melted

4 tablespoons diced onion

4 teaspoons minced garlic

40 small shrimp, peeled and deveined

1 cup half-and-half

2 teaspoons ground black pepper

6 tablespoons grated Parmesan cheese

4 sprigs fresh parsley

4 slices lemon, for garnish

DIRECTIONS

1. Cook pasta in a large pot of boiling water until al dente; drain.

2. Meanwhile, melt butter in a large saucepan. Sauté onion and garlic over medium heat until tender. Add shrimp; sauté over high heat for 1 minute, stirring constantly. Stir in half-and-half. Cook, stirring constantly, until sauce thickens.

3. Place pasta in a serving dish, and cover with shrimp sauce. Sprinkle with black pepper and Parmesan cheese. Garnish with parsley and lemon slices.

Arrabbiata Sauce

Submitted by: **Ellen**

Makes: 3 cups

Preparation: 15 minutes

Cooking: 20 minutes

Total: 35 minutes

"Spicy and delicious. Ideal on penne pasta."

INGREDIENTS

1 teaspoon olive oil

1 cup chopped onion

4 cloves garlic, minced

3/8 cup red wine

1 tablespoon white sugar

1 tablespoon chopped fresh basil

1 teaspoon crushed red pepper flakes

2 tablespoons tomato paste

1 tablespoon lemon juice

1/2 teaspoon Italian seasoning

1/4 teaspoon ground black pepper

2 (14.5 ounce) cans peeled and diced tomatoes

2 tablespoons chopped fresh parsley

DIRECTIONS

1. Heat oil in a large skillet or saucepan over medium heat. Sauté onion and garlic in oil for 5 minutes.

2. Stir in wine, sugar, basil, red pepper, tomato paste, lemon juice, Italian seasoning, black pepper and tomatoes; bring to a boil. Reduce heat to medium, and simmer uncovered about 15 minutes.

3. Stir in parsley. Ladle over the hot cooked pasta of your choice.

Fra Diavolo Sauce With Pasta

Submitted by: **Holly**

Makes: 4 servings

Preparation: 20 minutes

Cooking: 20 minutes

Total: 40 minutes

"This sauce includes shrimp and scallops, best served with linguine pasta."

INGREDIENTS

4 tablespoons olive oil

6 cloves garlic, crushed

3 cups whole peeled tomatoes with liquid, chopped

1½ teaspoons salt

1 teaspoon crushed red pepper flakes

1 (16 ounce) package linguine pasta

8 ounces small shrimp, peeled and deveined

8 ounces bay scallops

1 tablespoon chopped fresh parsley

DIRECTIONS

1. In a large saucepan, heat 2 tablespoons of the olive oil with the garlic over medium heat. When the garlic starts to sizzle, pour in the tomatoes. Season with salt and red pepper. Bring to a boil. Lower the heat, and simmer for 30 minutes, stirring occasionally.

2. Meanwhile, bring a large pot of lightly salted water to a boil. Cook pasta for 8 to 10 minutes, or until al dente; drain.

3. In another skillet, heat the remaining 2 tablespoons of olive oil over high heat. Add the shrimp and scallops. Cook for about 2 minutes, stirring frequently, or until the shrimp turn pink. Add shrimp and scallops to the tomato mixture, and stir in the parsley. Cook for 3 to 4 minutes, or until the sauce just begins to bubble. Serve sauce over pasta.

American Lasagna

Submitted by: **Rosemary Stoker**

Makes: 8 servings

Preparation: 30 minutes

Cooking: 1 hour 30 minutes

Total: 4 hours 30 minutes

"Making this lasagna a day ahead and refrigerating overnight allows the spices to meld, and gives it exceptional flavor."

INGREDIENTS

1½ pounds ground beef

1 onion, chopped

2 cloves garlic, minced

1 tablespoon chopped fresh basil

1 teaspoon dried oregano

2 tablespoons brown sugar

1½ teaspoons salt

1 (29 ounce) can diced tomatoes

2 (6 ounce) cans tomato paste

12 dry lasagna noodles

2 eggs, beaten

1 pint part-skim ricotta cheese

½ cup grated Parmesan cheese

2 tablespoons dried parsley

1 teaspoon salt

1 pound mozzarella cheese, shredded

2 tablespoons grated Parmesan cheese

DIRECTIONS

1. In a medium skillet over medium heat, brown ground beef, onion and garlic; drain fat. Mix in basil, oregano, brown sugar, 1½ teaspoons salt, diced tomatoes and tomato paste. Simmer for 30 to 45 minutes, stirring occasionally.

2. Preheat oven to 375°F (190°C). Bring a large pot of lightly salted water to a boil. Add lasagna noodles, and cook for 5 to 8 minutes, or until al dente; drain. Lay noodles flat on towels, and blot dry.

3. In a medium bowl, mix together eggs, ricotta, Parmesan cheese, parsley and 1 teaspoon salt.

4. Layer ⅓ of the lasagna noodles in the bottom of a 9x13 inch baking dish. Cover noodles with ½ ricotta mixture, ½ of the mozzarella cheese and ⅓ of the sauce. Repeat. Top with remaining noodles and sauce. Sprinkle additional Parmesan cheese over the top.

5. Bake in the preheated oven 30 minutes. Let stand 10 minutes before serving.

Bob's Awesome Lasagna

Submitted by: **Bob**

Makes: 1 - 9x13 inch pan
Preparation: 30 minutes
Cooking: 1 hour
Total: 1 hour 30 minutes

"This is a traditional baked lasagna that is a favorite in our family. Ground beef, cottage cheese, and mozzarella make it rich and filling."

INGREDIENTS

8 ounces lasagna noodles

1 pound ground beef

¼ cup minced onions

1 teaspoon salt

½ teaspoon garlic salt

1 (32 ounce) jar spaghetti sauce

1 (16 ounce) package large curd cottage cheese

1 pound mozzarella cheese, shredded

DIRECTIONS

1. Bring a large pot of lightly salted water to a boil. Cook noodles in boiling water for 8 to 10 minutes, or until al dente; drain.

2. In a large skillet over medium heat, sauté ground beef, onions, salt and garlic salt until meat is brown. Drain excess fat, add spaghetti sauce to beef mixture, and bring to a boil. Reduce heat, and simmer for 15 to 20 minutes.

3. Preheat oven to 350°F (175°C). Grease a 9x13 inch glass baking pan.

4. Line bottom of pan with three lasagna noodles. Spread ⅓ of sauce mixture over noodles. Layer ⅓ of the cottage cheese over the sauce. Sprinkle ⅓ of the mozzarella over the cottage cheese. Repeat this layering process until all ingredients are used up.

5. Bake in the preheated oven for one hour. Let stand for 10 minutes before serving.

Baked Spaghetti

Submitted by: **LaDonna**

Makes: 8 servings

Preparation: 10 minutes

Cooking: 45 minutes

Total: 1 hour 5 minutes

"Make this tasty dish ahead of time, and cook it when needed. Allow a little extra cooking time if you make this ahead and refrigerate."

INGREDIENTS

12 ounces spaghetti

1 cup chopped onions

1 cup chopped green bell peppers

1 pound ground beef

1 (16 ounce) can diced tomatoes

1 (4.5 ounce) can mushrooms, drained

1 teaspoon dried oregano

2 cups shredded mild Cheddar cheese

1 (10.75 ounce) can condensed cream of mushroom soup

¼ cup water

¼ cup grated Parmesan cheese

DIRECTIONS

1. Bring a large pot of lightly salted water to a boil. Add spaghetti, and cook for 8 to 10 minutes, or until al dente. Drain, and set aside.

2. In a large skillet over medium-high heat, sauté the onions, green peppers and ground beef. Once beef is brown and onions and peppers softened, add the tomatoes, mushrooms and oregano. Simmer uncovered for 10 minutes.

3. Preheat oven to 350°F (175°C). Grease a 9x13 inch baking dish. Place half of the cooked spaghetti into the prepared dish. Top with half of the meat mixture. Sprinkle with 1 cup of the mild Cheddar cheese. Repeat. In a medium bowl, mix together cream of mushroom soup and water until smooth; pour over casserole. Sprinkle with Parmesan cheese.

4. Bake in preheated oven for 30 to 35 minutes. Let stand 10 minutes before serving.

Baked Ziti

Submitted by: **Colleen B. Smith**

Makes: 8 servings

Preparation: 20 minutes

Cooking: 30 minutes

Total: 50 minutes

"A lady I worked with brought this in one day, and it was a hit. Now it is the favorite of all my dinner guests. It's great for a covered dish dinner too. I have made this also without the meat, and it is well received."

INGREDIENTS

1 pound dry ziti pasta

1 onion, chopped

1 pound ground beef

2 (26 ounce) jars spaghetti sauce

6 ounces Provolone cheese, sliced

1½ cups sour cream

6 ounces mozzarella cheese, shredded

2 tablespoons grated Parmesan cheese

DIRECTIONS

1. Bring a large pot of lightly salted water to a boil. Add ziti pasta, and cook until al dente, about 8 minutes; drain.

2. In a large skillet, brown onion and ground beef over medium heat. Add spaghetti sauce, and simmer 15 minutes.

3. Preheat the oven to 350°F (175°C). Butter a 9x13 inch baking dish. Layer as follows: ½ of the ziti, Provolone cheese, sour cream, ½ sauce mixture, remaining ziti, mozzarella cheese and remaining sauce mixture. Top with grated Parmesan cheese.

4. Bake for 30 minutes in the preheated oven, or until cheeses are melted.

Make Ahead Manicotti

Submitted by: **Sandir**

Makes: 6 servings
Preparation: 30 minutes
Cooking: 1 hour
Total: 1 hour 30 minutes

"I have used this basic principle and adapted it to make stuffed shells and lasagna. If making lasagna, I buy a second, smaller jar of spaghetti sauce. I always feel like I need a bit more. Merry Manicotti!"

INGREDIENTS

1 pint ricotta cheese

2 eggs

1 (10 ounce) package frozen chopped spinach, thawed and drained

1 cup shredded mozzarella cheese

1/2 cup grated Parmesan cheese

1 1/2 tablespoons white sugar

1/8 teaspoon salt

1/4 teaspoon ground black pepper

12 manicotti shells

1 (32 ounce) jar spaghetti sauce

DIRECTIONS

1. In a medium bowl, mix together ricotta cheese and eggs until blended. Stir in spinach, mozzarella cheese, 1/4 cup of the Parmesan cheese, sugar, salt and pepper. Stuff mixture into uncooked pasta shells.

2. Spread 1/2 cup spaghetti sauce in the bottom of a medium baking dish. Arrange stuffed pasta shells in a single layer over the sauce. Pour the remainder of the sauce over the shells, cover dish, and chill in the refrigerator for 8 hours, or overnight.

3. Preheat oven to 400°F (200°C). Bake covered for 40 minutes. Sprinkle with remaining Parmesan cheese, and bake for another 15 minutes.

Mexican Lasagna

Submitted by: **Shannon R.**

"A different twist on lasagna! Easy to make!"

Makes: 12 servings

Preparation: 30 minutes

Cooking: 1 hour 30 minutes

Total: 2 hours

INGREDIENTS

1 pound extra-lean ground beef

1 (16 ounce) can refried beans

2 teaspoons dried oregano

1 teaspoon ground cumin

3/4 teaspoon garlic powder

12 dry lasagna noodles

2½ cups water

2½ cups salsa

2 cups sour cream

3/4 cup chopped green onions

1 (2 ounce) can sliced black olives

1 cup shredded Pepper Jack cheese

DIRECTIONS

1. In a large skillet, cook the ground beef over medium-high heat until evenly brown. Drain off excess fat. In a large bowl, combine the cooked beef, refried beans, oregano, cumin and garlic powder.

2. Place four of the uncooked lasagna noodles in the bottom of a 9x13 inch baking dish. Spread half of the beef mixture over the noodles. Top with 4 more uncooked noodles and the remaining half of the beef mixture. Cover with remaining noodles. Combine the water and the salsa in a medium bowl, and pour over all.

3. Cover tightly with foil. Bake at 350°F (175°C) for 1½ hours, or until noodles are tender.

4. In a medium bowl, combine the sour cream, green onions and olives. Spoon over casserole, and top with shredded cheese. Return to the oven, and bake for an additional 5 to 10 minutes, or until cheese is melted.

Best Tuna Casserole

Submitted by: **Jennifer**

Makes: 6 servings

Preparation: 15 minutes

Cooking: 20 minutes

Total: 35 minutes

"This is a tuna casserole that even my picky family loves! The potato chips give the casserole a crunchy crust."

INGREDIENTS

1 (12 ounce) package egg noodles

¼ cup chopped onion

2 cups shredded Cheddar cheese

1 cup frozen green peas

2 (6 ounce) cans tuna, drained

2 (10.75 ounce) cans condensed cream of mushroom soup

½ (4.5 ounce) can sliced mushrooms

1 cup crushed potato chips

DIRECTIONS

1. Bring a large pot of lightly salted water to a boil. Cook pasta in boiling water for 8 to 10 minutes, or until al dente; drain.

2. Preheat oven to 425°F (220°C).

3. In a large bowl, thoroughly mix noodles, onion, 1 cup cheese, peas, tuna, soup and mushrooms. Transfer to a 9x13 inch baking dish, and top with potato chip crumbs and remaining 1 cup cheese.

4. Bake for 15 to 20 minutes in the preheated oven, or until cheese is bubbly.

beef & pork

Whether you're seeking special occasion indulgences or quick, easy weeknight cooking, this collection of recipes for beef and pork will serve you well. In the pages that follow, you'll find some traditional and beloved stand-bys in top form, fancy and festive dishes that are surprisingly easy to make at home, plus lots of thrilling new recipes that you may not have tried before!

Beef Wellington

Submitted by: **Normala**

Makes: 6 servings

Preparation: 30 minutes

Cooking: 30 minutes

Total: 1 hour

"This is a very easy recipe that I learned when I was living in England. Note that Beef Wellington should always be served with the center slightly pink. Enjoy!"

INGREDIENTS

2½ pounds beef tenderloin

2 tablespoons butter, softened

2 tablespoons butter

1 onion, chopped

½ cup sliced fresh mushrooms

2 ounces liver pâté

2 tablespoons butter, softened

salt and pepper to taste

1 (17.5 ounce) package frozen puff pastry, thawed

1 egg yolk, beaten

1 (10.5 ounce) can beef broth

2 tablespoons red wine

DIRECTIONS

1. Preheat oven to 425°F (220°C). Place beef in a small baking dish, and spread with 2 tablespoons softened butter. Bake for 10 to 15 minutes, or until browned. Remove from pan, and allow to cool completely. Reserve pan juices.

2. Melt 2 tablespoons butter in a skillet over medium heat. Sauté onion and mushrooms in butter for 5 minutes. Remove from heat, and let cool.

3. Mix together pâté and 2 tablespoons softened butter, and season with salt and pepper. Spread pâté over beef. Top with onion and mushroom mixture.

4. Roll out the puff pastry dough, and place beef in the center. Fold up, and seal all the edges, making sure the seams are not too thick. Place beef in a 9x13 inch baking dish, cut a few slits in the top of the dough, and brush with egg yolk.

5. Bake at 450°F (230°C) for 10 minutes, then reduce heat to 425°F (220°C) for 10 to 15 more minutes, or until pastry is a rich, golden brown. Set aside, and keep warm.

6. Place all reserved juices in a small saucepan over high heat. Stir in beef stock and red wine; boil for 10 to 15 minutes, or until slightly reduced. Strain, and serve with beef.

Lover's Beef Burgundy Filet

Submitted by: **Penelope Holmes**

Makes: 8 servings

Preparation: 40 minutes

Cooking: 20 minutes

Total: 6 hours 40 minutes

"One must be very careful who this is prepared for. Like a magic love potion, it brings out the lover in ANYone. Through trial and error, I learned very quickly not to prepare this for a mere 'casual date' UNLESS you want that 'casual date' to become 'more'...."

INGREDIENTS

4 cups Burgundy wine

1½ cups canola oil

1½ cups soy sauce

2 cups oyster sauce

1 tablespoon minced garlic

1½ teaspoons dried oregano

8 (6 ounce) filets mignons

½ cup butter, softened

1 teaspoon Burgundy wine

1 tablespoon minced shallots

1 tablespoon minced green onions

1 teaspoon ground white pepper

DIRECTIONS

1. In a medium saucepan, mix together Burgundy wine, canola oil, soy sauce, oyster sauce, garlic and oregano. Bring to a boil, and then remove from heat. Place in the refrigerator 1 hour, or until chilled.

2. Place filet mignon filets in a 9x13 inch baking dish, and pour the chilled marinade over them. Cover tightly with foil, and refrigerate for a minimum of 5 hours.

3. In a medium bowl, cream butter and 1 teaspoon of Burgundy wine with a hand mixer. Mix in shallots, green onions and white pepper by hand; cover tightly, and refrigerate.

4. Preheat an outdoor grill for high heat, and lightly oil grate. Preheat oven to 200°F (95°C).

5. Grill marinated filets to desired doneness, turning once. Place filets in a clean 9x13 inch baking dish. Dollop with the Burgundy butter mixture, and place in the preheated oven for a minute, or until butter is melted.

Sirloin Steak with Garlic Butter

Submitted by: **Solana**

Makes: 8 servings

Preparation: 20 minutes

Cooking: 10 minutes

Total: 30 minutes

"I have never tasted any other steak that came even close to the ones made with this recipe. If you are having steak, don't skimp on flavor to save a few calories. The butter makes this steak melt in your mouth wonderful."

INGREDIENTS

½ cup butter

2 teaspoons garlic powder

4 cloves garlic, minced

4 pounds beef top sirloin steak

salt and pepper to taste

DIRECTIONS

1. Preheat an outdoor grill for high heat.

2. In a small saucepan, melt butter over medium-low heat with garlic powder and minced garlic. Set aside.

3. Sprinkle both sides of each steak with salt and pepper.

4. Grill steaks 4 to 5 minutes per side, or to desired doneness. When done, transfer to warmed plates. Brush tops liberally with garlic butter, and allow to rest for 2 to 3 minutes before serving.

Savory Garlic Marinated Steaks

Submitted by: **Angie Zayac**

Makes: 2 servings

Preparation: 15 minutes

Cooking: 15 minutes

Total: 24 hours 30 minutes

"This beautiful marinade adds an exquisite flavor to these already tender steaks. The final result will be so tender and juicy, it will melt in your mouth."

INGREDIENTS

½ cup balsamic vinegar

¼ cup soy sauce

3 tablespoons minced garlic

2 tablespoons honey

2 tablespoons olive oil

2 teaspoons ground black pepper

1 teaspoon Worcestershire sauce

1 teaspoon onion powder

½ teaspoon salt

½ teaspoon liquid smoke flavoring

1 pinch cayenne pepper

2 (1/2 pound) beef rib eye steaks

DIRECTIONS

1. In a medium bowl, combine the vinegar, soy sauce, garlic, honey, olive oil, ground black pepper, Worcestershire sauce, onion powder, salt, liquid smoke and cayenne pepper.

2. Place steaks in a shallow, nonporous dish, and pour marinade over steaks. For optimum flavor, rub the liquid into the meat. Cover, and let marinate in the refrigerator for 24 to 48 hours.

3. Preheat an outdoor grill for medium-high to high heat.

4. Grill steaks for 7 to 8 minutes per side on a lightly oiled grate, or until internal temperature reaches at least 145°F (63°C).

Barbequed Marinated Flank Steak

Submitted by: Martha Dibblee

Makes: 4 servings

Preparation: 20 minutes

Cooking: 20 minutes

Total: 8 hours 40 minutes

"My butcher Harry at the Eastmoreland Grocery gave me this recipe about 30 years ago. It's easy to make, uses ordinary ingredients, and is delicious barbequed or oven broiled."

INGREDIENTS

¼ cup soy sauce

3 tablespoons honey

2 tablespoons distilled white vinegar

½ teaspoon ground ginger

½ teaspoon garlic powder

½ cup vegetable oil

1½ pounds flank steak

DIRECTIONS

1. In a blender, combine soy sauce, honey, vinegar, ginger, garlic powder and vegetable oil. Blend for 15 seconds.

2. Lay steak in a shallow glass or ceramic dish. Pierce flesh all over front and back with a sharp fork. Pour marinade over steak, then turn and coat the other side. Cover, and chill in the refrigerator 8 hours, or overnight.

3. Preheat an outdoor grill for high heat.

4. Place grate on highest level, and brush lightly with oil. Grill steak for 15 to 20 minutes, turning once, to desired doneness.

China Lake Barbequed Steak

Submitted by: **Bobbie**

Makes: 4 servings

Preparation: 10 minutes

Cooking: 10 minutes

Total: 4 hours 20 minutes

"I made this for my family when I was a Navy wife with three children with healthy appetites. This recipe will make the most inexpensive cuts very tender."

INGREDIENTS

1½ pounds flank steak

½ cup soy sauce

1 lemon, juiced

½ tablespoon garlic powder

¼ cup vegetable oil

DIRECTIONS

1. Mix soy sauce, lemon juice and oil together in a large resealable plastic bag. Rub garlic power into meat, and add to bag. Marinate in the refrigerator for at least 4 hours; turn bag over every 2 hours.

2. Preheat grill for medium heat.

3. Oil grate lightly, and place meat on grill. Cook over medium heat for 5 to 7 minutes per side, or until done.

London Broil II

Submitted by: **Jill**

Makes: 8 servings

Preparation: 30 minutes

Cooking: 15 minutes

Total: 5 hours 45 minutes

"The marinade is so flavorful you'll skip the steak sauce."

INGREDIENTS

1 clove garlic, minced

1 teaspoon salt

3 tablespoons soy sauce

1 tablespoon ketchup

1 tablespoon vegetable oil

1/2 teaspoon ground black pepper

1/2 teaspoon dried oregano

4 pounds flank steak

DIRECTIONS

1. In a small bowl, mix together garlic, salt, soy sauce, ketchup, vegetable oil, black pepper and oregano.

2. Score both sides of the meat, diamond cut, about 1/8 inch deep. Rub garlic mixture into both sides of the meat. Wrap tightly in aluminum foil, and refrigerate for 5 to 6 hours, or overnight. Flip meat every few hours.

3. Preheat an outdoor grill for high heat, and lightly oil grate.

4. Place meat on the prepared grill. Cook for 3 to 7 minutes per side, or to desired doneness.

Chicken Fried Steak

Submitted by: **Barbara**

Makes: 4 servings

Preparation: 15 minutes

Cooking: 30 minutes

Total: 45 minutes

"Breaded and deep fried beef cutlets are known as chicken fried steak because of the similarity in cooking method to fried chicken. This is a family recipe that we have used for years. Vegetable oil may be used in place of shortening for frying."

INGREDIENTS

1 pound boneless beef top loin

2 cups shortening

1 egg, beaten

1 cup buttermilk

salt and pepper to taste

¼ teaspoon garlic powder

1 cup all-purpose flour

¼ cup all-purpose flour

1 quart milk

salt and pepper to taste

DIRECTIONS

1. Cut top loin crosswise into 4 (4 ounce) cutlets. Using a glancing motion, pound each cutlet thinly with a moistened mallet or the side of a cleaver.

2. In a large, heavy skillet, heat ½ inch shortening to 365°F (185°C).

3. While the shortening is heating, prepare cutlets. In a shallow bowl, beat together egg, buttermilk, salt and pepper. In another shallow dish, mix together garlic powder and 1 cup flour. Dip cutlets in flour, turning to evenly coat both sides. Dip in egg mixture, coating both sides, then in flour mixture once again.

4. Place cutlets in heated shortening. Cook until golden brown, turning once. Transfer to a plate lined with paper towels. Repeat with remaining cutlets.

5. Using the drippings in the pan, prepare gravy over medium heat. To ½ cup drippings, blend in ¼ cup flour to form a paste. Gradually add milk to desired consistency, stirring constantly. For a thicker gravy add less milk; for a thinner gravy stir in more. Heat through, and season with salt and pepper to taste. Serve over chicken fried steak.

Salisbury Steak

Submitted by: **Kelly Berenger**

Makes: 6 servings

Preparation: 20 minutes

Cooking: 20 minutes

Total: 40 minutes

"This recipe has been in my family for years. It's easy to cook, but tastes like it took hours to make! I usually make enough extra sauce to pour over mashed potatoes. YUM!"

INGREDIENTS

1 (10.5 ounce) can condensed French onion soup

1½ pounds ground beef

½ cup dry bread crumbs

1 egg

¼ teaspoon salt

⅛ teaspoon ground black pepper

1 tablespoon all-purpose flour

¼ cup ketchup

¼ cup water

1 tablespoon Worcestershire sauce

½ teaspoon mustard powder

DIRECTIONS

1. In a large bowl, mix together ⅓ cup condensed French onion soup with ground beef, bread crumbs, egg, salt and black pepper. Shape into 6 oval patties.

2. In a large skillet over medium-high heat, brown both sides of patties. Pour off excess fat.

3. In a small bowl, blend flour and remaining soup until smooth. Mix in ketchup, water, Worcestershire sauce and mustard powder. Pour over meat in skillet. Cover, and cook for 20 minutes, stirring occasionally.

Sweet and Sour Meatballs II

Submitted by: **Cathy**

Makes: 5 servings

Preparation: 5 minutes

Cooking: 15 minutes

Total: 20 minutes

"I got this recipe from my mother-in-law shortly after I was married. Now it is a favorite of our kids. I like to serve it over rice."

INGREDIENTS

1 pound ground beef

1 egg

1 onion, chopped

1 cup dry bread crumbs

salt and pepper to taste

1 cup water

½ cup cider vinegar

½ cup ketchup

2 tablespoons cornstarch

1 cup brown sugar

2 tablespoons soy sauce

DIRECTIONS

1. In a large bowl, combine beef, egg, onion, bread crumbs, salt and pepper. Roll into meatballs about 1 to 1½ inches in size.

2. In a large skillet over medium heat, sauté the meatballs until browned on all sides.

3. In a separate medium bowl, mix together the water, vinegar, ketchup, cornstarch, sugar and soy sauce. Pour over the meatballs, and allow sauce to thicken. Continue to heat until the sauce just starts to bubble.

Tantalizingly Tangy Meatloaf

Submitted by: **Stacy B.**

Makes: 8 servings
Preparation: 15 minutes
Cooking: 30 minutes
Total: 45 minutes

"Meatloaf with a sauce that will keep them coming back for more. The sauce contains pineapple preserves, brown sugar and ketchup. It glazes up real nice over the meatloaf. I've NEVER had leftovers even when I've tripled the recipe!"

INGREDIENTS

1 pound ground beef

1/2 cup dry bread crumbs

1 egg

garlic powder to taste

1 dash Worcestershire sauce

1/3 cup ketchup

1/4 cup packed brown sugar

1/4 cup pineapple preserves

DIRECTIONS

1. Preheat oven to 350°F (175°C).

2. In a large bowl, combine the ground beef, bread crumbs, egg, garlic powder and Worcestershire sauce. Mix well, and place into a 9x5 inch loaf pan.

3. Bake in preheated oven for 30 to 50 minutes.

4. Meanwhile, in a separate medium bowl, stir together the ketchup, brown sugar and pineapple preserves. Pour over the meatloaf about 20 minutes before removing from oven.

Italian Style Meatloaf

Submitted by: **Stefanie Sierk**

Makes: 6 servings

Preparation: 15 minutes

Cooking: 1 hour

Total: 1 hour 15 minutes

"Made with mozzarella cheese and Italian seasoning, this is a different twist on everyday meatloaf! Enjoy!"

INGREDIENTS

1½ pounds ground beef

2 eggs, beaten

¾ cup dry bread crumbs

¼ cup ketchup

1 teaspoon Italian-style seasoning

1 teaspoon dried oregano

1 teaspoon dried basil

1 teaspoon garlic salt

1 (14.5 ounce) can diced tomatoes, drained

1½ cups shredded mozzarella cheese

DIRECTIONS

1. Preheat oven to 350°F (175°C).

2. In a large bowl, mix together ground beef, eggs, bread crumbs and ketchup. Season with Italian-style seasoning, oregano, basil, garlic salt, diced tomatoes and cheese. Press into a 9x5 inch loaf pan, and cover loosely with foil.

3. Bake in the preheated oven approximately 1 hour, or until internal temperature reaches 160°F (70°C).

Emily's Famous Sloppy Joes

Submitted by: **Emily**

Makes: 8 servings

Preparation: 10 minutes

Cooking: 20 minutes

Total: 30 minutes

"This is just a good old-fashioned Sloppy Joe recipe. Just slap some on a bun and enjoy!"

INGREDIENTS

1½ pounds ground beef

1 onion, chopped

1 red bell pepper, chopped

1 (6 ounce) can tomato paste

1 cup water

3 cloves garlic, minced

1 tablespoon chili powder

1 teaspoon paprika

1 teaspoon ground cumin

1 teaspoon distilled white vinegar

3 tablespoons brown sugar

1 teaspoon dried oregano

½ teaspoon salt

½ teaspoon ground black pepper

DIRECTIONS

1. In a large skillet over medium-high heat, sauté the ground beef for 5 minutes. Add the onion and red bell pepper; sauté for 5 more minutes, or until onion is tender. Drain the fat.

2. Mix in tomato paste and water, stirring until paste is dissolved. Stir in garlic, chili powder, paprika, cumin, vinegar, brown sugar, oregano, salt and pepper. Continue to heat for 5 to 10 minutes, or until mixture is thick and stewy.

Burrito Pie

Submitted by: **Kathi J. McClaren**

Makes: 7 servings

Preparation: 30 minutes

Cooking: 30 minutes

Total: 1 hour

"This is a lot like a lasagna, only Mexican-style! Serve like a pie and garnish with sour cream, salsa, lettuce and tomato. Make sure you like spicy foods before trying this one. It's hot!"

INGREDIENTS

2 pounds ground beef

1 onion, chopped

2 teaspoons minced garlic

1 (2 ounce) can black olives, sliced

1 (4 ounce) can diced green chili peppers

1 (16 ounce) jar taco sauce

1 (10 ounce) can diced tomatoes with green chile peppers

2 (16 ounce) cans refried beans

12 (8 inch) flour tortillas

9 ounces shredded Colby cheese

DIRECTIONS

1. Preheat oven to 350°F (175°C).

2. In a large skillet over medium heat, sauté the ground beef for 5 minutes. Add the onion and garlic, and sauté for 5 more minutes. Drain any excess fat, if desired. Mix in the olives, green chile peppers, tomatoes with green chile peppers, taco sauce and refried beans. Stir mixture thoroughly, reduce heat to low, and let simmer for 15 to 20 minutes.

3. Spread a thin layer of the meat mixture in the bottom of a 4 quart casserole dish. Cover with a layer of tortillas followed by more meat mixture, then a layer of cheese. Repeat tortilla, meat, cheese pattern until all the tortillas are used, topping off with a layer of meat mixture and cheese.

4. Bake for 20 to 30 minutes in the preheated oven, or until cheese is slightly brown and bubbly.

Taco Bake

Submitted by: **Leslie**

Makes: 8 servings

Preparation: 15 minutes

Cooking: 25 minutes

Total: 40 minutes

"This is a wonderful Tex-Mex dish to serve to guests or your family. Serve with tortilla chips."

INGREDIENTS

1½ pounds ground beef

1 (1.25 ounce) package taco seasoning mix

1 (16 ounce) can refried beans

1 (16 ounce) jar salsa

2 cups shredded Monterey Jack cheese

DIRECTIONS

1. Preheat oven to 325°F (160°C).

2. In a large, heavy skillet over medium-high heat, brown ground beef, and drain fat. Mix in dry taco seasoning.

3. Spoon browned meat into a 9x13 inch glass baking dish. Spoon a layer of refried beans over meat, then salsa. Top with shredded cheese.

4. Bake about 20 to 25 minutes in the preheated oven.

Stuffed Green Peppers

Submitted by: **Suzanne M. Munson**

Makes: 6 servings

Preparation: 30 minutes

Cooking: 30 minutes

Total: 1 hour

"Here's a delicious stuffed pepper recipe that's easy to make. Each green bell pepper contains ground beef, onion, tomatoes, rice and cheese, and is cooked in tomato soup."

INGREDIENTS

6 green bell peppers

salt to taste

1 pound ground beef

1/3 cup chopped onion

salt and pepper to taste

1 (14.5 ounce) can whole peeled tomatoes, chopped

1 teaspoon Worcestershire sauce

1/2 cup uncooked rice

1/2 cup water

1 cup shredded Cheddar cheese

2 (10.75 ounce) cans condensed tomato soup

water as needed

DIRECTIONS

1. Bring a large pot of salted water to a boil. Cut the tops off the peppers, and remove the seeds. Cook peppers in boiling water for 5 minutes; drain. Sprinkle salt inside each pepper, and set aside.

2. In a large skillet, sauté beef and onions for 5 minutes, or until beef is browned. Drain off excess fat, and season with salt and pepper. Stir in the tomatoes, rice, 1/2 cup water and Worcestershire sauce. Cover, and simmer for 15 minutes, or until rice is tender. Remove from heat, and stir in the cheese.

3. Preheat the oven to 350°F. (175°C). Stuff each pepper with the beef and rice mixture, and place peppers open side up in a baking dish. In a medium bowl, combine tomato soup with just enough water to make the soup a gravy consistency. Pour over the peppers.

4. Bake covered for 25 to 35 minutes, until heated through and cheese is melted and bubbly.

Tater Tot Bake

Submitted by: **Charlie**

Makes: 6 servings

Preparation: 20 minutes

Cooking: 40 minutes

Total: 1 hour

"This is ground beef and onions covered with tater tots, creamy mushroom soup and shredded Cheddar cheese. Even picky eaters love it!"

INGREDIENTS

1 pound ground beef

1 onion, chopped

salt and pepper to taste

½ (32 ounce) package tater tots

1 (10.75 ounce) can condensed cream of mushroom soup

½ cup milk

1½ cups shredded Cheddar cheese

DIRECTIONS

1. Preheat oven to 350°F (175°C).

2. In a large skillet over medium-high heat, brown the ground beef with the onions. Drain excess fat, and season with salt and pepper to taste.

3. Spread the beef mixture evenly over the bottom of a 2 quart casserole dish. Arrange tater tots evenly over beef layer. In a small bowl, stir the soup into the milk until smooth; pour over tater tot and beef layers. Sprinkle Cheddar cheese evenly over the top.

4. Bake in preheated oven for 30 to 40 minutes, until cheese is bubbly and slightly brown.

Cola Pot Roast II

Submitted by: **Sher Garfield**

Makes: 16 servings

Preparation: 15 minutes

Cooking: 5 hours

Total: 5 hours 15 minutes

"The rich brown gravy this makes is wonderful, with just a slight hint of sweetness. Everyone asks for the recipe, and NO ONE ever guesses the secret ingredient...cola!"

INGREDIENTS

4 pounds beef sirloin roast

3 carrots, chopped

3 stalks celery, chopped

1 clove garlic, minced

1/2 (.75 ounce) package dry brown gravy mix

2 tablespoons water

1 (1 ounce) package dry onion soup mix

1 (10.75 ounce) can condensed cream of mushroom soup

10 fluid ounces cola-flavored carbonated beverage

DIRECTIONS

1. Preheat oven to 350°F (175°C).

2. Place meat in a roasting pan. Sprinkle carrots, celery and minced garlic around roast.

3. In a small bowl, combine the brown gravy mix and water, mixing into a smooth paste. Add onion soup mix, cream of mushroom soup and cola-flavored carbonated beverage. Pour over the roast.

4. Cover pan, and cook 1 hour in the preheated oven.

5. Reduce oven temperature to 225°F (110°C), and continue cooking 2 hours. Remove from oven, and turn roast over so that the top is now covered with the gravy. Cover pan, and return to oven for a minimum of 2 hours.

6. Remove from oven, and let meat rest for 10 minutes before slicing.

Pot Roast in Beer

Submitted by: **Christine Johnson**

Makes: 6 servings

Preparation: 15 minutes

Cooking: 2 hours 15 minutes

Total: 2 hours 30 minutes

"What could be better together than beer and meat? Beer helps to make this roast moist, succulent and flavorful."

INGREDIENTS

2 pounds top round steak, trimmed

2 tablespoons vegetable oil

1 onion, chopped

2 stalks celery, chopped

1 clove garlic, minced

1 (10.75 ounce) can condensed cream of mushroom soup

1 (12 fluid ounce) can or bottle beer

2 bay leaves

2 whole cloves

DIRECTIONS

1. Heat a roasting pan over high heat, and coat bottom with oil. Sear meat on all sides. Remove from pan, and set aside.

2. Reduce heat to low, sauté onion, celery and garlic, scraping up browned bits. Cover, and cook on low for 15 minutes.

3. Mix in cream of mushroom soup and beer. Wrap bay leaves and cloves in cheesecloth, tie with string, and add to pan. Place roast on top of vegetables, spooning some sauce over meat. Cover with foil, and place lid over foil to seal well. Reduce heat, and simmer 1½ hours.

4. Remove meat from pan, and slice. Return to the pan, and spoon sauce over. Cook an additional 30 minutes.

Awesome Slow Cooker Pot Roast

Submitted by: **Brenda Arnold**

Makes: 12 servings

Preparation: 10 minutes

Cooking: 8 hours

Total: 8 hours 10 minutes

"This is a very easy recipe for a delicious pot roast. It makes its own gravy. It's designed especially for the working person who does not have time to cook all day, but it tastes like you did. You'll want the cut to be between 5 and 6 pounds."

INGREDIENTS

2 (10.75 ounce) cans condensed cream of mushroom soup

1 (1 ounce) package dry onion soup mix

1¼ cups water

5½ pounds pot roast

DIRECTIONS

1. In a slow cooker, mix cream of mushroom soup, dry onion soup mix and water. Place pot roast in slow cooker and coat with soup mixture.

2. Cook on High setting for 3 to 4 hours, or on Low setting for 8 to 9 hours.

Slow Cooker Barbeque

Submitted by: **Brandy**

Makes: 8 servings

Preparation: 25 minutes

Cooking: 9 hours

Total: 9 hours 25 minutes

"This is an old recipe my mom used to make for us kids. It is so good it almost melts in your mouth! Serve on sub rolls."

INGREDIENTS

3 pounds beef chuck roast

1 teaspoon garlic powder

1 teaspoon onion powder

salt and pepper to taste

1 (18 ounce) bottle barbeque sauce

DIRECTIONS

1. Place beef chuck roast into slow cooker. Sprinkle with garlic powder and onion powder, and season with salt and pepper. Pour barbeque sauce over meat. Cook on Low for 6 to 8 hours.

2. Remove meat from slow cooker, shred, and return to slow cooker. Cook for 1 more hour. Serve hot.

Barbecued Beef

Submitted by: **Corwynn Darkholme**

Makes: 12 servings

Preparation: 20 minutes

Cooking: 10 hours

Total: 10 hours 20 minutes

"This dish is zesty and yummy! It is very easy to make, as well as very deserving of 3 exclamation points!!! Spoon meat onto toasted sandwich buns, and top with additional barbecue sauce."

INGREDIENTS

1½ cups ketchup

¼ cup packed brown sugar

¼ cup red wine vinegar

2 tablespoons prepared Dijon-style mustard

2 tablespoons Worcestershire sauce

1 teaspoon liquid smoke flavoring

½ teaspoon salt

¼ teaspoon ground black pepper

¼ teaspoon garlic powder

4 pounds boneless chuck roast

DIRECTIONS

1. In a large bowl, combine ketchup, brown sugar, red wine vinegar, Dijon-style mustard, Worcestershire sauce and liquid smoke. Stir in salt, pepper and garlic powder.

2. Place chuck roast in a slow cooker. Pour ketchup mixture over chuck roast. Cover, and cook on Low for 8 to 10 hours.

3. Remove chuck roast from slow cooker, shred with a fork, and return to the slow cooker. Stir meat to evenly coat with sauce. Continue cooking approximately 1 hour.

Easy Slow Cooker French Dip

Submitted by: **Robyn Bloomquist**

Makes: 6 servings

Preparation: 10 minutes

Cooking: 7 hours

Total: 7 hours 10 minutes

"This makes a delicious French dip sandwich, perfect for the working mom! Nobody, not even teetotalers, have been able to detect the presence of beer in this recipe, but it adds a wonderful flavor! French fries make a great side dish, and they are good for dipping, too."

INGREDIENTS

4 pounds rump roast

1 (10.5 ounce) can beef broth

1 (10.5 ounce) can condensed French onion soup

1 (12 fluid ounce) can or bottle beer

6 French rolls

2 tablespoons butter

DIRECTIONS

1. Trim excess fat from the rump roast, and place in a slow cooker. Add the beef broth, onion soup and beer. Cook on Low setting for 7 hours.

2. Preheat oven to 350°F (175°C).

3. Split French rolls, and spread with butter. Bake 10 minutes, or until heated through.

4. Slice the meat on the diagonal, and place on the rolls. Serve the sauce for dipping.

Slow Cooker Beef Stroganoff

Submitted by: **Jessica**

Makes: 4 servings

Preparation: 10 minutes

Cooking: 8 hours

Total: 8 hours 10 minutes

"This is an easy variation of a favorite. I used to prepare it the traditional way, with sour cream, but I didn't have any one night, so I used cream cheese instead. My husband and I liked it even better! Serve over hot, cooked egg noodles or rice."

INGREDIENTS

1 pound cubed beef stew meat

1 (10.75 ounce) can condensed golden mushroom soup

1/2 cup chopped onion

1 tablespoon Worcestershire sauce

1/4 cup water

4 ounces cream cheese

DIRECTIONS

1. In a slow cooker, combine the meat, soup, onion, Worcestershire sauce and water.

2. Cook on Low setting for 8 hours, or on High setting for about 5 hours. Stir in cream cheese just before serving.

Broiled Pork Chops

Submitted by: **Jan Taylor**

Makes: 6 servings

Preparation: 20 minutes

Cooking: 15 minutes

Total: 35 minutes

"These are fabulous pork chops. Pork is very lean, and this quick broiling method keeps the meat juicy and succulent. Serve with steamed veggies and mashed potatoes for a complete meal."

INGREDIENTS

3/4 cup ketchup

3/4 cup water

2 tablespoons distilled white vinegar

1 tablespoon Worcestershire sauce

2 teaspoons brown sugar

1 teaspoon salt

1/2 teaspoon paprika

1/2 teaspoon chili powder

1/8 teaspoon ground black pepper

6 (3/4 inch) thick pork chops

DIRECTIONS

1. In a medium saucepan, combine the ketchup, water, vinegar, Worcestershire sauce, brown sugar, salt, paprika, chili powder and pepper. Bring to a boil. Reduce heat to low, and simmer for 5 minutes, stirring occasionally. Set aside half of the sauce.

2. Preheat broiler.

3. Brush both sides of the chops with sauce. Place chops on broiling pan rack. Broil about 4 inches from the heat for 4 minutes on each side. Brush with more sauce. Continue broiling, turning and basting every 3 to 4 minutes, until juices run clear. Serve with reserved sauce.

Baked Pork Chops

Submitted by: **Dawn Edberg**

Makes: 6 servings

Preparation: 30 minutes

Cooking: 1 hour 30 minutes

Total: 2 hours

"A pork chop recipe that is quick and easy. You may have all the ingredients already in the house. Try serving over rice."

INGREDIENTS

6 pork chops

1 teaspoon garlic powder

1 teaspoon seasoning salt

2 eggs, beaten

1/4 cup all-purpose flour

2 cups Italian-style seasoned bread crumbs

4 tablespoons olive oil

1 (10.75 ounce) can condensed cream of mushroom soup

1/2 cup milk

1/3 cup white wine

DIRECTIONS

1. Preheat oven to 350°F (175°C).

2. Rinse pork chops, pat dry, and season with garlic powder and seasoning salt to taste. Place the beaten eggs in a small bowl. Dredge the pork chops lightly in flour, dip in the egg, and coat liberally with bread crumbs.

3. Heat the oil in a medium skillet over medium-high heat. Fry the pork chops 5 minutes per side, or until the breading appears well browned. Transfer the chops to a 9x13 inch baking dish, and cover with foil.

4. Bake in the preheated oven for 1 hour. While baking, combine the cream of mushroom soup, milk and white wine in a medium bowl. After the pork chops have baked for an hour, cover them with the soup mixture. Replace foil, and bake for another 30 minutes.

Caramel Apple Pork Chops

Submitted by: **Karena H. Denton**

Makes: 4 servings

Preparation: 20 minutes

Cooking: 10 minutes

Total: 45 minutes

"Warm, spicy, and sweet, this wonderful Fall recipe is a guaranteed favorite for kids, and is great with smashed potatoes and buttered green beans."

INGREDIENTS

4 (3/4 inch) thick pork chops

1 teaspoon vegetable oil

2 tablespoons brown sugar

salt and pepper to taste

1/8 teaspoon ground cinnamon

1/8 teaspoon ground nutmeg

2 tablespoons unsalted butter

2 tart apples - peeled, cored and sliced

3 tablespoons pecans

DIRECTIONS

1. Preheat oven to 175°F (80°C). Place a medium dish in the oven to warm.

2. Heat a large skillet over medium-high heat. Brush chops lightly with oil, and place in hot pan. Cook for 5 to 6 minutes, turning occasionally, until evenly browned. Transfer to the warm dish, and keep warm in the preheated oven.

3. In a small bowl, combine brown sugar, salt and pepper, cinnamon and nutmeg. Add butter to skillet, and stir in brown sugar mixture and apples. Cover, and cook for 3 to 4 minutes, or just until apples are tender. Remove apples with a slotted spoon, and arrange on top of chops. Keep warm in the preheated oven.

4. Continue cooking mixture uncovered in skillet, until sauce thickens slightly. Spoon sauce over apples and chops. Sprinkle with pecans, if desired.

Easy Teriyaki Chops

Submitted by: **Kathy Statham**

Makes: 4 servings

Preparation: 5 minutes

Cooking: 10 minutes

Total: 4 hours 15 minutes

"This is an extremely easy recipe! The marinade also works great with chicken breasts."

INGREDIENTS

½ cup soy sauce

2 tablespoons red wine vinegar

2 teaspoons honey

2 teaspoons garlic powder

4 pork chops

DIRECTIONS

1. In a shallow dish, combine the soy sauce, vinegar, honey and garlic powder. Place chops in dish, and turn to coat. Cover, and marinate for 2 to 4 hours in the refrigerator.

2. Preheat grill to high heat, and lightly oil grate.

3. Grill steaks 5 to 8 minutes per side, or to desired doneness.

Skillet Chops with Mushroom Gravy

Submitted by: **Kathy Statham**

Makes: 4 servings

Preparation: 20 minutes

Cooking: 20 minutes

Total: 40 minutes

"This is a very comforting, satisfying dish, and makes a great meal when served with rice or mashed potatoes and a tossed salad."

INGREDIENTS

½ cup dry bread crumbs

2 tablespoons grated Parmesan cheese

4 pork chops

1 tablespoon vegetable oil

1 (10.75 ounce) can condensed cream of mushroom soup

½ cup milk

DIRECTIONS

1. Combine bread crumbs and Parmesan cheese in a large zippered plastic bag. Add chops two at a time, and shake to coat.

2. Heat oil in a large skillet over medium-high heat, and cook chops until brown on both sides. Remove chops from skillet, and reduce heat to medium.

3. Blend soup and milk in the skillet, stirring to scrape up the bits of breading left over from the chops. You can adjust the amount of milk depending on how thick you want the gravy to be (it will thin a bit during the cooking process). Bring to a gentle boil, raising heat slightly if necessary. When soup mixture is bubbling, return chops to skillet. Cover; reduce heat to low and simmer for 20 minutes, or until chops are cooked through.

Easy Pork Chop Casserole

Submitted by: **Karen K.**

Makes: 4 servings

Preparation: 20 minutes

Cooking: 2 hours

Total: 2 hours 20 minutes

"This is delicious and easy to prepare. Serve with rice. You can also try baking it with other vegetables, or potatoes."

INGREDIENTS

1 (10.5 ounce) can condensed cream of mushroom soup

1 packet dry onion soup mix

10½ fluid ounces water

1 cup diced mushrooms

4 pork chops

2 tablespoons vegetable oil

DIRECTIONS

1. Preheat oven to 350°F (175°C).

2. In a medium bowl, combine the mushroom soup, onion soup mix, water and mushrooms.

3. In a large skillet over medium-high heat, brown the pork chops on each side. Transfer chops to a 9x9 inch baking dish, and cover with the mushroom soup mixture.

4. Bake in the preheated oven for 1½ hours, or until internal pork temperature reaches 160°F (70°C).

Pork Chop and Potato Casserole

Submitted by: **Wendy**

Makes: 5 servings

Preparation: 20 minutes

Cooking: 1 hour

Total: 1 hour 20 minutes

"My family loves this recipe. It is easy and delicious. Pork chops are browned, then baked in a creamy mushroom sauce with potatoes, onion and cheese."

INGREDIENTS

1 tablespoon vegetable oil

6 boneless pork chops

1 (10.75 ounce) can condensed cream of
  mushroom soup

1 cup milk

4 potatoes, thinly sliced

½ cup chopped onion

1 cup shredded Cheddar cheese

DIRECTIONS

1. Preheat oven to 400°F (200°C).

2. Heat oil in a large skillet over medium high-heat. Place the pork chops in the oil, and sear.

3. In a medium bowl, combine the soup and the milk. Arrange the potatoes and onions in a 9x13 inch baking dish. Place the browned chops over the potatoes and onions, then pour the soup mixture over all.

4. Bake 30 minutes in the preheated oven. Top with the cheese, and bake for 30 more minutes.

Cantonese Dinner

Submitted by: **Amy Eckert**

Makes: 5 servings

Preparation: 15 minutes

Cooking: 8 hours

Total: 8 hours 15 minutes

"This is a great slow cooker recipe given to me by my Mom. While not strictly authentic, it does have a great sweet and sour taste that goes so well with pork. Serve over cooked white rice. My kids all love it!!! Recipe can be doubled, and it freezes well."

INGREDIENTS

2 pounds pork steaks, cut into strips

2 tablespoons vegetable oil

1 onion, thinly sliced

1 (4.5 ounce) can mushrooms, drained

1 (8 ounce) can tomato sauce

3 tablespoons brown sugar

1½ teaspoons distilled white vinegar

1½ teaspoons salt

2 tablespoons Worcestershire sauce

DIRECTIONS

1. In a large heavy skillet, heat oil over medium-high heat. Brown pork in oil. Drain off excess fat.

2. Place pork, onion, mushrooms, tomato sauce, brown sugar, vinegar, salt and Worcestershire sauce in a slow cooker. Cook on High for 4 hours, or on Low for 6 to 8 hours.

Honey Garlic Ribs

Submitted by: **Loll**

Makes: 4 servings

Preparation: 20 minutes

Cooking: 1 hour

Total: 1 hour 20 minutes

"Easy to make, these ribs are delicious served either hot or at room temperature. So this is a great recipe for a casual dinner party that you can make ahead. The sauce is great served over rice."

INGREDIENTS

4 pounds pork spareribs

1/2 cup honey

1/4 cup soy sauce

1/4 cup distilled white vinegar

2 cloves garlic, minced

2 tablespoons brown sugar

1 teaspoon baking soda

1 teaspoon garlic salt

DIRECTIONS

1. Preheat oven to 375 °F (190°C).

2. Slice the ribs into individual pieces. In a large bowl, combine the honey, soy sauce, vinegar, garlic and brown sugar. Stir until honey and sugar are completely dissolved, then stir in the baking soda. The mixture will begin to foam. Transfer ribs to the bowl, and turn to coat.

3. Cover a cookie sheet with foil, and arrange the ribs meat side up on the sheet. Pour excess sauce over all, and sprinkle with the garlic salt.

4. Bake for 1 hour, turning every 20 minutes.

Maple Glazed Ribs

Submitted by: **Karen Toellner**

Makes: 4 servings

Preparation: 10 minutes

Cooking: 1 hour 35 minutes

Total: 3 hours 45 minutes

"Basted with a savory sweet sauce, these ribs are definitely finger-licking good!"

INGREDIENTS

3 pounds pork baby back ribs

3/4 cup maple syrup

2 tablespoons packed brown sugar

2 tablespoons ketchup

1 tablespoon cider vinegar

1 tablespoon Worcestershire sauce

1/2 teaspoon salt

1/2 teaspoon mustard powder

DIRECTIONS

1. Place ribs in a large pot, and cover with water. Simmer covered for about 1 hour. Drain when meat is tender, and place in a shallow dish.

2. In a small saucepan, combine maple syrup, brown sugar, ketchup, vinegar, Worcestershire sauce, salt and mustard powder. Bring to a boil. Pour over ribs, and marinate in the refrigerator for about 2 hours.

3. Prepare grill for cooking with indirect heat. Remove ribs from glaze. In a small saucepan, bring marinade to a boil, and cook for several minutes.

4. Transfer ribs to grill. Cook over medium heat for about 20 minutes, or until tender and glazed; baste with marinating liquid, and turn occasionally.

Simple BBQ Ribs

Submitted by: **Lloyd Rushing**

Makes: 4 servings

Preparation: 30 minutes

Cooking: 1 hour 30 minutes

Total: 2 hours

"Country-style ribs are cut from the loin, one of the leanest areas of pork. These ribs are seasoned, boiled until tender, then baked with your favorite barbeque sauce. That's it! Back to simplicity, back to the country life. Sigh."

INGREDIENTS

2½ pounds country style pork ribs

1 tablespoon garlic powder

1 teaspoon ground black pepper

2 tablespoons salt

1 cup barbeque sauce

DIRECTIONS

1. Place ribs in a large pot with enough water to cover. Season with garlic powder, black pepper and salt. Bring water to a boil, and cook ribs until tender.

2. Preheat oven to 325°F (165°C).

3. Remove ribs from pot, and place them in a 9x13 inch baking dish. Pour barbeque sauce over ribs. Cover dish with aluminum foil, and bake in the preheated oven for 1 to 1½ hours, or until internal temperature of pork has reached 160°F (70°C).

Burgundy Pork Tenderloin

Submitted by: **Kathleen White**

Makes: 4 servings

Preparation: 30 minutes

Cooking: 1 hour

Total: 1 hour 30 minutes

"My husband doesn't care for pork much, but he loves this. It is very easy to fix, and it is very rich tasting. Serve with baked potato."

INGREDIENTS

2 pounds pork tenderloin

1/2 teaspoon salt

1/2 teaspoon ground black pepper

1/2 teaspoon garlic powder

1/2 onion, thinly sliced

1 stalk celery, chopped

2 cups red wine

1 (.75 ounce) package dry brown gravy mix

DIRECTIONS

1. Preheat oven to 350°F (175°C).

2. Place pork in a 9x13 inch baking dish, and sprinkle meat with salt, pepper and garlic powder. Top with onion and celery, and pour wine over all.

3. Bake in the preheated oven for 45 minutes.

4. When done baking, remove meat from baking dish, and place on a serving platter. Pour gravy mix into baking dish with wine and cooking juices, and stir until thickened. Slice meat, and cover with the gravy.

Pork Roast with Thyme

Submitted by: **Teresa C. Rouzer**

Makes: 12 servings

Preparation: 20 minutes

Cooking: 3 hours

Total: 3 hours 20 minutes

"This savory recipe is easy and delicious. It is my favorite recipe for cooking a pork roast. Serve with autumn apples and sweet potatoes."

INGREDIENTS

5 pounds pork roast, trimmed

3 cloves garlic, sliced

1 teaspoon salt

½ tablespoon ground black pepper

3 bay leaves

½ cup cider vinegar

1 teaspoon dried thyme

DIRECTIONS

1. Preheat oven to 325°F (165°C).

2. With a small knife, pierce top of roast. Force garlic slices into the cuts. Sprinkle the roast with salt and pepper. Place bay leaves in the bottom of the roasting pan, and set roast on top of bay leaves, fat side up. Mix vinegar and thyme in a small bowl, and pour over the top of the roast.

3. Bake in the preheated oven 3 hours, or until an internal temperature of 160°F (70°C) is reached. Using a baster or spoon, baste the drippings over the roast frequently while it is cooking. Let the roast rest for 10 minutes when done before slicing.

Herbed Pork and Apples

Submitted by: **Michelle Chapman**

Makes: 14 servings

Preparation: 1 hour 20 minutes

Cooking: 2 hours 30 minutes

Total: 10 hours 50 minutes

"Whenever I make this roast for company they always ask for the recipe. I have also made this with a pork tenderloin and it comes out great!"

INGREDIENTS

1 teaspoon dried sage

1 teaspoon dried thyme

1 teaspoon dried rosemary

1 teaspoon dried marjoram

salt and pepper to taste

6 pounds pork loin roast

4 tart apples - peeled, cored, cut into 1 inch chunks

1 red onion, chopped

3 tablespoons brown sugar

1 cup apple juice

2/3 cup real maple syrup

DIRECTIONS

1. In a small bowl, combine the sage, thyme, rosemary, marjoram, salt and pepper. Rub over roast. Cover, and refrigerate roast for 6 to 8 hours, or overnight.

2. Preheat oven to 325°F (165°C).

3. Place roast in a shallow roasting pan, and bake in the preheated oven for 1 to 1½ hours. Drain fat.

4. In a medium bowl, mix apples and onion with brown sugar. Spoon around roast, and continue to cook for 1 hour more, or until the internal temperature of the roast is 160°F (70°C). Transfer the roast, apples and onion to a serving platter, and keep warm.

5. To make the gravy, skim excess fat from meat juices. Pour drippings into a medium heavy skillet. Stir in apple juice and syrup. Cook and stir over medium-high heat until liquid has been reduced by half, about 1 cup. Slice the roast, and serve with gravy.

Slow Cooker Cranberry Pork

Submitted by: **Dawn**

Makes: 6 servings

Preparation: 10 minutes

Cooking: 4 hours

Total: 4 hours 10 minutes

"Sweet, tangy and easy. The sauce is also good with chicken instead of pork. Try serving with rice and onion rings."

INGREDIENTS

1 (16 ounce) can cranberry sauce

⅓ cup French salad dressing

1 onion, sliced

3 pounds pork tenderloin

DIRECTIONS

1. In a medium bowl, combine the cranberry sauce, salad dressing and onion. Place pork in a slow cooker and cover with the sauce mixture.

2. Cook on High setting for 4 hours, or on Low setting for 8 hours. Pork is done when the internal temperature has reached 160°F (70°C).

Heavenly Potatoes and Ham

Submitted by: **Terri Martin**

Makes: 12 servings

Preparation: 30 minutes

Cooking: 30 minutes

Total: 1 hour

"This recipe is an all-time family favorite that is filling and delicious."

INGREDIENTS

5 pounds red potatoes, quartered

1 (16 ounce) container sour cream

½ cup butter

1 (10.75 ounce) can condensed cream of chicken soup

2 cups shredded Cheddar cheese

¼ cup chopped green onion

2 cups cooked, chopped ham

salt and pepper to taste

1½ cups Parmesan cheese flavored bread crumbs

¼ cup melted butter

DIRECTIONS

1. Preheat oven to 350°F (175°C). Lightly grease a 9x13 inch baking dish.

2. Place potatoes in a large pot of water, and bring to a boil. Boil until slightly tender, about 12 minutes. Drain, and transfer to a large bowl.

3. Mix sour cream, butter, cream of chicken soup, Cheddar cheese, green onions, ham, salt and pepper with the potatoes. Spread mixture in the prepared baking dish. Sprinkle with bread crumbs, and drizzle with butter.

4. Bake 30 minutes in the preheated oven.

Quiche Lorraine

Submitted by: **Jennifer**

Makes: 1 - 9 inch pie

Preparation: 15 minutes

Cooking: 55 minutes

Total: 1 hour 20 minutes

"Bacon, Swiss cheese and onions mingle in perfect harmony amidst the eggs and cream in this timeless classic. Perfect for breakfast, brunch, lunch, dinner or just an indulgent snack!"

INGREDIENTS

1 recipe pastry for a 9 inch single crust pie

12 slices bacon

1 cup shredded Swiss cheese

1/3 cup minced onion

4 eggs, beaten

2 cups light cream

3/4 teaspoon salt

1/4 teaspoon white sugar

1/8 teaspoon cayenne pepper

DIRECTIONS

1. Preheat oven to 425°F (220°C).

2. Place bacon in a large skillet, and fry over medium-high heat until crisp. Drain on paper towels, then chop coarsely. Sprinkle bacon, cheese and onion into pastry shell.

3. In a medium bowl, whisk together eggs, cream, salt, sugar and cayenne pepper. Pour mixture into pastry shell.

4. Bake 15 minutes in the preheated oven. Reduce heat to 300°F (150°C), and bake an additional 30 minutes, or until a knife inserted 1 inch from edge comes out clean. Allow quiche to sit 10 minutes before cutting into wedges.

Sausage Gravy

Submitted by: **Rene**

Makes: 8 servings

Cooking: 30 minutes

Total: 30 minutes

"My mother learned how to make this while we lived in Nashville many years ago, and it is now a family favorite. Good old-fashioned sausage gravy. It's her most requested recipe from family and friends alike. Serve over biscuits or toast."

INGREDIENTS

1 pound ground pork sausage

3 tablespoons bacon grease

1/4 cup all-purpose flour

3 cups milk

1/2 teaspoon salt

1/4 teaspoon ground black pepper

DIRECTIONS

1. Brown sausage in a large skillet over medium-high heat. Set aside, leaving the drippings in the skillet.

2. Mix bacon grease into the sausage drippings. Reduce heat to medium, combine with the flour, and stir constantly until mixture just turns golden brown.

3. Thoroughly whisk milk into skillet. When the mixture is smooth, thickened and begins to bubble, return the sausage to skillet. Season with salt and pepper. Reduce heat, and simmer for about 15 minutes.

Christmas Breakfast Sausage Casserole

Submitted by: **M.K. Meredith**

Makes: 5 servings

Preparation: 20 minutes

Cooking: 1 hour 30 minutes

Total: 9 hours 50 minutes

"My mom has always made this for us on Christmas morning, and since we only have it once a year it makes it even more good. It is so delicious, and everyone enjoys it! When I double the recipe I use 1 pound regular sausage and 1 pound sage sausage."

INGREDIENTS

1 pound ground pork sausage

6 slices white bread, toasted and cut into cubes

8 ounces mild Cheddar cheese, shredded

1 teaspoon mustard powder

½ teaspoon salt

4 eggs, beaten

2 cups milk

DIRECTIONS

1. Crumble sausage into a medium skillet. Cook over medium heat until evenly brown; drain.

2. In a medium bowl, mix together cooked sausage, toasted white bread, Cheddar cheese, mustard powder, salt, eggs and milk. Pour into a greased 9x13 inch baking dish. Cover, and chill in the refrigerator 8 hours, or overnight.

3. Preheat oven to 350°F (175°C).

4. Cover, and bake 45 to 60 minutes. Uncover, and reduce temperature to 325°F (165°C). Bake for an additional 30 minutes, or until set.

chicken & turkey

Chicken is a dinnertime favorite. Its mild character makes it the perfect blank canvas on which to create your own personal collage of flavors. Everyone's imagination runs out of steam now and then, so let us inspire you with some great ideas to put the spark back into your relationship with chicken. And don't forget about turkey! Once you try these phenomenal recipes, you'll know it's not just for Thanksgiving anymore.

Braised Balsamic Chicken

Submitted by: **Beth**

Makes: 6 servings

Preparation: 10 minutes

Cooking: 20 minutes

Total: 30 minutes

"This chicken is good with either rice or pasta. Green beans make a nice side dish."

INGREDIENTS

6 skinless, boneless chicken breast halves

ground black pepper to taste

1 teaspoon garlic salt

2 tablespoons olive oil

1 onion, thinly sliced

1/2 cup balsamic vinegar

1 (14.5 ounce) can diced tomatoes

1 teaspoon dried basil

1 teaspoon dried oregano

1 teaspoon dried rosemary

1/2 teaspoon dried thyme

DIRECTIONS

1. Season chicken breasts with ground black pepper and garlic salt. Heat olive oil in a medium skillet, and brown the onion and seasoned chicken breasts.

2. Pour tomatoes and balsamic vinegar over chicken, and season with basil, oregano, rosemary and thyme. Simmer until chicken is no longer pink and the juices run clear, about 15 minutes.

Chicken Marsala

Submitted by: **Lisa**

Makes: 4 servings

Preparation: 10 minutes

Cooking: 20 minutes

Total: 30 minutes

"A delicious, classic chicken dish — lightly coated chicken breasts braised with Marsala wine and mushrooms. Easy and ideal for both a quick weeknight entree AND serving to company."

INGREDIENTS

¼ cup all-purpose flour for coating

½ teaspoon salt

¼ teaspoon ground black pepper

½ teaspoon dried oregano

4 skinless, boneless chicken breast halves - pounded ¼ inch thick

4 tablespoons butter

4 tablespoons olive oil

1 cup sliced mushrooms

½ cup Marsala wine

¼ cup cooking sherry

DIRECTIONS

1. In a shallow dish or bowl, mix together the flour, salt, pepper and oregano. Coat chicken pieces in flour mixture.

2. In a large skillet, melt butter in oil over medium heat. Place chicken in the pan, and lightly brown. Turn over chicken pieces, and add mushrooms. Pour in wine and sherry. Cover skillet; simmer chicken 10 minutes, turning once, until no longer pink and juices run clear.

Romantic Chicken with Artichokes and Mushrooms

Submitted by: **Caity-O**

Makes: 4 servings

Preparation: 10 minutes

Cooking: 35 minutes

Total: 45 minutes

"Easy, moist, flavorful and aromatic — the white wine, artichokes and mushrooms make this chicken dish the to way to any man's heart! Delicious served with buttered noodles and fresh greens."

INGREDIENTS

4 skinless, boneless chicken breast halves

salt and pepper to taste

1 tablespoon olive oil

1 tablespoon butter

1 cup sliced fresh mushrooms

1 (14 ounce) can marinated quartered artichoke hearts, drained, liquid reserved

1 cup white wine

1 tablespoon capers

DIRECTIONS

1. Season chicken with salt and pepper. Heat oil and butter in a large skillet over medium heat. Brown chicken in oil and butter for 5 to 7 minutes per side; remove from skillet, and set aside.

2. Place artichoke hearts and mushrooms in the skillet, and sauté until mushrooms are brown and tender. Return chicken to skillet, and pour in reserved artichoke liquid and wine. Reduce heat to low, and simmer for about 10 to 15 minutes, until chicken is no longer pink and juices run clear.

3. Stir in capers, and simmer for another 5 minutes. Remove from heat; serve immediately.

Alice Chicken

Submitted by: **Misty**

Makes: 4 servings

Preparation: 5 minutes

Cooking: 15 minutes

Total: 1 hour 20 minutes

"Marinated chicken breasts broiled with bacon and cheese, then served with sautéed mushrooms and honey mustard dressing. Fantastic way to broil chicken that adds that extra something!"

INGREDIENTS

4 skinless, boneless chicken breast halves

5 fluid ounces Worcestershire sauce

8 slices bacon

2 tablespoons butter

8 ounces fresh mushrooms, sliced

1 (8 ounce) package Monterey Jack cheese, shredded

1 (16 ounce) container honey mustard salad dressing

DIRECTIONS

1. Place chicken in a glass dish or bowl; poke with a fork several times, then pour Worcestershire sauce in and turn to coat. Cover dish or bowl and refrigerate for about 1 hour.

2. Place bacon in a large, deep skillet. Cook over medium high heat until evenly brown. Drain, and set aside.

3. Heat butter in a small skillet over medium heat. Add mushrooms, and sauté for about 10 minutes, or until soft; set aside.

4. Preheat oven to Broil.

5. Remove chicken from marinade (discard any remaining liquid), and broil for about 5 minutes each side. When chicken is almost finished, top each breast with 2 slices bacon, then cheese. Continue to broil until cheese has melted, then remove from oven. Serve with mushrooms and salad dressing for topping.

Chicken Cordon Bleu II

Submitted by: **Behr Kleine**

Makes: 6 servings

Preparation: 15 minutes

Cooking: 45 minutes

Total: 1 hour

"'Cordon Bleu' is a French term, literally translated as 'blue ribbon', that originally referred to an award for culinary excellence given to women cooks! The term can now apply to any superior cook (yes, men too), and also to this dish (chicken, ham and Swiss cheese slices, breaded and sautéed). This yummy version adds paprika and a creamy white wine sauce worthy of it's own blue ribbon. Two blue ribbon tastes in wedded bliss — Chicken Cordon Bleu II!"

INGREDIENTS

6 skinless, boneless chicken breast halves

6 slices Swiss cheese

6 slices ham

3 tablespoons all-purpose flour

1 teaspoon paprika

6 tablespoons butter

1/2 cup dry white wine

1 teaspoon chicken bouillon

1 tablespoon cornstarch

1 cup heavy whipping cream

DIRECTIONS

1. Pound chicken breasts if they are too thick. Place a cheese and ham slice on each breast within 1/2 inch of the edges. Fold the edges of the chicken over the filling, and secure with toothpicks. Mix the flour and paprika in a small bowl, and coat the chicken pieces.

2. Heat the butter in a large skillet over medium-high heat, and cook the chicken until browned on all sides. Add the wine and bouillon. Reduce heat to low, cover, and simmer for 30 minutes, until chicken is no longer pink and juices run clear.

3. Remove the toothpicks, and transfer the breasts to a warm platter. Blend the cornstarch with the cream in a small bowl, and whisk slowly into the skillet. Cook, stirring until thickened, and pour over the chicken. Serve warm.

Chicken Breasts Pierre

Submitted by: **Nancy**

Makes: 6 servings

Preparation: 30 minutes

Cooking: 40 minutes

Total: 1 hour 10 minutes

"One of my husband's favorites. I've been making this for over fifteen years, and he's not sick of it yet! Serve with pan sauces, crusty French bread and a tossed green salad."

INGREDIENTS

6 skinless, boneless chicken breast halves

¼ cup all-purpose flour

½ teaspoon salt

1 pinch ground black pepper

3 tablespoons butter

1 (14.5 ounce) can stewed tomatoes, with liquid

½ cup water

2 tablespoons brown sugar

2 tablespoons distilled white vinegar

2 tablespoons Worcestershire sauce

1 teaspoon salt

2 teaspoons chili powder

1 teaspoon mustard powder

½ teaspoon celery seed

1 clove garlic, minced

⅛ teaspoon hot pepper sauce

DIRECTIONS

1. In a shallow dish or bowl, combine flour, ½ teaspoon salt and ground black pepper. Coat chicken breasts with flour mixture. Melt butter in a large skillet over medium heat, and brown chicken on all sides. Remove from skillet, and drain on paper towels.

2. In the same skillet, combine the tomatoes, water, brown sugar, vinegar and Worcestershire sauce. Season with salt, chili powder, mustard, celery seed, garlic and hot pepper sauce. Bring to a boil; reduce heat, and return chicken to skillet. Cover, and simmer for 35 to 40 minutes, or until chicken is tender, no longer pink and juices run clear.

Lemon Mushroom Herb Chicken

Submitted by: **Valerie Serao**

Makes: 4 servings

Preparation: 5 minutes

Cooking: 20 minutes

Total: 25 minutes

"Easy chicken and herbs in a creamy lemon and mushroom sauce. The sauce is excellent over rice — my kids can't get enough!"

INGREDIENTS

1 cup all-purpose flour

1/2 tablespoon dried thyme

2 tablespoons dried basil

1 tablespoon dried parsley

1 teaspoon paprika

1 teaspoon salt

1/2 teaspoon ground black pepper

1 teaspoon garlic powder

4 boneless, skinless chicken breast halves

1/2 cup butter

1 (10.75 ounce) can condensed cream of mushroom soup

1 (10.75 ounce) can chicken broth

1/4 cup dry white wine

1 lemon, juiced

1 tablespoon chopped fresh parsley

2 tablespoons capers

1 tablespoon grated lemon zest

DIRECTIONS

1. In a shallow dish or bowl, combine the flour, thyme, basil, parsley, paprika, salt, ground black pepper and garlic powder. Dredge chicken in the mixture to coat, patting off any excess flour.

2. Melt butter in a large skillet over medium heat, and sauté chicken until no longer translucent, about 10 minutes. In a medium bowl, mix together the cream of mushroom soup, chicken broth, wine and lemon juice; pour over chicken. Cover skillet, and simmer 20 minutes, or until chicken is no longer pink and juices run clear. Garnish with parsley, capers and lemon zest.

Breaded Chicken Fingers

Submitted by: **Janet Shannon**

Makes: 8 servings

Preparation: 20 minutes

Cooking: 10 minutes

Total: 2 hours 30 minutes

"If you like the taste of garlic, this recipe is for you. It is easy to make, but requires time to marinate."

INGREDIENTS

6 skinless, boneless chicken breast halves - cut into ½ inch strips

1 egg, beaten

1 cup buttermilk

1½ teaspoons garlic powder

1 cup all-purpose flour

1 cup seasoned bread crumbs

1 teaspoon salt

1 teaspoon baking powder

1 quart oil for frying

DIRECTIONS

1. Place chicken strips into a large, resealable plastic bag. In a small bowl, mix the egg, buttermilk and garlic powder. Pour mixture into bag with chicken. Seal, and refrigerate 2 to 4 hours.

2. In another large, resealable plastic bag, mix together the flour, bread crumbs, salt and baking powder. Remove chicken from refrigerator, and drain, discarding buttermilk mixture. Place chicken in flour mixture bag. Seal, and shake to coat.

3. Heat oil in a large, heavy skillet to 375°F (190°C).

4. Carefully place coated chicken in hot oil. Fry until golden brown and juices run clear. Drain on paper towels.

Fried Chicken with Creamy Gravy

Submitted by: **Gina**

Makes: 4 servings

Preparation: 25 minutes

Cooking: 30 minutes

Total: 55 minutes

"Seasoned fried chicken is served with a rich gravy made from the pan drippings. It's down home goodness that's definitely not for dieters! Takes some preparation, but is definitely worth it. Enjoy!"

INGREDIENTS

½ cup milk

1 egg, beaten

1 cup all-purpose flour

2 teaspoons garlic salt

1 teaspoon paprika

1 teaspoon ground black pepper

¼ teaspoon poultry seasoning

1 (4 pound) whole chicken, cut into pieces

3 cups vegetable oil

1 cup chicken broth

1 cup milk

DIRECTIONS

1. In a medium bowl, beat together ½ cup milk and egg. In a resealable plastic bag, mix together the flour, garlic salt, paprika, pepper and poultry seasoning. Place chicken in bag, seal, and shake to coat. Dip chicken in milk and egg mixture, then once more in flour mixture. Reserve any remaining flour mixture.

2. In a large skillet, heat oil to 365°F (185°C). Place coated chicken in the hot oil, and brown on all sides. Reduce heat to medium-low, and continue cooking chicken until tender, about 30 minutes. Remove chicken from skillet, and drain on paper towels.

3. Discard all but 2 tablespoons of the frying oil. Over low heat, stir in 2 tablespoons of the reserved flour mixture. Stirring constantly, cook about 2 minutes. Whisk in chicken stock, scraping browned bits off bottom of skillet. Stir in 1 cup milk, and bring all to a boil over high heat, stirring constantly. Reduce heat to low, and simmer for about 5 minutes. Serve immediately with the chicken.

Honey Fried Chicken

Submitted by: **SmKat**

Makes: 8 pieces

Preparation: 30 minutes

Cooking: 40 minutes

Total: 1 hour 10 minutes

"This has been a favorite in my family for many years — we first had it at a small restaurant in New England and wanted to try to make it ourselves. I think we came very close! Hope you enjoy it!"

INGREDIENTS

1 (4 pound) whole chicken, cut into pieces

salt and pepper to taste

1/2 cup honey

1 tablespoon garlic powder

1 packet chicken bouillon

2 cups all-purpose flour

1 quart vegetable oil for frying

DIRECTIONS

1. Season chicken pieces with salt and pepper, then coat each seasoned chicken piece with honey.

2. In a shallow dish or bowl, mix together the garlic powder, chicken bouillon granules and flour. Dredge honey coated chicken pieces in flour mixture, coating completely.

3. Fill a large, heavy skillet with oil to a depth of one inch. Heat over medium-high heat.

4. Fry chicken for at least 5 minutes per side, until no longer pink and juices run clear.

Gourmet Chicken Pizza

Submitted by: **Lessalee**

Makes: 1 pizza
Preparation: 15 minutes
Cooking: 40 minutes
Total: 55 minutes

"Here is a chicken pizza recipe that you may love. We do. We used to purchase this already prepared for the oven, so now I have come up with my own recipe. A perfect piece of pizza!"

INGREDIENTS

2 skinless, boneless chicken breast halves

1 (10 ounce) can refrigerated pizza crust dough

½ cup Ranch-style salad dressing

1 cup shredded mozzarella cheese

1 cup shredded Cheddar cheese

1 cup chopped tomatoes

¼ cup chopped green onions

DIRECTIONS

1. Preheat oven to 425°F (220°C). Lightly grease a pizza pan or medium baking sheet.

2. Place chicken in a large skillet over medium-high heat. Cook until no longer pink and juices run clear. Cool, then either shred or chop into small pieces.

3. Unroll dough and press into the prepared pizza pan or baking sheet. Bake crust for 7 minutes in the preheated oven, or until it begins to turn golden brown. Remove from oven.

4. Spread ranch dressing over partially baked crust. Sprinkle on mozzarella cheese. Place tomatoes, green onion and chicken on top of mozzarella cheese, then top with Cheddar cheese. Return to the oven for 20 to 25 minutes, until cheese is melted and bubbly.

Pollo Fajitas

Submitted by: **Teresa C. Rouzer**

Makes: 5 servings

Preparation: 15 minutes

Cooking: 10 minutes

Total: 55 minutes

"Chicken thighs are used in this recipe, but boneless, skinless breasts could be used instead. Be careful not to overcook, as the result could be rather dry chicken. Serve with warm flour tortillas, salsa and sour cream."

INGREDIENTS

1 tablespoon Worcestershire sauce

1 tablespoon cider vinegar

1 tablespoon soy sauce

1 teaspoon chili powder

1 clove garlic, minced

1 dash hot pepper sauce

1½ pounds boneless, skinless chicken thighs, cut into strips

1 tablespoon vegetable oil

1 onion, thinly sliced

1 green bell pepper, sliced

½ lemon, juiced

DIRECTIONS

1. In a medium bowl, combine Worcestershire sauce, vinegar, soy sauce, chili powder, garlic and hot pepper sauce. Place chicken in sauce, and turn once to coat. Marinate for 30 minutes at room temperature, or cover and refrigerate for several hours.

2. Heat oil in a large skillet over high heat. Add chicken strips to the pan, and sauté for 5 minutes. Add the onion and green pepper, and sauté another 3 minutes. Remove from heat, and sprinkle with lemon juice.

Amy's Garlic Egg Chicken

Submitted by: **Amy Miazga**

Makes: 4 servings

Preparation: 5 minutes

Cooking: 40 minutes

Total: 4 hours 45 minutes

"An easy dish for garlic lovers. Golden looking, golden tasting!"

INGREDIENTS

1 egg yolk

6 cloves garlic, chopped

4 skinless, boneless chicken breast halves

6 tablespoons butter

1 cup dry bread crumbs

1 cup grated Parmesan cheese

1 tablespoon dried parsley

1 tablespoon garlic powder

½ tablespoon salt

1 tablespoon ground black pepper

DIRECTIONS

1. In a glass dish, beat egg yolk with garlic. Place chicken in egg mixture, and turn to coat. Cover dish and refrigerate for at least 4 hours, or overnight if possible.

2. Preheat oven to 400°F (200°C).

3. Melt butter and pour into the bottom of a 9x13 inch baking dish. Mix together the bread crumbs, Parmesan cheese, parsley, garlic powder, salt and pepper. Dip marinated chicken in crumb mixture. Place coated chicken in baking dish, and pour remaining egg mixture over.

4. Bake in preheated oven for 15 to 20 minutes on each side, or until chicken is no longer pink and juices run clear.

Chicken With Mushrooms

Submitted by: **Kim Fischer**

Makes: 4 servings

Preparation: 15 minutes

Cooking: 30 minutes

Total: 45 minutes

"This is one of the best ways that I have ever prepared chicken. This recipe has been requested many times after I have served it. Serve chicken over hot cooked rice or noodles."

INGREDIENTS

3 cups sliced mushrooms

4 skinless, boneless chicken breast halves

2 eggs, beaten

1 cup seasoned bread crumbs

2 tablespoons butter

6 ounces mozzarella cheese, sliced

3/4 cup chicken broth

DIRECTIONS

1. Preheat oven to 350°F (175°C).

2. Place half of the mushrooms in a 9x13 inch pan. Dip chicken into beaten eggs, then roll in bread crumbs.

3. In skillet, melt butter over medium heat. Brown both sides of chicken in skillet. Place chicken on top of mushrooms, arrange remaining mushrooms on chicken, and top with mozzarella cheese. Add chicken broth to pan.

4. Bake in preheated oven for 30 to 35 minutes, or until chicken is no longer pink and juices run clear.

Chicken Cordon Bleu

Submitted by: **Kiersten**

Makes: 4 servings

Preparation: 10 minutes

Cooking: 35 minutes

Total: 45 minutes

"This entree is easy and delicious! It's one of my husband's favorites! Try to use the largest chicken breasts you can find so you'll be able to roll them easier."

INGREDIENTS

4 skinless, boneless chicken breast halves

1/4 teaspoon salt

1/8 teaspoon ground black pepper

6 slices Swiss cheese

4 slices cooked ham

1/2 cup seasoned bread crumbs

DIRECTIONS

1. Preheat oven to 350°F (175°C). Coat a 7x11 inch baking dish with nonstick cooking spray.

2. Pound chicken breasts to 1/4 inch thickness.

3. Sprinkle each piece of chicken on both sides with salt and pepper. Place 1 cheese slice and 1 ham slice on top of each breast. Roll up each breast, and secure with a toothpick. Place in baking dish, and sprinkle chicken evenly with bread crumbs.

4. Bake for 30 to 35 minutes, or until chicken is no longer pink. Remove from oven, and place 1/2 cheese slice on top of each breast. Return to oven for 3 to 5 minutes, or until cheese has melted. Remove toothpicks, and serve immediately.

Tomato Chicken Parmesan

Submitted by: **Alicia Navarro**

Makes: 6 servings

Preparation: 15 minutes

Cooking: 30 minutes

Total: 45 minutes

"A delicious Italian breaded chicken smothered with cheese and tomato sauce!"

INGREDIENTS

2 eggs, beaten

1 cup grated Parmesan cheese

7 ounces seasoned bread crumbs

6 skinless, boneless chicken breast halves

1 tablespoon vegetable oil

12 ounces pasta sauce

6 slices Monterey Jack cheese

DIRECTIONS

1. Preheat oven to 375°F (190°C).

2. Pour beaten eggs into a shallow dish or bowl. In another shallow dish or bowl, mix together the grated Parmesan cheese and bread crumbs. Dip chicken breasts into beaten egg, then into bread crumb mixture to coat.

3. In a large skillet, heat oil over medium high heat. Add coated chicken and sauté for about 8 to 10 minutes each side, or until chicken is cooked through and juices run clear.

4. Pour tomato sauce into a lightly greased 9x13 inch baking dish. Add chicken, then place a slice of Monterey Jack cheese over each breast, and bake in the preheated oven for 20 minutes or until cheese is completely melted.

Cheddar Chicken

Submitted by: **Karen Bush**

Makes: 8 servings

Preparation: 30 minutes

Cooking: 40 minutes

Total: 1 hour 10 minutes

"A quick and easy coated chicken recipe for busy people on the go!"

INGREDIENTS

1 cup crushed cornflakes cereal

³/₄ cup grated Parmesan cheese

¹/₄ cup shredded Cheddar cheese

¹/₂ cup butter, melted

8 skinless, boneless chicken breast halves

DIRECTIONS

1. Preheat oven to 350°F (175°C).

2. In a medium bowl, mix the cornflake crumbs, Parmesan cheese and Cheddar cheese.

3. Dip the chicken breasts in the melted butter, and roll them in the cornflake crumb mixture. Place chicken in a lightly greased 9x13 inch baking dish.

4. Bake in the preheated oven for 30 to 40 minutes, until chicken is no longer pink and juices run clear.

Candied Chicken Breasts

Submitted by: **Judi Johnston**

Makes: 10 servings

Preparation: 15 minutes

Cooking: 1 hour

Total: 1 hour 15 minutes

"Breaded chicken breasts baked with a sweet, sticky sauce with a bite. Very easy to prepare. This is a family favorite, and if you want to impress someone, this is just the thing!"

INGREDIENTS

10 skinless, boneless chicken breast halves

2 cups dry bread crumbs

2 tablespoons all-purpose flour

1 tablespoon dried oregano

2 teaspoons salt

2 teaspoons ground black pepper

1 tablespoon vegetable oil

1½ cups packed brown sugar

¼ cup prepared mustard

½ cup ketchup

1 tablespoon Worcestershire sauce

1 tablespoon soy sauce

¼ cup grated onion

½ teaspoon salt

¾ cup water

10 pineapple rings

DIRECTIONS

1. Rinse chicken breasts and pat dry. In a shallow dish or bowl, mix together the bread crumbs, flour, oregano, 2 teaspoons salt and pepper. Heat oil in a large skillet over medium high heat; dredge chicken in bread crumb mixture and brown in skillet, about 3 to 4 minutes each side. Layer chicken in 2 lightly greased 9x13 inch baking dishes.

2. Preheat oven to 350°F (175°C).

3. In a large saucepan over low heat, combine the brown sugar, mustard, ketchup, Worcestershire sauce, soy sauce, onion, ½ teaspoon salt and water. Bring to a boil, and pour over chicken. Cover baking dishes with aluminum foil.

4. Bake in preheated oven for 1 hour, or until chicken is no longer pink and juices run clear. Top each piece with a pineapple ring, and serve.

Garlic Parmesan Chicken

Submitted by: **Jennifer**

Makes: 8 servings

Preparation: 15 minutes

Cooking: 30 minutes

Total: 45 minutes

"Awesome baked Chicken Parmesan! Chicken is dipped in garlic butter, then rolled in a cheese and bread crumb mixture, and baked to perfection."

INGREDIENTS

2 cups dry bread crumbs

1/2 cup grated Parmesan cheese

1 (3 ounce) can French-fried onions

1 teaspoon mustard powder

1/2 cup butter

2 cloves garlic, chopped

1 tablespoon Worcestershire sauce

4 bone-in chicken breasts

DIRECTIONS

1. Preheat oven to 350°F (175°C). Lightly grease a 9x13 inch baking dish.

2. In a medium, shallow dish or bowl, combine the bread crumbs, cheese, onions and mustard; set aside. Melt butter in a small saucepan; add garlic and Worcestershire sauce, and sauté garlic until tender. Remove from heat.

3. Dip chicken breasts in garlic butter mixture, then roll in bread crumb and cheese mixture, coating thoroughly. Place coated chicken in the prepared baking dish. Drizzle with any remaining garlic butter mixture.

4. Bake in the preheated oven for 20 to 30 minutes, or until chicken is no longer pink and juices run clear.

Aussie Chicken

Submitted by: **Rebecca A. Armes**

Makes: 4 servings

Preparation: 25 minutes

Cooking: 25 minutes

Total: 1 hour 20 minutes

"This recipe is very similar to a chicken dish served at a local well-known restaurant. A friend of mine was kind enough to share it. It includes chicken breasts topped with mushrooms, bacon and cheese cooked in a honey-mustard sauce."

INGREDIENTS

4 skinless, boneless chicken breast halves, pounded to ½ inch thickness

2 teaspoons seasoning salt

6 slices bacon, cut in half

½ cup prepared mustard

½ cup honey

¼ cup light corn syrup

¼ cup mayonnaise

1 tablespoon onion powder

1 tablespoon vegetable oil

1 cup sliced fresh mushrooms

2 cups shredded Colby-Monterey Jack cheese

2 tablespoons chopped fresh parsley

DIRECTIONS

1. Rub the chicken breasts with the seasoning salt, cover and refrigerate for 30 minutes.

2. Preheat oven to 350°F (175°C). Place bacon in a large, deep skillet. Cook over medium high heat until crisp. Set aside.

3. In a medium bowl, combine the mustard, honey, corn syrup, mayonnaise and dried onion flakes. Remove half of sauce, cover and refrigerate to serve later.

4. Heat oil in a large skillet over medium heat. Place the breasts in the skillet and sauté for 3 to 5 minutes per side, or until browned. Remove from skillet and place the breasts into a 9x13 inch baking dish. Apply the honey mustard sauce to each breast, then layer each breast with mushrooms and bacon. Sprinkle top with shredded cheese.

5. Bake in preheated oven for 15 minutes, or until cheese is melted and chicken juices run clear. Garnish with parsley and serve with the reserved honey mustard sauce.

Baked Teriyaki Chicken

Submitted by: **Marian Collins**

Makes: 6 servings

Preparation: 30 minutes

Cooking: 1 hour

Total: 1 hour 30 minutes

"A much requested chicken recipe! Easy to double for a large group. Delicious!"

INGREDIENTS

1 tablespoon cornstarch

1 tablespoon cold water

1/2 cup white sugar

1/2 cup soy sauce

1/4 cup cider vinegar

1 clove garlic, minced

1/2 teaspoon ground ginger

1/4 teaspoon ground black pepper

12 skinless chicken thighs

DIRECTIONS

1. In a small saucepan over low heat, combine the cornstarch, cold water, sugar, soy sauce, vinegar, garlic, ginger and ground black pepper. Let simmer, stirring frequently, until sauce thickens and bubbles.

2. Preheat oven to 425°F (220°C).

3. Place chicken pieces in a lightly greased 9x13 inch baking dish. Brush chicken with the sauce. Turn pieces over, and brush again.

4. Bake in the preheated oven for 30 minutes. Turn pieces over, and bake for another 30 minutes, until no longer pink and juices run clear. Brush with sauce every 10 minutes during cooking.

Bacon Mushroom Chicken

Submitted by: Sara Blanchard

Makes: 2 servings

Preparation: 15 minutes

Cooking: 1 hour

Total: 1 hour 15 minutes

"Really good, really easy with the great flavor of bacon! Serve with rice or buttered noodles. Note: If you don't want to use heavy cream in the recipe, use 1 teaspoon flour mixed with 2 teaspoons water instead!"

INGREDIENTS

2 tablespoons butter, melted

2 bone-in chicken breast halves

2 teaspoons salt

1 clove garlic, crushed

2 thick slices bacon

1/2 cup halved mushrooms

1/4 cup heavy cream

DIRECTIONS

1. Preheat oven to 350°F (175°C).

2. Pour melted butter into a 9x13 inch baking dish. Add chicken, skin side down; sprinkle with seasoning salt and garlic. Turn chicken over, season, and lay bacon strips on top. Sprinkle with mushrooms.

3. Bake in preheated oven for 45 minutes to 60 minutes, or until chicken is no longer pink and juices run clear.

4. Remove chicken, bacon and mushrooms to a platter and keep warm. Pour juices from baking dish into a small saucepan and whisk together with cream over low heat until thickened. Pour sauce over chicken and serve warm.

Anniversary Chicken

Submitted by: **Vicki Frew**

Makes: 6 servings

Preparation: 30 minutes

Cooking: 35 minutes

Total: 1 hour 5 minutes

"I made this chicken for 100 people at my in-laws' 50th wedding anniversary party. Boy, was it a hit!"

INGREDIENTS

2 tablespoons vegetable oil

6 skinless, boneless chicken breast halves

½ cup teriyaki basting sauce

½ cup Ranch-style salad dressing

1 cup shredded Cheddar cheese

3 green onions, chopped

½ (3 ounce) can bacon bits

1 tablespoon chopped fresh parsley, for garnish

DIRECTIONS

1. Preheat oven to 350°F (175°C).

2. In a large skillet, heat oil over medium-high heat. Add chicken breasts, and sauté 4 to 5 minutes each side, until lightly browned.

3. Place browned chicken breasts in a 9x13 inch baking dish. Brush with teriyaki sauce, then spoon on salad dressing. Sprinkle with cheese, green onions and bacon bits.

4. Bake for 25 to 35 minutes, or until chicken is no longer pink and juices run clear. Garnish with parsley and serve.

Caramelized Baked Chicken

Submitted by: Sandy

Makes: 6 servings

Preparation: 15 minutes

Cooking: 1 hour

Total: 1 hour 15 minutes

"Roast chicken pieces with sticky, sweet and tangy coating."

INGREDIENTS

3 pounds chicken wings

2 tablespoons olive oil

½ cup soy sauce

2 tablespoons ketchup

1 cup honey

1 clove garlic, minced

salt and pepper to taste

DIRECTIONS

1. Preheat oven to 375°F (190°C).

2. Place chicken in a 9x13 inch baking dish. Mix together the oil, soy sauce, ketchup, honey, garlic, salt and pepper. Pour over the chicken.

3. Bake in preheated oven for one hour, or until sauce is caramelized.

Roasted Lemon Herb Chicken

Submitted by: **Barbara**

Makes: 8 servings

Preparation: 15 minutes

Cooking: 1 hour 30 minutes

Total: 1 hour 45 minutes

"My family loves this. My husband even requests it."

INGREDIENTS

1 (3 pound) whole chicken

2 teaspoons Italian seasoning

½ teaspoon seasoning salt

½ teaspoon mustard powder

1 teaspoon garlic powder

½ teaspoon ground black pepper

2 lemons

2 tablespoons olive oil

DIRECTIONS

1. Preheat oven to 325°F (165°C).

2. Combine the seasoning, salt, dry mustard, garlic powder and black pepper; set aside. Rinse the chicken thoroughly, and remove the giblets. Place chicken in a 9x13 inch baking dish. Sprinkle 1½ teaspoons of the spice mixture inside the chicken. Rub the remaining mixture on the outside of the chicken.

3. Squeeze the juice of the 2 lemons into a small bowl or cup, and mix with the olive oil. Drizzle this oil/juice mixture over the chicken.

4. Bake in the preheated oven for 30 to 45 minutes, until juices run clear, basting several times with the remaining oil mixture.

Easy Cheesy Chicken

Submitted by: **Leslye Miyashiro**

Makes: 6 servings

Preparation: 15 minutes

Cooking: 8 hours

Total: 8 hours 15 minutes

"Put this in a slow cooker in the morning, and dinner is easy and delicious. Serve over rice or noodles."

INGREDIENTS

6 skinless, boneless chicken breast halves

salt and pepper to taste

1 teaspoon garlic powder

1 (10.75 ounce) can condensed cream of mushroom soup

1 (10.75 ounce) can condensed cream of chicken soup

1 (11 ounce) can condensed cream of Cheddar cheese soup

1 (8 ounce) container sour cream

DIRECTIONS

1. Rinse chicken, and pat dry. Sprinkle with salt, pepper and garlic powder. Place in slow cooker.

2. In a medium bowl, mix together cream of chicken soup, cream of mushroom soup and cream of Cheddar cheese soup.

3. Cook on Low for 6 to 8 hours. Stir in sour cream just before serving.

Baked Slow Cooker Chicken

Submitted by: **'Cotton' Couch**

Makes: 4 servings

Preparation: 20 minutes

Cooking: 10 hours

Total: 10 hours 20 minutes

"Baked chicken in a slow cooker for busy people! Put the chicken on in the morning, and have golden brown baked chicken for dinner."

INGREDIENTS

1 (2 to 3 pound) whole chicken, cut into pieces

salt and pepper to taste

1 teaspoon paprika

DIRECTIONS

1. Wad three pieces of aluminum foil into 3 to 4 inch balls, and place them in the bottom of the slow cooker.

2. Rinse the chicken, inside and out, under cold running water. Pat dry with paper towels. Season the chicken with the salt, pepper and paprika, and place in the slow cooker on top of the crumbled aluminum foil.

3. Set the slow cooker to High for 1 hour, then turn down to Low for about 8 to 10 hours, or until the chicken is no longer pink and the juices run clear.

Jenny's Grilled Chicken Breasts

Submitted by: **Jenny English**

Makes: 4 servings

Preparation: 15 minutes

Cooking: 30 minutes

Total: 45 minutes

"This is the recipe that my friends and family still beg me to make when the grill is brought out. It's so easy and versatile, and can be tried on several different meats. I like it with scalloped potatoes, baked potatoes or rice pilaf. Try it with cilantro or oregano instead of parsley. Save leftovers for salad the next day."

INGREDIENTS

4 skinless, boneless chicken breast halves

½ cup lemon juice

½ teaspoon onion powder

ground black pepper to taste

seasoning salt to taste

2 teaspoons dried parsley

DIRECTIONS

1. Preheat an outdoor grill for medium-high heat, and lightly oil grate.

2. Dip chicken in lemon juice, and sprinkle with the onion powder, ground black pepper, seasoning salt and parsley. Discard any remaining lemon juice.

3. Cook on the prepared grill 10 to 15 minutes per side, or until no longer pink and juices run clear.

RamJam Chicken

Submitted by: **Laura Ramanjooloo**

Makes: 8 servings

Preparation: 20 minutes

Cooking: 10 minutes

Total: 3 hours 30 minutes

"This is my absolute favorite marinade for chicken. I could eat this every night! The longer you let it marinate, the more intense the flavor. I usually let it sit overnight in the refrigerator, but a few hours will do."

INGREDIENTS

¼ cup soy sauce

3 tablespoons dry white wine

2 tablespoons lemon juice

2 tablespoons vegetable oil

¾ teaspoon dried Italian-style seasoning

1 teaspoon grated fresh ginger root

1 clove garlic, crushed

¼ teaspoon onion powder

1 pinch ground black pepper

8 skinless, boneless chicken breast halves - cut into strips

DIRECTIONS

1. In a large, resealable plastic bag, combine the soy sauce, wine, lemon juice, oil, Italian-style seasoning, ginger, garlic, onion powder and ground black pepper. Place chicken in the bag. Seal, and let marinate in the refrigerator for at least 3 hours, or overnight.

2. Preheat an outdoor grill for medium-high heat, and lightly oil grate.

3. Thread the chicken onto skewers, and set aside. Pour marinade into a small saucepan, and bring to a boil over high heat.

4. Cook chicken on the prepared grill for approximately 5 minutes per side, basting with the sauce several times. Chicken is done when no longer pink and juices run clear.

Grilled Asian Chicken

Submitted by: **Janet M.**

Makes: 4 servings

Preparation: 15 minutes

Cooking: 15 minutes

Total: 50 minutes

"Great for last minute company or a quick dinner by rounding it out with a baked potato and tossed salad."

INGREDIENTS

¼ cup soy sauce

4 teaspoons sesame oil

2 tablespoons honey

3 slices fresh ginger root

2 cloves garlic, crushed

4 boneless chicken breasts

DIRECTIONS

1. In a small microwave-safe bowl, combine the soy sauce, oil, honey, ginger root and garlic. Heat in microwave on medium for 1 minute, then stir. Heat again for 30 seconds, watching closely to prevent boiling.

2. Pour soy sauce mixture over chicken breasts in a shallow medium dish or bowl, and marinate in refrigerator for 15 minutes.

3. Preheat an outdoor grill for medium-high heat, and lightly oil grate.

4. Cook chicken on the prepared grill 5 to 8 minutes per side, or until no longer pink and juices run clear. Baste frequently with remaining marinade. Chicken will turn a beautiful golden brown.

Pineapple Chicken Tenders

Submitted by: **Hillary Roberts**

Makes: 10 appetizer servings
Preparation: 30 minutes
Cooking: 10 minutes
Total: 1 hour 10 minutes

"Delicious little bites for an appetizer or a light meal with a salad!"

INGREDIENTS

1 cup unsweetened pineapple juice

1/2 cup packed brown sugar

1/3 cup light soy sauce

2 pounds chicken breast tenders, raw

DIRECTIONS

1. In a small saucepan over medium heat, mix pineapple juice, brown sugar and soy sauce. Remove from heat just before the mixture comes to a boil.

2. Place chicken tenders in a medium bowl. Cover with juice mixture, and marinate in the refrigerator at least 30 minutes.

3. Preheat an outdoor grill for medium heat, and lightly oil grate. Thread chicken onto wooden skewers.

4. Grill chicken tenders about 5 minutes per side, until no longer pink and juices run clear. They cook quickly, so watch them closely.

Beer Butt Chicken

Submitted by: **Barrie Tapp**

Makes: 4 servings

Preparation: 30 minutes

Cooking: 3 hours

Total: 4 hours

"A whole chicken is seasoned and slowly cooked on the grill. This is a bit unorthodox, but the end result is moist, flavorful and amazing. All you'll need is some chicken, butter, beer and seasonings."

INGREDIENTS

1 cup butter

2 tablespoons garlic salt

2 tablespoons paprika

salt and pepper to taste

1 (12 fluid ounce) can beer

1 (4 pound) whole chicken

DIRECTIONS

1. Preheat an outdoor grill for low heat, and lightly oil grate.

2. In a small skillet, melt ½ cup butter. Mix in 1 tablespoon garlic salt, 1 tablespoon paprika, salt and pepper.

3. Discard ½ the beer, leaving the remainder in the can. Add remaining butter, garlic salt, paprika and desired amount of salt and pepper to beer can. Place can on a disposable baking sheet. Set chicken on can, inserting can into the cavity of the chicken. Baste chicken with the melted, seasoned butter.

4. Place baking sheet with beer and chicken on the prepared grill. Cook over low heat for about 3 hours, or until chicken is no longer pink and juices run clear.

Chicken and Biscuit Casserole

Submitted by: **Cyndi Smith**

Makes: 6 servings

Preparation: 30 minutes

Cooking: 40 minutes

Total: 1 hour 10 minutes

"A kind of marriage between the traditional chicken pot pie and chicken and dumplings. My family begs me to make this!"

INGREDIENTS

¼ cup butter

2 cloves garlic, minced

½ cup chopped onion

½ cup chopped celery

½ cup chopped baby carrots

½ cup all-purpose flour

2 teaspoons white sugar

1 teaspoon salt

1 teaspoon dried basil

½ teaspoon ground black pepper

4 cups chicken broth

1 (10 ounce) can peas, drained

4 cups diced, cooked chicken meat

2 cups buttermilk baking mix

2 teaspoons dried basil

⅔ cup milk

DIRECTIONS

1. Preheat oven to 350°F (175°C). Lightly grease a 9x13 inch baking dish.

2. In a medium skillet, melt the butter over medium-high heat, and sauté the garlic, onion, celery and carrots. Stir in the flour, sugar, salt, 1 teaspoon dried basil, and pepper. Add broth, and bring to a boil. Stirring constantly, boil 1 minute, reduce heat, and stir in peas. Simmer 5 minutes, then mix in chicken. Transfer mixture to the prepared baking dish.

3. Combine the baking mix and 2 teaspoons dried basil. Stir in milk to form a dough. Divide the dough into 6 to 8 balls. On floured wax paper, use the palm of your hand to flatten each ball of dough into a circular shape; place on top of chicken mixture.

4. Bake uncovered in the preheated oven for 30 minutes. Cover with foil, and bake for 10 more minutes. To serve, spoon chicken mixture over biscuits.

Swiss Chicken Casserole

Submitted by: **Melanie Burton**

Makes: 6 servings

Preparation: 10 minutes

Cooking: 50 minutes

Total: 1 hour

"A tasty spin on the usual chicken and stuffing casserole. Great served with rice or egg noodles."

INGREDIENTS

6 skinless, boneless chicken breast halves

6 slices Swiss cheese

1 (10.75 ounce) can condensed cream of chicken soup

¼ cup milk

1 (8 ounce) package dry bread stuffing mix

½ cup melted butter

DIRECTIONS

1. Preheat oven to 350°F (175°C). Lightly grease a 9x13 inch baking dish.

2. Arrange chicken breasts in the baking dish. Place one slice of Swiss cheese on top of each chicken breast. Combine cream of chicken soup and milk in a medium bowl, and pour over chicken breasts. Sprinkle with stuffing mix. Pour melted butter over top, and cover with foil.

3. Bake 50 minutes, or until chicken is no longer pink and juices run clear.

Chicken Enchiladas

Submitted by: **Debbie Donham**

Makes: 8 servings

Preparation: 30 minutes

Cooking: 30 minutes

Total: 1 hour 30 minutes

"This is a quick and easy recipe. Good for quick suppers."

INGREDIENTS

4 skinless, boneless chicken breast halves

1 onion, chopped

1/2 pint sour cream

1 cup shredded Cheddar cheese

1 tablespoon dried parsley

1/2 teaspoon dried oregano

1/2 teaspoon ground black pepper

1/2 teaspoon salt (optional)

1 (15 ounce) can tomato sauce

1/2 cup water

1 tablespoon chili powder

1/3 cup chopped green bell pepper

1 clove garlic, minced

8 (10 inch) flour tortillas

1 (12 ounce) jar taco sauce

3/4 cup shredded Cheddar cheese

DIRECTIONS

1. Preheat oven to 350°F (175°C).

2. In a medium, non-stick skillet over medium heat, cook chicken until no longer pink and juices run clear. Drain excess fat. Cube the chicken and return it to the skillet. Add the onion, sour cream, Cheddar cheese, parsley, oregano and ground black pepper. Heat until cheese melts. Stir in salt, tomato sauce, water, chili powder, green pepper and garlic.

3. Roll even amounts of the mixture in the tortillas. Arrange in a 9x13 inch baking dish. Cover with taco sauce and 3/4 cup Cheddar cheese. Bake uncovered in the preheated oven 20 minutes. Cool 10 minutes before serving.

Homestyle Turkey, the Michigander Way

Submitted by: **Robin C.**

Makes: 10 servings

Preparation: 10 minutes

Cooking: 5 hours

Total: 5 hours 10 minutes

"A simple, down to basics recipe when it comes to the good old tom turkey."

INGREDIENTS

12 pounds whole turkey

6 tablespoons butter, divided

4 cups warm water

3 tablespoons chicken bouillon

2 tablespoons dried parsley

2 tablespoons dried minced onion

2 tablespoons seasoning salt

DIRECTIONS

1. Preheat oven to 350°F (175°C). Rinse and wash turkey. Discard the giblets, or add to pan if they are anyone's favorites.

2. Place turkey in a Dutch oven or roasting pan. Separate the skin over the breast to make little pockets. Put 3 tablespoons of the butter on both sides between the skin and breast meat. This makes for very juicy breast meat.

3. In a medium bowl, combine the water with the bouillon. Sprinkle in the parsley and minced onion. Pour over the top of the turkey. Sprinkle seasoning salt over the turkey.

4. Cover with foil, and bake in the preheated oven 4 to 5 hours, until the internal temperature of the turkey reaches 180°F (80°C). For the last 45 minutes or so, remove the foil so the turkey will brown nicely.

Rosemary Roasted Turkey

Submitted by: **Star Pooley**

Makes: 1 turkey

Preparation: 25 minutes

Cooking: 4 hours

Total: 4 hours 45 minutes

"This recipe makes your turkey moist and full of flavor. You can also use this recipe for Cornish game hens, chicken breasts or roasting chicken. Select a turkey sized according to the amount of people you will be serving."

INGREDIENTS

¾ cup olive oil

3 tablespoons minced garlic

2 tablespoons chopped fresh rosemary

1 tablespoon chopped fresh basil

1 tablespoon Italian seasoning

1 teaspoon ground black pepper

salt to taste

12 pounds whole turkey

DIRECTIONS

1. Preheat oven to 325°F (165°C).

2. In a small bowl, mix the olive oil, garlic, rosemary, basil, Italian seasoning, black pepper and salt. Set aside.

3. Wash the turkey inside and out; pat dry. Remove any large fat deposits. Loosen the skin from the breast. This is done by slowly working your fingers between the breast and the skin. Work it loose to the end of the drumstick, being careful not to tear the skin.

4. Using your hand, spread a generous amount of the rosemary mixture under the breast skin and down the thigh and leg. Rub the remainder of the rosemary mixture over the outside of the breast. Use toothpicks to seal skin over any exposed breast meat.

5. Place the turkey on a rack in a roasting pan. Add about ¼ inch of water to the bottom of the pan. Roast in the preheated oven 3 to 4 hours, or until the internal temperature of the bird reaches 180°F (80°C).

Turkey Pot Pie

Submitted by: **Linda**

Makes: 1 - 10 inch pie
Preparation: 20 minutes
Cooking: 1 hour
Total: 1 hour 20 minutes

"A perfect way to use leftover turkey. This pie tastes yummy, and will feed up to eight hungry people."

INGREDIENTS

1 recipe pastry for a (10 inch) double crust pie	salt and pepper to taste
4 tablespoons butter, divided	2 cubes chicken bouillon
1 onion, minced	2 cups water
2 stalks celery, chopped	3 potatoes, peeled and cubed
2 carrots, diced	1 1/2 cups cubed cooked turkey
3 tablespoons dried parsley	3 tablespoons all-purpose flour
1 teaspoon dried oregano	1/2 cup milk

DIRECTIONS

1. Preheat oven to 425°F (220°C). Roll out bottom pie crust, place into a 10 inch pie pan and set aside.

2. Place 2 tablespoons of the butter in a large skillet. Add the onion, celery, carrots, parsley, oregano, salt and pepper. Cook and stir until the vegetables are soft. Stir in the bouillon and water. Bring mixture to a boil. Stir in the potatoes, and cook until tender but still firm.

3. In a medium saucepan, melt the remaining 2 tablespoons butter. Stir in the turkey and flour. Add the milk, and heat through. Stir the turkey mixture into the vegetable mixture, and cook until thickened. Pour mixture into the unbaked pie shell. Roll out the top crust, and place on top of filling. Flute edges, and make 4 slits in the top crust to let out steam.

4. Bake in the preheated oven for 15 minutes. Reduce oven temperature to 350°F (175°C) and continue baking for 20 minutes, or until crust is golden brown.

seafood

Even those who turn up their noses at anything that swims, have been know to devour these seafood dishes and ask for more. Whether you're a certified fish fiend looking for fresh ideas or you're staring down a case of crustaceans wishing you knew what on earth to do with them, these recipes will provide a delicious, savory solution.

Charbroiled Salmon

Submitted by: **Alan Harasimowicz**

Makes: 4 servings

Preparation: 5 minutes

Cooking: 10 minutes

Total: 2 hours 15 minutes

"This seafood treat is best prepared over a charcoal fire, but in bad weather the oven broiler will do. The secret is in the marinade."

INGREDIENTS

1 cup soy sauce

2 tablespoons red wine

1/2 teaspoon ground ginger

1/2 teaspoon ground black pepper

2 pounds salmon steaks

4 sprigs fresh parsley, for garnish

4 slices lemon, for garnish

DIRECTIONS

1. Combine soy sauce, red wine, ginger, and black pepper in a large, resealable plastic bag. Seal, and shake vigorously to mix ingredients. Add salmon steaks, squeeze out excess air, and seal. Refrigerate, turning frequently to keep all sides in contact with the liquid, for no less than 2 hours.

2. Preheat an outdoor grill for medium high heat.

3. Cook on a hot grill for about 5 minutes per side, basting freely with extra marinade. Serve with parsley garnish and lemon slices.

Baked Dijon Salmon

Submitted by: **Arnie Williams**

Makes: 4 servings

Preparation: 15 minutes

Cooking: 15 minutes

Total: 30 minutes

"This is a wonderful way to prepare fresh salmon filets in the oven. Be sure to make extra, your family will be begging for more!"

INGREDIENTS

¼ cup butter, melted

3 tablespoons prepared Dijon-style mustard

1½ tablespoons honey

¼ cup dry bread crumbs

¼ cup finely chopped pecans

4 teaspoons chopped fresh parsley

4 (4 ounce) filets salmon

1 lemon, for garnish

salt and pepper to taste

DIRECTIONS

1. Preheat oven to 400°F (200°C).

2. In a small bowl, stir together butter, mustard and honey. Set aside. In another bowl, mix together bread crumbs, pecans and parsley.

3. Brush each salmon filet lightly with honey mustard mixture, and sprinkle the top of the filets with the bread crumb mixture.

4. Bake salmon in preheated oven until it flakes easily with a fork, approximately 10 to 15 minutes. Season with salt and pepper, and garnish with a wedge of lemon.

Barbecue Halibut Steaks

Submitted by: **Duane Glende**

Makes: 2 servings

Preparation: 5 minutes

Cooking: 15 minutes

Total: 20 minutes

"A simple recipe for barbecued halibut. Soy sauce and brown sugar add a special zip that is uncommonly delicious."

INGREDIENTS

2 tablespoons butter

2 tablespoons brown sugar

2 cloves garlic, minced

1 tablespoon lemon juice

2 teaspoons soy sauce

½ teaspoon ground black pepper

1 pound halibut steaks

DIRECTIONS

1. Preheat an outdoor grill for medium high heat.

2. Combine butter, brown sugar, garlic, lemon juice, soy sauce and pepper in a small saucepan. Stir ingredients over medium heat until the sugar dissolves.

3. Coat the halibut with sauce, and place on the grill. Baste, and cook about 5 minutes. Turn, baste, and cook another 5 minutes.

Morgan's Grilled Fish

Submitted by: **Morgan**

Makes: 4 servings

Preparation: 10 minutes

Cooking: 10 minutes

Total: 50 minutes

"A great summertime recipe for grilled salmon filets. These are marinated in lemon and herbs. Very light and flavorful. Grilled onions would be an excellent addition!"

INGREDIENTS

¼ cup olive oil

1 tablespoon dried parsley

2 tablespoons dried thyme

1 tablespoon dried rosemary

1 clove garlic, minced

4 salmon filets

2 tablespoons fresh lemon juice

DIRECTIONS

1. Preheat an outdoor grill for medium heat.

2. In a shallow glass dish, mix the oil, parsley, thyme, rosemary and garlic. Place the salmon in the dish, turning to coat the fish evenly. Squeeze the juice from the lemon over each filet. Cover the dish, and marinate in the refrigerator for 30 minutes.

3. Grill the fish over medium heat for 8 to 10 minutes, turning once. Fish is done when it flakes easily with a fork.

Mexican Baked Fish

Submitted by: **Christine Johnson**

Makes: 6 servings

Preparation: 15 minutes

Cooking: 15 minutes

Total: 30 minutes

"A baked fish dish. You get to choose the heat. Use mild salsa for a little heat and extra hot salsa for lots of heat! Serve with rice, black beans, warm tortillas and lime Margaritas for a festive meal!"

INGREDIENTS

1½ pounds cod

1 cup salsa

1 cup shredded sharp Cheddar cheese

½ cup coarsely crushed corn chips

1 avocado - peeled, pitted and sliced

¼ cup sour cream

DIRECTIONS

1. Preheat oven to 400°F (200°C). Lightly grease one 8x12 inch baking dish.

2. Rinse fish fillets under cold water, and pat dry with paper towels. Lay fillets side by side in the prepared baking dish. Pour the salsa over the top, and sprinkle evenly with the shredded cheese. Top with the crushed corn chips.

3. Bake, uncovered, in the preheated oven for 15 minutes, or until fish is opaque and flakes with a fork. Serve topped with sliced avocado and sour cream.

Cheesy Catfish

Submitted by: **Deborah Westbrook**

Makes: 8 servings

Preparation: 20 minutes

Cooking: 15 minutes

Total: 35 minutes

"This savory catfish dish is coated in Parmesan cheese and baked. Excellent for an easy family dinner! A fish dish even your kids will love!"

INGREDIENTS

1 egg

1 tablespoon milk

3/4 cup grated Parmesan cheese

1 1/4 cups all-purpose flour

1 1/2 teaspoons salt

1 1/2 teaspoons ground black pepper

1 teaspoon paprika

8 (4 ounce) filets catfish

1/4 cup margarine, melted

DIRECTIONS

1. Preheat oven to 350°F (175°C).

2. Beat the egg together with the milk in a medium bowl. In another bowl, stir together the cheese, flour, salt, pepper and paprika.

3. Dip catfish in the egg and milk mixture, then dredge in the cheese mixture until coated. Arrange fish in a single layer in the bottom of a 9x13 inch baking dish. Pour melted margarine over the fish.

4. Bake for 15 minutes, or until golden brown.

Fish Chowder

Submitted by: **Amy The**

Makes: 8 servings

Preparation: 30 minutes

Cooking: 30 minutes

Total: 1 hour

"The fishermen of Bodega Bay, California shared this favorite, quick and easy recipe with my sister during a Fish Festival. It is one of the best chowders I've had, and my kids love it too! We top with bacon bits and a few shakes of hot sauce for a little spice. Enjoy!"

INGREDIENTS

2 tablespoons butter

2 cups chopped onion

4 fresh mushrooms, sliced

1 stalk celery, chopped

4 cups chicken stock

4 cups diced potatoes

2 pounds cod, diced into ½ inch cubes

salt to taste

ground black pepper to taste

⅛ teaspoon Old Bay Seasoning™, or to taste

1 cup clam juice

½ cup all-purpose flour

2 (12 fluid ounce) cans evaporated milk

DIRECTIONS

1. In a large stockpot, melt 2 tablespoons butter over medium heat. Sauté onions, mushrooms and celery in butter until tender.

2. Add chicken stock and potatoes; simmer for 10 minutes.

3. Add fish, and simmer another 10 minutes.

4. Season to taste with Old Bay seasoning, salt and pepper. Mix together clam juice and flour until smooth; stir into soup. Remove from heat, and stir in evaporated milk. Serve.

Coconut Shrimp

Submitted by: **Linda Vergura**

Makes: 4 servings

Preparation: 10 minutes

Cooking: 20 minutes

Total: 1 hour

"These crispy shrimp are rolled in a coconut beer batter before frying. For dipping sauce, I use orange marmalade, mustard and horseradish mixed to taste."

INGREDIENTS

1 egg

½ cup all-purpose flour

⅔ cup beer

1½ teaspoons baking powder

¼ cup all-purpose flour

2 cups flaked coconut

24 shrimp

3 cups oil for frying

DIRECTIONS

1. In medium bowl, combine egg, ½ cup flour, beer and baking powder. Place ¼ cup flour and coconut in two separate bowls.

2. Hold shrimp by tail, and dredge in flour, shaking off excess flour. Dip in egg/beer batter; allow excess to drip off. Roll shrimp in coconut, and place on a baking sheet lined with wax paper. Refrigerate for 30 minutes. Meanwhile, heat oil to 350°F (175°C) in a deep-fryer.

3. Fry shrimp in batches: cook, turning once, for 2 to 3 minutes, or until golden brown. Using tongs, remove shrimp to paper towels to drain. Serve warm with your favorite dipping sauce.

Grilled Shrimp Scampi

Submitted by: **Holly Murphy**

Makes: 6 servings

Preparation: 35 minutes

Cooking: 6 minutes

Total: 1 hour 11 minutes

"Shrimp marinated in lemon, garlic, and parsley for 30 minutes, then grilled. Can be used as an appetizer or main dish. Scallops can also be used."

INGREDIENTS

¼ cup light olive oil

¼ cup lemon juice

3 tablespoons chopped fresh parsley

1 tablespoon minced garlic

ground black pepper to taste

¼ teaspoon crushed red pepper

1½ pounds shrimp

DIRECTIONS

1. In a medium, non-reactive bowl, combine the olive oil, lemon juice, parsley, garlic, black pepper and crushed red pepper. Stir in shrimp to coat. Marinate for 30 minutes or less.

2. Preheat grill for high heat.

3. Remove shrimp from marinade, and thread onto skewers. Grill for about 2 to 3 minutes on each side, or until done.

Shrimp Scampi

Submitted by: **Deborah Corda**

Makes: 4 servings

Preparation: 5 minutes

Cooking: 25 minutes

Total: 30 minutes

"A delicious and quick way to enjoy shrimp - even on a busy weeknight!"

INGREDIENTS

1 pound linguini pasta

¼ cup butter

5 cloves garlic, minced

1 pound medium shrimp - peeled and deveined

1 cup bread crumbs

½ cup white wine

1 lemon, juiced

¼ cup light olive oil

DIRECTIONS

1. Preheat oven to 350°F (175°C).

2. Bring a large pot of salted water to a boil, add pasta, and cook until al dente. Drain pasta, and set aside.

3. In a large skillet, melt butter over medium heat. Add most of the garlic, keeping some for later. Coat the garlic completely with butter. Do not let the garlic brown. Add shrimp, and toss to coat. Immediately remove pan from heat; shrimp will not be cooked yet.

4. Sprinkle the shrimp with breadcrumbs (enough to coat the shrimp), and transfer the entire mixture to a medium casserole dish. Pour wine and the lemon juice over the shrimp. Cover, and bake at 350°F (175°C) for 10 minutes.

5. Remove cover, and bake an additional 5 minutes.

6. In a small saucepan heat olive oil with remaining garlic. Toss the pasta with the olive oil and garlic mixture. Serve the shrimp over the pasta with additional lemon slices on the side.

Basil Shrimp

Submitted by: **Gail Laulette**

Makes: 4 servings

Preparation: 25 minutes

Cooking: 5 minutes

Total: 1 hour 30 minutes

"This was given to me by my friend Elaine. It is one of the most delicious shrimp recipes for the BBQ I have ever had, and it is so easy. My son would eat the whole recipe if I didn't watch him."

INGREDIENTS

2½ tablespoons olive oil

¼ cup butter, melted

1½ lemons, juiced

3 tablespoons coarse grained prepared mustard

4 ounces fresh basil, minced

3 cloves garlic, minced

salt to taste

1 pinch white pepper

3 pounds fresh shrimp, peeled and deveined

DIRECTIONS

1. In a shallow, non-porous dish or bowl, mix together olive oil and melted butter. Then stir in lemon juice, mustard, basil and garlic, and season with salt and white pepper. Add shrimp, and toss to coat. Cover, and refrigerate for 1 hour.

2. Preheat grill to high heat.

3. Remove shrimp from marinade, and thread on skewers.

4. Lightly oil grate, and arrange skewers on grill. Cook for 4 minutes, turning once, until done.

Baked Seafood Au Gratin

Submitted by: **Katy B. Minchew**

Makes: 8 servings

Preparation: 20 minutes

Cooking: 1 hour

Total: 1 hour 20 minutes

"This was my Mom's favorite seafood recipe, she is now 88, I am 60 and this is my all time favorite seafood recipe also. I have had guests, who, when invited to dinner, specifically request this to be served."

INGREDIENTS

1 onion, chopped

1 green bell pepper, chopped

1 cup butter, divided

1 cup all-purpose flour, divided

1 pound fresh crabmeat

4 cups water

1 pound shrimp

1/2 pound small scallops

1/2 pound flounder filets

3 cups milk

1 cup shredded sharp Cheddar cheese

1 tablespoon distilled white vinegar

1 teaspoon Worcestershire sauce

1/2 teaspoon salt

1 pinch ground black pepper

1 dash hot pepper sauce

1/2 cup grated Parmesan cheese

DIRECTIONS

1. In a heavy skillet, sauté the onion and the pepper in 1/2 cup of butter. Cook until tender. Mix in 1/2 cup of the flour, and cook over medium heat for 10 minutes, stirring frequently. Stir in crabmeat, remove from heat, and set aside.

2. In a large Dutch oven, bring the water to a boil. Add the shrimp, scallops and flounder, and simmer for 3 minutes. Drain, reserving 1 cup of the cooking liquid, and set the seafood aside.

3. In a heavy saucepan, melt the remaining 1/2 cup butter over low heat. Stir in remaining 1/2 cup flour. Cook and stir constantly for 1 minute. Gradually add the milk plus the 1 cup reserved cooking liquid. Raise heat to medium; cook, stirring constantly, until the mixture is thickened and bubbly. Mix in the shredded Cheddar cheese, vinegar, Worcestershire sauce, salt, pepper and hot sauce. Stir in cooked seafood.

4. Preheat oven to 350°F (175°C). Lightly grease one 9x13 inch baking dish. Press crabmeat mixture into the bottom of the prepared pan. Spoon the seafood mixture over the crabmeat crust, and sprinkle with the Parmesan cheese.

5. Bake in the preheated oven for 30 minutes or until lightly browned. Serve immediately.

Seafood Enchiladas

Submitted by: **Cathy**

Makes: 6 servings

Preparation: 15 minutes

Cooking: 40 minutes

Total: 55 minutes

"These crab and shrimp stuffed enchiladas taste like the ones served at a popular Mexican restaurant in my area. My husband just loves them. After sprinkling the cheese over the enchiladas before baking, you can also garnish with tomatoes, cilantro, olive slices, or whatever other garnish you enjoy."

INGREDIENTS

1 onion, chopped

1 tablespoon butter

1/2 pound fresh crabmeat

1/4 pound shrimp - peeled, deveined and coarsely chopped

8 ounces Colby cheese

1 cup half-and-half cream

1/2 cup sour cream

1/4 cup butter, melted

1 1/2 teaspoons dried parsley

1/2 teaspoon garlic salt

6 (10 inch) flour tortillas

DIRECTIONS

1. Preheat oven to 350°F (175°C).

2. In a large skillet, sauté onions in 1 tablespoon butter until transparent. Remove the skillet from heat, and stir in crabmeat and shrimp. Mix in 1 cup shredded cheese. Place a large spoonful of the mixture into each tortilla. Roll the tortillas up around the mixture, and arrange the rolled tortillas in a 9x13 inch baking dish.

3. In saucepan, combine half and half, sour cream, 1/4 cup butter, parsley and garlic salt. Stir until the mixture is lukewarm and blended. Pour this sauce over the enchiladas, and sprinkle with remaining cheese.

4. Bake in preheated oven for 30 minutes.

My Best Clam Chowder

Submitted by: **Sharon Johnson**

Makes: 8 servings

Preparation: 25 minutes

Cooking: 25 minutes

Total: 50 minutes

"A delicious, traditional, cream based chowder, this recipe calls for the standard chowder ingredients: onion, celery, potatoes, diced carrots, clams, and cream. A little red wine vinegar is added before serving for extra flavor."

INGREDIENTS

3 (6.5 ounce) cans minced clams

1 cup minced onion

1 cup diced celery

2 cups cubed potatoes

1 cup diced carrots

¾ cup butter

¾ cup all-purpose flour

1 quart half-and-half cream

2 tablespoons red wine vinegar

1½ teaspoons salt

ground black pepper to taste

DIRECTIONS

1. Drain juice from clams into a large skillet over the onions, celery, potatoes and carrots. Add water to cover, and cook over medium heat until tender.

2. Meanwhile, in a large, heavy saucepan, melt the butter over medium heat. Whisk in flour until smooth. Whisk in cream and stir constantly until thick and smooth. Stir in vegetables and clam juice. Heat through, but do not boil.

3. Stir in clams just before serving. If they cook too much they get tough. When clams are heated through, stir in vinegar, and season with salt and pepper.

vegetarian

Veggie is in! Discover the delights of eggplant, beans, tofu, sweet potatoes, and more — rolled up in tortillas, smothered in hearty tomato sauce, baked into a delicate quiche, or simmered with enticing spices. This is meatless eating at its best. And guess what? You don't need to be a vegetarian to love these recipes!

Addictive Sweet Potato Burritos

Submitted by: **Karena H. Denton**

Makes: 12 burritos

Preparation: 25 minutes

Cooking: 12 minutes

Total: 40 minutes

"Once you've had one - you'll want another. The recipe is a little different from most burrito recipes, but I've had many, many requests for it. Serve these with sour cream, chopped green onions and salsa. For vegan burritos, omit the cheese and sour cream. These may be made ahead of time, individually frozen, then heated. For an interesting variation, try deep frying these tasty burritos."

INGREDIENTS

3 teaspoons vegetable oil

1 onion, chopped

4 cloves garlic, minced

6 cups canned kidney beans, drained

2 cups water

3 tablespoons chili powder

2 teaspoons ground cumin

4 teaspoons prepared mustard

1 pinch cayenne pepper, or to taste

3 tablespoons soy sauce

4 cups cooked and mashed sweet potatoes

12 (10 inch) flour tortillas, warmed

8 ounces Cheddar cheese, shredded

DIRECTIONS

1. Preheat oven to 350°F (175°C).

2. Heat oil in a medium skillet, and sauté onion and garlic in until soft. Stir in beans, and mash. Gradually stir in water, and heat until warm. Remove from heat, and stir in the chili powder, cumin, mustard, cayenne pepper and soy sauce.

3. Divide bean mixture and mashed sweet potatoes evenly between the warm flour tortillas. Top with cheese. Fold up tortillas burrito style.

4. Bake for 12 minutes in the preheated oven, and serve.

Eggplant Parmesan

Submitted by: **Karen K.**

Makes: 8 servings

Preparation: 25 minutes

Cooking: 45 minutes

Total: 1 hour 40 minutes

"This makes a delicious entree served with a salad and garlic bread."

INGREDIENTS

1 eggplant, cut into ¾ inch slices

1½ tablespoons salt

8 tablespoons olive oil

8 ounces ricotta cheese

6 ounces mozzarella cheese, shredded

½ cup grated Parmesan cheese

1 egg, beaten

½ cup chopped fresh basil

4 cups pasta sauce

DIRECTIONS

1. Sprinkle both sides of the eggplant slices with salt. Place slices in a colander, and place a dish underneath the colander to capture liquid that will sweat out of the eggplant. Allow to sit for 30 minutes.

2. Preheat oven to 350°F (175°C). In a medium bowl, mix the ricotta, mozzarella cheese and ¼ cup Parmesan cheese. Mix in egg and basil.

3. Rinse the eggplant in cold water until all salt is removed. In a large skillet, heat 4 tablespoons olive oil over medium heat. Place one layer of eggplant in the pan, brown each side. Repeat with remaining eggplant slices, using additional oil if necessary.

4. In a 9x13 inch baking dish, evenly spread 1½ cups of spaghetti sauce. Arrange a single layer of eggplant slices on top of the sauce. Top the eggplant with½ of the cheese mixture. Repeat layering process until all the eggplant and cheese mixture is used. Pour remaining sauce on top of layers, and sprinkle with remaining Parmesan cheese.

5. Bake 30 to 45 minutes in the preheated oven, until sauce is bubbly.

Tofu Parmigiana

Submitted by: **Jill B. Mittelstadt**

Makes: 4 servings

Preparation: 25 minutes

Cooking: 20 minutes

Total: 45 minutes

"Breaded tofu alla parmigiana. You'll just about swear this is eggplant or veal! One of my husband's favorites, and he doesn't even suspect! Serve with a simple crisp green salad, angel hair pasta and garlic bread."

INGREDIENTS

½ cup seasoned bread crumbs

5 tablespoons grated Parmesan cheese

2 teaspoons dried oregano

salt to taste

ground black pepper to taste

1 (12 ounce) package firm tofu

2 tablespoons olive oil

1 (8 ounce) can tomato sauce

½ teaspoon dried basil

1 clove garlic, minced

4 ounces mozzarella cheese, shredded

DIRECTIONS

1. In a small bowl, combine bread crumbs, 2 tablespoons Parmesan cheese, 1 teaspoon oregano, salt and black pepper.

2. Slice tofu into ¼ inch thick slices, and place in bowl of cold water. One at a time, press tofu slices into crumb mixture, turning to coat all sides.

3. Heat oil in a medium skillet over medium heat. Cook tofu slices until crisp on one side. Drizzle with a bit more olive oil, turn, and brown on the other side.

4. Combine tomato sauce, basil, garlic and remaining oregano. Place a thin layer of sauce in an 8 inch square baking pan. Arrange tofu slices in the pan. Spoon remaining sauce over tofu. Top with shredded mozzarella and remaining 3 tablespoons Parmesan.

5. Bake at 400°F (205°C) for 20 minutes.

Grandma's Slow Cooker Vegetarian Chili

Submitted by: **Kevin S. Weiss**

Makes: 8 servings

Preparation: 10 minutes

Cooking: 2 hours

Total: 2 hours 10 minutes

"This is a simple crowd pleasing recipe that can sit in a slow cooker until it is time to serve."

INGREDIENTS

1 (11 ounce) can condensed black bean soup

1 (15 ounce) can kidney beans, drained and rinsed

1 (15 ounce) can garbanzo beans, drained and rinsed

1 (16 ounce) can vegetarian baked beans

1 (14.5 ounce) can chopped tomatoes in puree

1 (15 ounce) can whole kernel corn, drained

1 onion, chopped

1 green bell pepper, chopped

2 stalks celery, chopped

2 cloves garlic, chopped

1 tablespoon chili powder

1 tablespoon dried parsley

1 tablespoon dried oregano

1 tablespoon dried basil

DIRECTIONS

1. In a slow cooker, combine black bean soup, kidney beans, garbanzo beans, baked beans, tomatoes, corn, onion, bell pepper and celery. Season with garlic, chili powder, parsley, oregano and basil.

2. Cook for at least two hours on High.

Seven Layer Tortilla Pie

Submitted by: **Karen C. Greenlee**

Makes: 6 servings

Preparation: 15 minutes

Cooking: 40 minutes

Total: 55 minutes

"Looks like a pie, cuts like a pie, and tastes like a little bit of Southwestern heaven. This casserole is made from pinto and black beans layered with tortillas and cheese. Picante sauce gives it just the right kick. You can replace the Cheddar cheese with Monterey Jack if you like."

INGREDIENTS

2 (15 ounce) cans pinto beans, drained and rinsed

1 cup salsa, divided

2 cloves garlic, minced

2 tablespoons chopped fresh cilantro

1 (15 ounce) can black beans, rinsed and drained

½ cup chopped tomatoes

7 (8 inch) flour tortillas

2 cups shredded reduced-fat Cheddar cheese

1 cup salsa

½ cup sour cream

DIRECTIONS

1. Preheat oven to 400°F (200°C).

2. In a large bowl, mash pinto beans. Stir in ¾ cup salsa and garlic.

3. In a separate bowl, mix together ¼ cup salsa, cilantro, black beans and tomatoes.

4. Place 1 tortilla in a pie plate or tart dish. Spread ¾ cup pinto bean mixture over tortilla to within ½ inch of edge. Top with ¼ cup cheese, and cover with another tortilla. Spread with ⅔ cup black bean mixture, and top with ¼ cup cheese. Repeat layering twice. Cover with remaining tortilla, and spread with remaining pinto bean mixture and cheese.

5. Cover with foil, and bake in preheated oven for about 40 minutes. Cut into wedges, and serve with salsa and sour cream.

Spinach Quiche

Submitted by: **Bailey**

Makes: 1 - 9 inch quiche

Preparation: 20 minutes

Cooking: 40 minutes

Total: 1 hour

"Let me start by saying that I devised this recipe myself, and I just sort of add 'this and that.' This recipe is VERY forgiving, so you can add or remove ingredients according to your taste!"

INGREDIENTS

½ cup butter

3 cloves garlic, chopped

1 small onion, chopped

1 (10 ounce) package frozen chopped spinach, thawed and drained

1 (4.5 ounce) can mushrooms, drained

1 (6 ounce) package herb and garlic feta, crumbled

1 (8 ounce) package shredded Cheddar cheese

salt and pepper to taste

1 unbaked 9 inch pie crust

4 eggs, beaten

1 cup milk

salt and pepper to taste

DIRECTIONS

1. Preheat oven to 375°F (190°C).

2. In a medium skillet, melt butter over medium heat. Sauté garlic and onion in butter until lightly browned, about 7 minutes. Stir in spinach, mushrooms, feta and ½ cup Cheddar cheese. Season with salt and pepper. Spoon mixture into pie crust.

3. In a medium bowl, whisk together eggs and milk. Season with salt and pepper. Pour into the pastry shell, allowing egg mixture to thoroughly combine with spinach mixture.

4. Bake in preheated oven for 15 minutes. Sprinkle top with remaining Cheddar cheese, and bake an additional 35 to 40 minutes, until set in center. Allow to stand 10 minutes before serving.

Baked Vegetables

Submitted by: **Klara Yudovich**

Makes: 4 servings

Preparation: 15 minutes

Cooking: 45 minutes

Total: 1 hour

"Very simple vegetable dish seasoned with dry soup powder, and baked until tender and caramelized. Try different dry soup types to vary the flavor. I like onion or mushroom."

INGREDIENTS

2 potatoes, peeled and cubed

4 carrots, cut into 1 inch pieces

1 head fresh broccoli, cut into florets

4 zucchini, thickly sliced

salt to taste

¼ cup olive oil

1 (1 ounce) package dry onion soup mix

DIRECTIONS

1. Preheat oven to 400°F (200°C). Lightly oil a large, shallow baking dish.

2. Combine vegetables in prepared baking dish, and lightly salt. Brush with olive oil, and sprinkle with dry soup mix.

3. Bake for 30 to 45 minutes in the preheated oven, or until vegetables are tender. You can feel with a fork when they are ready.

Zucchini Patties

Submitted by: **Sherlie A. Magaret**

Makes: 4 servings

Preparation: 10 minutes

Cooking: 20 minutes

Total: 30 minutes

"Excellent way to use up that abundance of zucchini from the garden."

INGREDIENTS

2 cups grated zucchini

2 eggs, beaten

¼ cup chopped onion

½ cup all-purpose flour

½ cup grated Parmesan cheese

½ cup shredded mozzarella cheese

salt to taste

DIRECTIONS

1. In a medium bowl, combine the zucchini, eggs, onion, flour, Parmesan, mozzarella and salt.

2. Heat oil in a medium skillet over medium-high heat. Drop zucchini mixture by heaping tablespoonfuls, and cook for a few minutes on each side, until golden.

side dishes

Bring side dishes into the spotlight! Even the most spectacular main dish looks lonely without a complementary side dish or two. You've told us you love potatoes in every form, so here are some of the best recipes to help you mash, bake, grill, or roast them to perfection. You'll love to eat your veggies, too, when you discover how good green beans, carrots, asparagus, squash, and broccoli can be.

Oven Roasted Red Potatoes

Submitted by: **Donna Lasater**

Makes: 8 servings

Preparation: 15 minutes

Cooking: 40 minutes

Total: 55 minutes

"These roasted red potatoes are very easy to prepare and taste excellent!"

INGREDIENTS

1½ (1 ounce) packages dry onion soup mix

2 pounds red potatoes, halved

⅓ cup olive oil

DIRECTIONS

1. Preheat oven to 450°F (230°C).

2. In a large plastic bag, combine the soup mix, red potatoes and olive oil. Close bag, and shake until potatoes are fully covered.

3. Pour potatoes into a medium baking dish; bake 40 minutes in the preheated oven, stirring occasionally.

Grilled Potatoes and Onion

Submitted by: **Bob Cody**

Makes: 4 servings

Preparation: 15 minutes

Cooking: 30 minutes

Total: 45 minutes

"Always cook up a package of potatoes and onions with the rest of your grilled meal! Start early, because it takes about a half an hour to cook."

INGREDIENTS

4 potatoes, sliced

1 red onion, sliced

1 teaspoon salt

1 teaspoon ground black pepper

4 tablespoons butter

DIRECTIONS

1. Preheat a grill for indirect heat.

2. Measure out 2 or 3 sheets of aluminum foil large enough to easily wrap the vegetables, and layer one on top of the other. Place potatoes and onion in the center, sprinkle with salt and pepper, and dot with butter. Wrap into a flattened square, and seal the edges.

3. Place aluminum wrapped package over medium heat, and cover. Cook for approximately 30 minutes, turning once. Serve hot off the grill.

Creamy Au Gratin Potatoes

Submitted by: **Cathy Martin**

Makes: 4 servings

Preparation: 30 minutes

Cooking: 1 hour 30 minutes

Total: 2 hours

"This is my husband's favorite dish, and he considers it a special occasion every time I make it. The creamy cheese sauce and the tender potatoes in this classic French dish combine to make a deliciously addictive experience. It's a great side dish with a roast pork loin or beef tenderloin. Add a green salad and French bread, and you have found the magic path to a man's heart."

INGREDIENTS

4 russet potatoes, sliced into ¼ inch slices

1 onion, sliced into rings

salt and pepper to taste

3 tablespoons butter

3 tablespoons all-purpose flour

½ teaspoon salt

2 cups milk

1½ cups shredded Cheddar cheese

DIRECTIONS

1. Preheat oven to 400°F (200°C). Butter a 1 quart casserole dish.

2. Layer ½ of the potatoes into bottom of the prepared casserole dish. Top with the onion slices, and add the remaining potatoes. Season with salt and pepper to taste.

3. In a medium-size saucepan, melt butter over medium heat. Mix in the flour and salt, and stir constantly with a whisk for one minute. Stir in milk. Cook until mixture has thickened. Stir in cheese all at once, and continue stirring until melted, about 30 to 60 seconds. Pour cheese over the potatoes, and cover the dish with aluminum foil.

4. Bake 1½ hours in the preheated oven.

Day Before Mashed Potatoes

Submitted by: **Erin**

Makes: 8 servings

Preparation: 20 minutes

Cooking: 30 minutes

Total: 8 hours 50 minutes

"This recipe helps you plan ahead by allowing you to make your mashed potatoes in advance!"

INGREDIENTS

9 potatoes, peeled and cubed

6 ounces cream cheese

1 cup sour cream

2 teaspoons onion powder

1 teaspoon salt

¼ teaspoon ground black pepper

2 tablespoons butter

DIRECTIONS

1. Bring a large pot of salted water to a boil. Drop in potatoes, and cook until tender but still firm, about 15 minutes.

2. Transfer potatoes to a large bowl, and mash until smooth. Mix in the cream cheese, sour cream, onion powder, salt, pepper and butter. Cover, and refrigerate 8 hours, or overnight.

3. Preheat oven to 350°F (175°C). Lightly grease a medium baking dish.

4. Spread potato mixture into the prepared baking dish, and bake in the preheated oven about 30 minutes.

Cowboy Mashed Potatoes

Submitted by: **Bruticus**

Makes: 4 servings

Preparation: 20 minutes

Cooking: 20 minutes

Total: 40 minutes

"Quick, easy and delicious mashed potatoes with corn and carrots."

INGREDIENTS

1 pound red potatoes

1 pound Yukon Gold (yellow) potatoes

1 fresh jalapeno pepper, sliced

12 ounces baby carrots

4 cloves garlic

1 (10 ounce) package frozen white corn, thawed

1/4 cup butter

1/2 cup shredded Cheddar cheese

salt and pepper to taste

DIRECTIONS

1. Place red potatoes, yellow potatoes, jalapeno pepper, carrots and garlic cloves in a large pot. Cover with water, and bring to a boil over high heat. Cook 15 to 20 minutes, until potatoes are tender. Drain water from pot.

2. Stir in corn and butter. Mash the mixture with a potato masher until butter is melted and potatoes have reached desired consistency. Mix in cheese, salt and pepper. Serve hot.

Hash Brown Casserole II

Submitted by: **Courtney**

Makes: 1 - 3 quart casserole

Preparation: 20 minutes

Cooking: 40 minutes

Total: 1 hour

"Cheesy and delicious, this hash brown casserole has a crunchy topping."

INGREDIENTS

1 (2 pound) package frozen hash brown potatoes, thawed

½ cup melted butter

1 (10.75 ounce) can condensed cream of chicken soup

1 (8 ounce) container sour cream

½ cup chopped onions

2 cups shredded Cheddar cheese

1 teaspoon salt

¼ teaspoon ground black pepper

2 cups crushed cornflakes cereal

¼ cup melted butter

DIRECTIONS

1. Preheat oven to 350°F (175°C).

2. In a large bowl, combine hash browns, ½ cup melted butter, cream of chicken soup, sour cream, chopped onion, Cheddar cheese, salt and pepper. Place mixture in a 3 quart casserole dish.

3. In a medium saucepan over medium heat, sauté cornflakes in ¼ cup melted butter, and sprinkle the mixture over the top of the casserole.

4. Bake covered in preheated oven for 40 minutes.

Praline Sweet Potatoes

Submitted by: **Mike Kennon**

Makes: 6 servings

Preparation: 10 minutes

Cooking: 30 minutes

Total: 40 minutes

"The best sweet potatoes you will ever eat!"

INGREDIENTS

4 cups mashed sweet potatoes

½ cup white sugar

2 tablespoons vanilla extract

4 eggs, beaten

½ pint heavy cream

¼ pound butter

1 cup packed brown sugar

½ cup all-purpose flour

1¼ cups chopped pecans

DIRECTIONS

1. Butter one 2 quart casserole dish. Preheat oven to 350°F (175°C).

2. In a mixing bowl, combine the sweet potatoes, sugar, vanilla extract, eggs and cream. Blend well, and spread evenly in casserole dish.

3. Prepare the topping by combining the butter, brown sugar, flour and pecans. Mix until crumbly, and sprinkle over sweet potato mixture.

4. Bake for 30 minutes in the preheated oven.

Green Beans with Bread Crumbs

Submitted by: **Marie Kenney**

Makes: 4 servings

Preparation: 15 minutes

Cooking: 10 minutes

Total: 25 minutes

"My mom gave me this recipe. It's been in the family for years. Hope you enjoy it as much as we do - it's a sure way to get my kids to eat green beans. You can easily double this recipe."

INGREDIENTS

1 pound fresh green beans, washed and trimmed

1/2 cup water

1/4 cup Italian-style seasoned bread crumbs

1/4 cup olive oil

salt and pepper to taste

1/4 teaspoon garlic powder

1/4 teaspoon dried oregano

1/4 teaspoon dried basil

1/4 cup grated Parmesan cheese

DIRECTIONS

1. Combine green beans and 1/2 cup water in a medium pot. Cover, and bring to boil. Reduce heat to medium, and let beans cook for 10 minutes, or until tender. Drain well.

2. Place beans in a medium serving bowl, and mix in bread crumbs, olive oil, salt, pepper, garlic powder, oregano and basil. Toss mixture until the beans are coated. Sprinkle with Parmesan cheese, and serve.

Garlic Green Beans

Submitted by: **Ericka Ettinger**

Makes: 5 servings

Preparation: 5 minutes

Cooking: 30 minutes

Total: 35 minutes

"Caramelized garlic and cheese! Is there anything better with green beans? You'd better make plenty for everyone!"

INGREDIENTS

1 tablespoon butter

3 tablespoons olive oil

1 medium head garlic - peeled and sliced

2 (14.5 ounce) cans green beans, drained

salt and pepper to taste

¼ cup grated Parmesan cheese

DIRECTIONS

1. Melt butter in a large skillet, and stir in olive oil and garlic. Sauté over low heat until the garlic is slightly brown.

2. Stir in the green beans, and season with salt and pepper. Cook until beans are tender, about 10 minutes. Turn off heat, and sprinkle with Parmesan cheese.

Grilled Asparagus

Submitted by: **Larry Lampert**

Makes: 4 servings

Preparation: 15 minutes

Cooking: 10 minutes

Total: 25 minutes

"The special thing about this recipe is that it's so simple. Fresh asparagus with a little oil, salt and pepper is cooked quickly over high heat on the grill. Enjoy the natural flavor of your veggies."

INGREDIENTS

1 pound fresh asparagus

1 tablespoon olive oil

salt and pepper to taste

DIRECTIONS

1. Preheat an outdoor grill for high heat.

2. Trim bottoms of asparagus. Lightly coat the spears with the oil. Season with salt and pepper to taste.

3. Grill over high heat for 2 to 3 minutes, or to desired tenderness.

Buttery Cooked Carrots

Submitted by: **Rebecca A. Armes**

Makes: 4 servings

Preparation: 15 minutes

Cooking: 10 minutes

Total: 25 minutes

"Sweet cooked carrots that even my carrot hating family loves. There are never leftovers."

INGREDIENTS

1 pound baby carrots

¼ cup margarine

⅓ cup brown sugar

DIRECTIONS

1. Cook carrots in a large pot of boiling water until tender. Drain off most of the liquid, leaving bottom of pan covered with water. Set the carrots aside.

2. Stir margarine and brown sugar into the water. Simmer and stir until the margarine melts. Return carrots to the pot, and toss to coat. Cover, and let sit for a few minutes to allow flavors to mingle.

Broccoli Rice Casserole

Submitted by: **Gina Williams**

Makes: 10 servings

Preparation: 30 minutes

Cooking: 45 minutes

Total: 1 hour 15 minutes

"A creamy side dish that is baked in a delicious cheese sauce. This is the best broccoli rice casserole you will ever eat!"

INGREDIENTS

2 (10 ounce) packages frozen chopped broccoli

3 cups instant rice

1 (10.75 ounce) can condensed cream of mushroom soup

1 (10.75 ounce) can condensed cream of chicken soup

2½ cups water

1 (16 ounce) package processed American cheese, cubed

1 tablespoon butter

1 bunch celery, chopped

1 large onion, chopped

salt and pepper to taste

DIRECTIONS

1. Cook broccoli and rice according to package directions. Preheat oven to 350°F (175°C).

2. In a medium saucepan over low heat, mix cream of mushroom soup and cream of chicken soup with water. Gradually stir in cheese until melted. Be careful that the cheese doesn't burn.

3. Melt butter in a large skillet over medium-high heat, and sauté celery and onion until soft.

4. In a large mixing bowl, combine broccoli, rice, soup and cheese mixture, celery and onion. Pour mixture into a 9x13 inch baking dish.

5. Bake in the preheated oven for 15 minutes, until bubbly and lightly brown.

Awesome Broccoli-Cheese Casserole

Submitted by: **Stacy M. Polcyn**

"My mom used to make this easy recipe every Thanksgiving when I was little. We kids could never get enough! It was our very favorite Thanksgiving vegetable. If you have children, or have some coming to visit you as guests this Thanksgiving, I guarantee that they will eat (and enjoy) this veggie dish! Even though I rarely cook with canned condensed soups, I still make this yummy broccoli casserole during the holiday season. It's fabulous with a Christmas ham and potatoes au gratin too. (Note: Be sure to use sharp Cheddar cheese for a nice full flavor.) Mmmmmmm!"

INGREDIENTS

1 (10.75 ounce) can condensed cream of mushroom soup

1 cup mayonnaise

1 egg, beaten

¼ cup finely chopped onion

3 (10 ounce) packages frozen chopped broccoli

8 ounces shredded sharp Cheddar cheese

salt to taste

ground black pepper to taste

2 pinches paprika

DIRECTIONS

1. Preheat oven to 350°F (175°C). Butter a 9x13 inch baking dish.

2. In a medium bowl, whisk together condensed cream of mushroom soup, mayonnaise, egg and onion.

3. Place frozen broccoli into a very large mixing bowl. (I like to use my large stainless steel bowl to mix this recipe thoroughly.) Break up the frozen broccoli. Using a rubber spatula, scrape soup-mayonnaise mixture on top of broccoli, and mix well. Sprinkle on cheese and mix well. Spread mixture into prepared baking dish, and smooth top of casserole. Season to taste with salt, pepper and paprika.

4. Bake for 45 minutes to 1 hour in the preheated oven.

Awesome and Easy Creamy Corn Casserole

Submitted by: **Ruthie Crickmer**

Makes: 8 servings

Preparation: 5 minutes

Cooking: 45 minutes

Total: 50 minutes

"This truly is the most delicious stuff! A bit like a cross between corn souffle and a slightly sweet corn pudding! Try it, I know you will love the ease of preparation and especially the taste. Everyone always wants the recipe! Note: The ingredients can be doubled and baked in a 9x13 inch baking dish in almost the same amount of cooking time."

INGREDIENTS

½ cup butter, melted

2 eggs, beaten

1 (8.5 ounce) package dry corn bread mix

1 (15 ounce) can whole kernel corn, drained

1 (14.75 ounce) can creamed corn

1 cup sour cream

DIRECTIONS

1. Preheat oven to 350°F (175°C), and lightly grease a 9x9 inch baking dish.

2. In a medium bowl, combine butter, eggs, corn bread mix, whole and creamed corn and sour cream. Spoon mixture into prepared dish.

3. Bake for 45 minutes in the preheated oven, or until the top is golden brown.

Yellow Squash Casserole

Submitted by: **Rosalie Carter**

Makes: 1 - 9x13 inch pan

Preparation: 20 minutes

Cooking: 25 minutes

Total: 45 minutes

"Tender squash, gooey cheese and crunchy crackers make this a memorable side dish or a hearty main course. This is a great dish that can be made with low-fat ingredients and is still just as good!"

INGREDIENTS

4 cups sliced yellow squash

1/2 cup chopped onion

35 buttery round crackers, crushed

1 cup shredded Cheddar cheese

2 eggs, beaten

3/4 cup milk

1/4 cup butter, melted

1 teaspoon salt

ground black pepper to taste

2 tablespoons butter

DIRECTIONS

1. Preheat oven to 400°F (200°C).

2. Place squash and onion in a large skillet. Pour in just enough water to cover bottom of skillet. Cover with a lid, and cook over low heat until squash is tender, about 5 minutes. Drain well.

3. In a medium bowl, mix together cracker crumbs and cheese. Stir half of the cracker mixture into the cooked squash and onions. In a small bowl, mix together beaten eggs and milk. Stir egg mixture into squash mixture, followed by 1/4 cup melted butter, salt and pepper. Mix well, then spread into a 9x13 inch baking pan. Cover top with remaining cheese and cracker mixture. Dot with 2 tablespoons butter.

4. Bake in preheated oven for 25 minutes, or until heated through and browned on top.

breads

Surrender to the warm seduction of home-baked bread. Cinnamon rolls, bagels, and quick breads may make breakfast the best meal of the day. Then there's lunch — a sandwich on slices of the world's best yeasty loaves. With high hopes for a basket filled with rolls, biscuits, cornbread, or focaccia, everyone will rush home for dinner. It's okay, have another slice!

Soft, Moist and Gooey Cinnamon Buns

Submitted by: **Tania**

Makes: 2 dozen buns

Preparation: 15 minutes

Cooking: 20 minutes

Total: 3 hours 35 minutes

"I tried long and hard to find the ultimate cinnamon bun recipe for bread machines...this is it. They are so soft and yummy!"

INGREDIENTS

1 cup milk

1 egg, beaten

4 tablespoons melted butter

4 tablespoons water

1/2 (3.5 ounce) package instant vanilla pudding mix

4 cups bread flour

1 tablespoon white sugar

1/2 teaspoon salt

2 1/4 teaspoons bread machine yeast

1/2 cup butter, softened

1 cup packed brown sugar

2 teaspoons ground cinnamon

1/4 cup chopped walnuts (optional)

1/4 cup raisins (optional)

1 teaspoon milk

1 1/2 cups confectioners' sugar

4 tablespoons butter, softened

1 teaspoon vanilla extract

DIRECTIONS

1. In a bread machine pan, place the milk, beaten egg, melted butter, water, vanilla pudding mix, bread flour, sugar, salt and yeast in the order recommended by the manufacturer. Select the Dough cycle.

2. When cycle is finished, remove the dough, and knead for 3 to 5 minutes. Roll out to a large rectangle.

3. Mix together the softened butter, brown sugar and cinnamon. Spread over dough. Sprinkle with chopped walnuts and raisins, if desired. Starting with the widest end, roll the dough into a log. Pinch to seal seams. Cut into 1/2 inch to 1 inch slices, and place in a greased 9x13 inch pan. Place in a draft-free space, and allow to rise until doubled.

4. Preheat the oven to 350°F (175°C). Bake for 15 to 20 minutes. To make frosting, mix the milk, confectioners sugar, softened butter and vanilla in a small bowl. Spread over warm cinnamon rolls.

Cinnamon Rolls II

Submitted by: **Stephanie Knewasser**

Makes: 24 rolls

Preparation: 20 minutes

Cooking: 25 minutes

Total: 3 hours 20 minutes

"These are gobbled up as soon as family sees them. I'll never try another cinnamon roll recipe, because I think these are the best. Note: These are wonderful fresh, but they don't freeze well."

INGREDIENTS

1 cup milk

1 cup water

¼ cup butter

1½ teaspoons salt

6 cups all-purpose flour

1½ tablespoons active dry yeast

½ cup white sugar

2 eggs

⅓ cup butter, softened

1½ teaspoons ground cinnamon

¾ cup white sugar

¾ cup raisins (optional)

¾ cup chopped walnuts (optional)

2 cups confectioners' sugar

3 tablespoons butter, melted

½ teaspoon vanilla extract

3 tablespoons milk

DIRECTIONS

1. In saucepan, heat 1 cup milk, water and ¼ cup butter until very warm (butter doesn't need to be completely melted). Place all ingredients in the pan of the bread machine in the order suggested by the manufacturer. Select the Dough cycle. Press Start.

2. Once Dough cycle is complete, remove the dough from the bread machine. Punch down, and divide into 2 parts. On a floured surface, roll each part into a large rectangle. Smear each rectangle with the softened butter. Combine the cinnamon and ¾ cup sugar. Sprinkle over the rectangles. Generously sprinkle the raisins and/or chopped nuts over the top.

3. Roll the dough up into two logs starting at the long side. Cut each log into 12 slices. Place the rolls cut side down into two 9x13 inch greased baking pans. Cover, and let rise in a warm place until almost doubled (about 30 minutes).

4. Bake in a preheated 375°F (190°C) oven for 20 to 25 minutes, or until golden. Combine the confectioner's sugar, 3 tablespoons melted butter, vanilla and 3 tablespoons milk. Frosting should be thick. Spread over baked rolls and enjoy.

Monkey Bread

Submitted by: **LuAnn Connolly**

Makes: 1 10 inch tube pan

Preparation: 15 minutes

Cooking: 35 minutes

Total: 1 hour

"Refrigerated biscuits with cinnamon bake in a tube pan. My 7 year old daughter, Leah, loves her Monkey Bread. Enjoy!"

INGREDIENTS

3 (12 ounce) packages refrigerated biscuits

1 cup white sugar

2 teaspoons ground cinnamon

½ cup margarine

1 cup packed brown sugar

½ cup chopped walnuts (optional)

½ cup raisins

DIRECTIONS

1. Preheat oven to 350°F (175°C). Grease one 9 or 10 inch tube pan.

2. Mix white sugar and cinnamon in a plastic bag. Cut biscuits into quarters. Shake 6 to 8 biscuit pieces in the sugar cinnamon mix. Arrange pieces in the bottom of the prepared pan. Continue until all biscuits are coated and placed in pan. If using nuts and raisins, arrange them in and among the biscuit pieces as you go along.

3. In a small saucepan, melt the margarine with the brown sugar over medium heat. Boil for 1 minute. Pour over the biscuits.

4. Bake at 350°F (175°C) for 35 minutes. Let bread cool in pan for 10 minutes, then turn out onto a plate. Do not cut! The bread just pulls apart.

Cinnamon Bread

Submitted by: **Carol**

Makes: 1 - 9x5 inch loaf
Preparation: 20 minutes
Cooking: 50 minutes
Total: 1 hour 10 minutes

"This is a lovely way to start off your morning when you want a little something different than your usual. Note: If you don't have buttermilk you may substitute milk with 1 tablespoon vinegar to measure 1 cup."

INGREDIENTS

2 cups all-purpose flour

1 cup white sugar

2 teaspoons baking powder

½ teaspoon baking soda

1½ teaspoons ground cinnamon

1 teaspoon salt

1 cup buttermilk

¼ cup vegetable oil

2 eggs

2 teaspoons vanilla extract

2 tablespoons white sugar

1 teaspoon ground cinnamon

2 teaspoons margarine

DIRECTIONS

1. Preheat oven to 350°F (175°C). Grease one 9x5 inch loaf pan.

2. Measure flour, 1 cup sugar, baking powder, baking soda, 1½ teaspoons cinnamon, salt, buttermilk, oil, eggs and vanilla into large mixing bowl. Beat 3 minutes. Pour into prepared loaf pan. Smooth top.

3. Combine 2 tablespoons white sugar, 1 teaspoon cinnamon and butter, mixing until crumbly. Sprinkle topping over smoothed batter. Using knife, cut in a light swirling motion to give a marbled effect.

4. Bake for about 50 minutes. Test with toothpick. When inserted it should come out clean. Remove bread from pan to rack to cool.

Best Ever Muffins

Submitted by: **Lori**

Makes: 1 dozen
Preparation: 10 minutes
Cooking: 25 minutes
Total: 35 minutes

"Start with this basic recipe, and add one of several different ingredients for a variety of different muffins."

INGREDIENTS

2 cups all-purpose flour

3 teaspoons baking powder

1/2 teaspoon salt

3/4 cup white sugar

1 egg

1 cup milk

1/4 cup vegetable oil

DIRECTIONS

1. Preheat oven to 400°F (205°C).

2. Stir together the flour, baking powder, salt and sugar in a large bowl. Make a well in the center. In a small bowl or 2 cup measuring cup, beat egg with a fork. Stir in milk and oil. Pour all at once into the well in the flour mixture. Mix quickly and lightly with a fork until moistened, but do not beat. The batter will be lumpy. Pour the batter into paper lined muffin pan cups.

3. Variations: Blueberry Muffins: Add 1 cup fresh blueberries. Raisin Muffins: Add 1 cup finely chopped raisins. Date Muffins: Add 1 cup finely chopped dates. Cheese Muffins: Fold in 1 cup grated sharp yellow cheese. Bacon Muffins: Fold 1/4 cup crisp cooked bacon, broken into bits.

4. Bake for 25 minutes, or until golden.

Banana Crumb Muffins

Submitted by: **Lisa Kreft**

Makes: 10 muffins

Preparation: 15 minutes

Cooking: 20 minutes

Total: 35 minutes

"The crumb topping is what makes these banana muffins stand apart from the ordinary. They're scrumptious!"

INGREDIENTS

1 1/2 cups all-purpose flour

1 teaspoon baking soda

1 teaspoon baking powder

1/2 teaspoon salt

3 bananas, mashed

3/4 cup white sugar

1 eggs, lightly beaten

1/3 cup butter, melted

1/3 cup packed brown sugar

1/8 cup all-purpose flour

1/8 teaspoon ground cinnamon

1 tablespoon butter

DIRECTIONS

1. Preheat oven to 375°F (190°C). Lightly grease 10 muffin cups, or line with muffin papers.

2. In a large bowl, mix together flour, baking soda, baking powder and salt. In another bowl, beat together bananas, sugar, egg and melted butter. Stir the banana mixture into the flour mixture just until moistened. Spoon batter into prepared muffin cups.

3. In a small bowl, mix together brown sugar, flour and cinnamon. Cut in butter until mixture resembles coarse cornmeal. Sprinkle topping over muffins.

4. Bake in preheated oven for 18 to 20 minutes, until a toothpick inserted into center of a muffin comes out clean.

Alienated Blueberry Muffins

Submitted by: **Nora Donovan**

Makes: 2 dozen

Preparation: 15 minutes

Cooking: 25 minutes

Total: 40 minutes

"I got this recipe from my grandmother in New Jersey. They fit the title, because they are out of this world!"

INGREDIENTS

2 cups fresh blueberries

¼ cup all-purpose flour

2 cups all-purpose flour

4 teaspoons baking powder

1 teaspoon salt

¼ cup margarine

1½ cups white sugar

2 eggs

1 teaspoon vanilla extract

1 cup milk

DIRECTIONS

1. Preheat oven to 375°F (190°C). Grease muffins tins, or line cups with paper liners.

2. Sprinkle ¼ cup flour over blueberries, and stir to coat berries thoroughly.

3. In a small bowl, whisk together 2 cups flour, baking powder and salt.

4. In a large bowl, cream margarine, and gradually mix in sugar. Beat eggs, and stir into creamed mixture along with vanilla. Stir in milk alternately with flour mixture, mixing well after each addition. Fold in berries. Fill muffin cups ⅔ full with batter.

5. Bake for 25 minutes.

To Die For Blueberry Muffins

Submitted by: **Colleen**

Makes: 8 large muffins

Preparation: 15 minutes

Cooking: 25 minutes

Total: 40 minutes

"These muffins are extra large and yummy with the sugary-cinnamon crumb topping. I usually double the recipe and fill the muffin cups just to the top edge for a wonderful extra-generously-sized deli style muffin. Add extra blueberries too, if you want!"

INGREDIENTS

1½ cups all-purpose flour

¾ cup white sugar

½ teaspoon salt

2 teaspoons baking powder

⅓ cup vegetable oil

1 egg

⅓ cup milk

1 cup fresh blueberries

½ cup white sugar

⅓ cup all-purpose flour

¼ cup butter, cubed

1½ teaspoons ground cinnamon

DIRECTIONS

1. Preheat oven to 400°F (200°C). Grease muffin cups or line with muffin liners.

2. Combine 1½ cups flour, ¾ cup sugar, salt and baking powder. Place vegetable oil into a 1 cup measuring cup; add the egg and enough milk to fill the cup. Mix this with flour mixture. Fold in blueberries. Fill muffin cups right to the top, and sprinkle with crumb topping mixture.

3. To Make Crumb Topping: Mix together ½ cup sugar, ⅓ cup flour, ¼ cup butter, and 1½ teaspoons cinnamon. Mix with fork, and sprinkle over muffins before baking.

4. Bake for 20 to 25 minutes in the preheated oven, or until done.

Fluffy French Toast

Submitted by: **Bonnie**

Makes: 12 slices

Preparation: 10 minutes

Cooking: 20 minutes

Total: 30 minutes

"This French toast recipe is different because it uses flour. I have given it to some friends and they've all liked it better than the French toast they usually make!"

INGREDIENTS

¼ cup all-purpose flour

1 cup milk

1 pinch salt

3 eggs

½ teaspoon ground cinnamon

1 teaspoon vanilla extract

1 tablespoon white sugar

12 thick slices bread

DIRECTIONS

1. Measure flour into a large mixing bowl. Slowly whisk in the milk. Whisk in the salt, eggs, cinnamon, vanilla extract and sugar until smooth.

2. Heat a lightly oiled griddle or frying pan over medium heat.

3. Soak bread slices in mixture until saturated. Cook bread on each side until golden brown. Serve hot.

Baked French Toast

Submitted by: **Laura**

Makes: 12 servings

Preparation: 15 minutes

Cooking: 40 minutes

Total: 15 hours

"I got this recipe from my sister in law. She and my brother had it at their gift opening after the wedding. I make it any time we have people staying with us, and it is always a hit. You may sprinkle the top with pecans if you wish."

INGREDIENTS

1 (1 pound) loaf French bread, cut diagonally in 1 inch slices

8 eggs

2 cups milk

1½ cups half-and-half cream

2 teaspoons vanilla extract

¼ teaspoon ground cinnamon

¾ cup butter

1⅓ cups brown sugar

3 tablespoons light corn syrup

DIRECTIONS

1. Butter a 9x13 inch baking dish. Arrange the slices of bread in the bottom. In a large bowl, beat together eggs, milk, cream, vanilla and cinnamon. Pour over bread slices, cover, and refrigerate overnight.

2. The next morning, preheat oven to 350°F (175°C). In a small saucepan, combine butter, brown sugar and corn syrup; heat until bubbling. Pour over bread and egg mixture.

3. Bake in preheated oven, uncovered, for 40 minutes.

Blue Ribbon Overnight Rolls

Submitted by: **Pam Vienneau**

Makes: 2 dozen

Preparation: 30 minutes

Cooking: 15 minutes

Total: 25 hours

"Easy tasty recipe! Never any left when I make them."

INGREDIENTS

1 (.25 ounce) package active dry yeast

1 cup warm milk

½ cup white sugar

2 eggs, beaten

½ cup butter, melted

1 teaspoon salt

4 cups all-purpose flour

DIRECTIONS

1. In a large bowl, mix together yeast, milk and sugar. Let stand for 30 minutes.

2. Mix eggs, butter and salt into yeast mixture. Mix in flour, 2 cups at a time. Cover with wax paper. Let dough stand at room temperature overnight.

3. In the morning, divide the dough in half. Roll each half into a 9 inch round circle. Cut each round into 12 pie shaped wedges. Roll up each wedge starting from wide end to the tip. Place on greased cookie sheets. Let stand until ready to bake.

4. Bake at 375°F (190°C) for 12 to 15 minutes.

Unbelievable Rolls

Submitted by: **Sherlie Magaret**

Makes: 16 rolls

Preparation: 30 minutes

Cooking: 15 minutes

Total: 2 hours 15 minutes

"Simple dinner rolls that are easy to make. Dough is also a great base for cinnamon rolls."

INGREDIENTS

3/4 cup milk

3/4 cup water

1/2 cup white sugar

1 teaspoon salt

2 eggs

5 teaspoons active dry yeast

5 cups all-purpose flour

1/2 cup margarine, melted

DIRECTIONS

1. In a medium saucepan over medium heat, warm milk, water, sugar and salt. Remove from heat, and mix in the eggs and yeast.

2. Measure flour into a large bowl. Make a well in the flour, and pour milk mixture into it. Do not stir. Cover with a lid, and let stand for 20 to 30 minutes.

3. Pour melted margarine into flour, and mix well. Add more flour if too sticky. Knead lightly. Cover, and let rise for 20 to 30 minutes.

4. Shape the dough into rolls, and place on a baking sheet. Let rise again for 20 to 30 minutes.

5. Bake rolls in a preheated 400°F (205°C) oven for 15 minutes, or until done.

Tasty Buns

Submitted by: **Charlene Kaunert**

Makes: 12 buns

Preparation: 20 minutes

Cooking: 15 minutes

Total: 1 hour 20 minutes

"Excellent yeast buns that can be used for hamburgers or just plain dinner rolls. They don't take long to make and have never failed for me!!"

INGREDIENTS

5 cups all-purpose flour

2 (.25 ounce) packages dry yeast

1 cup milk

3/4 cup water

1/2 cup vegetable oil

1/4 cup white sugar

1 teaspoon salt

DIRECTIONS

1. Stir together 2 cups flour and the yeast. In a separate bowl, heat milk, water, oil, sugar and salt to lukewarm in microwave. Add all at once to the flour mixture, and beat until smooth, about 3 minutes.

2. Mix in enough flour to make a soft dough, 2 to 3 cups. Mix well. Dust a flat surface with flour, turn dough out onto floured surface, and let rest under bowl for about 10 minutes.

3. Shape dough into 12 slightly flat balls, and place on greased baking sheet to rise until doubled in size.

4. Bake in a preheated 400°F (200°C) oven for 12 to 15 minutes.

Burger or Hot Dog Buns

Submitted by: **Sally**

Makes: 1 dozen

Preparation: 20 minutes

Cooking: 10 minutes

Total: 1 hour 30 minutes

"This recipe can be used to make either hamburger buns or hot dog buns. My husband says they are 'top of the line.' Nice and soft."

INGREDIENTS

1 cup milk

½ cup water

¼ cup butter

4½ cups all-purpose flour

1 (.25 ounce) package instant yeast

2 tablespoons white sugar

1½ teaspoons salt

1 egg

DIRECTIONS

1. In a small saucepan, heat milk, water and butter until very warm, 120°F (50°C).

2. In a large bowl, mix together 1¾ cup flour, yeast, sugar and salt. Mix milk mixture into flour mixture, and then mix in egg. Stir in the remaining flour, ½ cup at a time, beating well after each addition. When the dough has pulled together, turn it out onto a lightly floured surface, and knead until smooth and elastic, about 8 minutes.

3. Divide dough into 12 equal pieces. Shape into smooth balls, and place on a greased baking sheet. Flatten slightly. Cover, and let rise for 30 to 35 minutes.

4. Bake at 400°F (200°C) for 10 to 12 minutes, or until golden brown.

5. For Hot Dog Buns: Shape each piece into a 6x4 inch rectangle. Starting with the longer side, roll up tightly, and pinch edges and ends to seal. Let rise about 20 to 25 minutes. Bake as above. These buns are pretty big. I usually make 16 instead of 12.

J.P.'s Big Daddy Biscuits

Submitted by: **John Pickett**

Makes: 6 grand sized biscuits

Preparation: 30 minutes

Cooking: 15 minutes

Total: 45 minutes

"This recipe will produce the biggest biscuits in the history of the world! Serve these gems with butter, preserves, honey, gravy or they can also be used as dinner rolls...you get the picture. The dough can also be prepared several hours, and up to a day ahead of time. If so, turn dough out onto aluminum foil that has been either floured, lightly buttered or lightly sprayed with cooking spray. Roll up foil until it is sealed, and refrigerate. Don't be surprised if your biscuits rise even higher because the baking powder has had more time to act in the dough. You may have to make a few batches before you get desired results: desired results equals huge mongo biscuits."

INGREDIENTS

2 cups all-purpose flour

1 tablespoon baking powder

1 teaspoon salt

1 tablespoon white sugar

1/3 cup shortening

1 cup milk

DIRECTIONS

1. Preheat oven to 425°F (220°C).

2. In a large bowl, whisk together the flour, sugar, baking powder, salt and sugar. Cut in the shortening until the mixture resembles coarse meal. Gradually stir in milk until dough pulls away from the side of the bowl.

3. Turn out onto a floured surface, and knead 15 to 20 times. Pat or roll dough out to 1 inch thick. Cut biscuits with a large cutter or juice glass dipped in flour. Repeat until all dough is used. Brush off the excess flour, and place biscuits onto an ungreased baking sheet.

4. Bake for 13 to 15 minutes in the preheated oven, or until edges begin to brown.

Cheese Biscuits

Submitted by: **Debbie Pleau**

Makes: 10 - 12 biscuits

Preparation: 10 minutes

Cooking: 10 minutes

Total: 20 minutes

"I got this recipe from a friend. Best if eaten warm!!!"

INGREDIENTS

2 cups baking mix

²/₃ cup milk

¹/₂ cup shredded Cheddar cheese

¹/₄ cup Parmesan cheese

¹/₄ cup butter

¹/₂ teaspoon garlic powder

1 teaspoon dried parsley

DIRECTIONS

1. Preheat oven to 450°F (230°C).

2. Stir together baking mix, milk and cheeses until soft dough forms. Drop by spoonfuls onto an ungreased cookie sheet.

3. Bake for 10 to 12 minutes, or until bottoms are lightly browned.

4. Melt butter, and stir in garlic powder and parsley flakes. Brush over warm biscuits.

White Bread

Submitted by: **Lisa**

Makes: 1 -1½ pound loaf
Preparation: 5 minutes
Cooking: 3 hours
Total: 3 hours 5 minutes

"The best white bread you'll ever have! Delicious warm with butter!"

INGREDIENTS

1¼ cups lukewarm milk

3 cups all-purpose flour

1½ tablespoons white sugar

1½ teaspoons salt

2 tablespoons butter

2 teaspoons active dry yeast

DIRECTIONS

1. Place ingredients in the pan of the bread machine in the order suggested by the manufacturer.

2. Select Basic or White Bread setting, and press Start. When done, place on wire rack for at least 10 minutes before slicing.

Amish White Bread

Submitted by: **Peg**

Makes: 2 - 9x5 inch loaves

Preparation: 20 minutes

Cooking: 40 minutes

Total: 2 hours 30 minutes

"I got this recipe from a friend. It is very easy, and doesn't take long to make."

INGREDIENTS

2 cups warm water (110°F / 45°C)

2/3 cup white sugar

1 1/2 tablespoons active dry yeast

1 1/2 teaspoons salt

1/4 cup vegetable oil

6 cups bread flour

DIRECTIONS

1. In a large bowl, dissolve the sugar in warm water, and then stir in yeast. Allow to proof until yeast resembles a creamy foam.

2. Mix salt and oil into the yeast. Mix in flour one cup at a time. Knead dough on a lightly floured surface until smooth. Place in a well oiled bowl, and turn dough to coat. Cover with a damp cloth. Allow to rise until doubled in bulk, about 1 hour.

3. Punch dough down. Knead for a few minutes, and divide in half. Shape into loaves, and place into two well oiled 9x5 inch loaf pans. Allow to rise for 30 minutes, or until dough has risen 1 inch above pans.

4. Bake at 350°F (175°C) for 30 minutes.

Best Bread Machine Bread

Submitted by: **Karen K.**

Makes: 1 - 1½ pound loaf

Preparation: 10 minutes

Cooking: 40 minutes

Total: 3 hours

"This recipe is easy and foolproof. It makes a very soft and tasty loaf of bread with a flaky crust."

INGREDIENTS

1 cup warm water (110°F / 45°C)

2 tablespoons white sugar

1 (.25 ounce) package bread machine yeast

¼ cup vegetable oil

3 cups bread flour

1 teaspoon salt

DIRECTIONS

1. Place the water, sugar and yeast in the pan of the bread machine. Let the yeast dissolve and foam for 10 minutes. Add the oil, flour and salt to the yeast. Select Basic or White Bread setting, and press Start.

French Bread

Submitted by: **Jenn Hall**

Makes: 2 large loaves
Preparation: 25 minutes
Cooking: 40 minutes
Total: 2 hours 40 minutes

"A crisp, crunchy crust and slightly chewy center make this bread as traditional as the breads served in France."

INGREDIENTS

6 cups all-purpose flour

2¹/₂ (.25 ounce) packages active dry yeast

1¹/₂ teaspoons salt

2 cups warm water (110°F / 45°C)

1 tablespoon cornmeal

1 egg white

1 tablespoon water

DIRECTIONS

1. In a large bowl, combine 2 cups flour, yeast and salt. Stir in 2 cups warm water, and beat until well blended using a stand mixer with a dough hook attachment. Using a wooden spoon, stir in as much of the remaining flour as you can.

2. On a lightly floured surface, knead in enough flour to make a stiff dough that is smooth and elastic. Knead for about 8 to 10 minutes total. Shape into a ball. Place dough in a greased bowl, and turn once. Cover, and let rise in a warm place until doubled.

3. Punch dough down, and divide in half. Turn out onto a lightly floured surface. Cover, and let rest for 10 minutes. Roll each half into large rectangle. Roll up, starting from a long side. Moisten edge with water and seal. Taper ends.

4. Grease a large baking sheet. Sprinkle with cornmeal. Place loaves, seam side down, on the prepared baking sheet. Lightly beat the egg white with 1 tablespoon of water, and brush on. Cover with a damp cloth. Let rise until nearly doubled, 35 to 40 minutes.

5. With a very sharp knife, make 3 or 4 diagonal cuts about ¼ inch deep across top of each loaf. Bake in a preheated 375°F (190°C) oven for 20 minutes. Brush again with egg white mixture. Bake for an additional 15 to 20 minutes, or until bread tests done. If necessary, cover loosely with foil to prevent over browning. Remove from baking sheet, and cool on a wire rack.

French Baguettes

Submitted by: **Judy Taubert**

Makes: 2 baguettes

Preparation: 15 minutes

Cooking: 25 minutes

Total: 1 hour 50 minutes

"Great eaten fresh from oven. Used to make sub sandwiches, etc."

INGREDIENTS

1 cup water

2¹/₂ cups bread flour

1 tablespoon white sugar

1 teaspoon salt

1¹/₂ teaspoons bread machine yeast

1 egg yolk

1 tablespoon water

DIRECTIONS

1. Place 1 cup water, bread flour, sugar, salt and yeast into bread machine pan in the order recommended by manufacturer. Select Dough cycle, and press Start.

2. When the cycle has completed, place dough in a greased bowl, turning to coat all sides. Cover, and let rise in a warm place for about 30 minutes, or until doubled in bulk. Dough is ready if indentation remains when touched.

3. Punch down dough. On a lightly floured surface, roll into a 16x12 inch rectangle. Cut dough in half, creating two 8x12 inch rectangles. Roll up each half of dough tightly, beginning at 12 inch side, pounding out any air bubbles as you go. Roll gently back and forth to taper end. Place 3 inches apart on a greased cookie sheet. Make deep diagonal slashes across loaves every 2 inches, or make one lengthwise slash on each loaf. Cover, and let rise in a warm place for 30 to 40 minutes, or until doubled in bulk.

4. Preheat oven to 375°F (190°C). Mix egg yolk with 1 tablespoon water; brush over tops of loaves.

5. Bake for 20 to 25 minutes in the preheated oven, or until golden brown.

Honey Wheat Bread

Submitted by: **Kristin Zaharias**

Makes: 2 - 9x5 inch loaves

Preparation: 25 minutes

Cooking: 35 minutes

Total: 2 hours 30 minutes

"This is a county fair blue ribbon winning loaf - it is delicate and soft."

INGREDIENTS

1 (.25 ounce) package rapid rise yeast

1 teaspoon white sugar

½ cup warm water (110°F / 45°C)

1 (12 fluid ounce) can evaporated milk

¼ cup water

¼ cup melted shortening

¼ cup honey

2 teaspoons salt

2 cups whole wheat flour

3 cups bread flour

2 tablespoons butter

DIRECTIONS

1. Dissolve yeast and sugar in ½ cup warm water.

2. Combine milk, ¼ cup water, shortening, honey, salt and wheat flour in food processor or bowl. Mix in yeast mixture, and let rest 15 minutes. Add white flour, and process until dough forms a ball. Knead dough by processing an additional 80 seconds in food processor, or mix and knead by hand 10 minutes. Place the dough in a buttered bowl, and turn to coat. Cover the bowl with plastic wrap. Let dough rise for 45 minutes, or until almost doubled.

3. Punch down, and divide dough in half. Roll out each half, and pound out the bubbles. Form into loaves, and place in buttered 9x5 inch bread pans. Butter the tops of the dough, and cover loosely with plastic wrap. Let rise in a warm area until doubled; second rise should take about 30 minutes.

4. Place a small pan of water on the bottom shelf of the oven. Preheat oven to 375°F (190°C).

5. Bake for 25 to 35 minutes, or until tops are dark golden brown. Butter crusts while warm. Slice when cool.

Whole Wheat Honey Bread

Submitted by: **Melinda Halvorson**

Makes: 1 - 1¹/₂ pound loaf

Preparation: 5 minutes

Cooking: 3 hours

Total: 3 hours 5 minutes

"This is our family favorite! Very moist."

INGREDIENTS

1¹/₈ cups water

3 cups whole wheat flour

1¹/₂ teaspoons salt

¹/₃ cup honey

1 tablespoon dry milk powder

1¹/₂ tablespoons shortening

1¹/₂ teaspoons active dry yeast

DIRECTIONS

1. Place ingredients in bread machine pan in the order suggested by the manufacturer. Select Whole Wheat setting, and then press Start.

Honey Of An Oatmeal Bread

Submitted by: **Merrilee**

Makes: 1 - 1 pound loaf

Preparation: 5 minutes

Cooking: 3 hours

Total: 3 hours 5 minutes

"Our family goes through a loaf of this every day. Slightly sweet, and light. Great with dinner, and a favorite for sandwiches."

INGREDIENTS

1 cup water

1 tablespoon vegetable oil

1/4 cup honey

1 teaspoon salt

1/2 cup rolled oats

2 cups bread flour

1 teaspoon active dry yeast

DIRECTIONS

1. Place ingredients in bread machine pan in the order suggested by the manufacturer.

2. Select Light Crust or Basic setting, and press Start.

Garlic Bread

Submitted by: **Jenny Kernan**

Makes: 1 - 2 pound loaf

Preparation: 5 minutes

Cooking: 3 hours

Total: 3 hours 5 minutes

"This is a fragrant and tasty bread machine recipe."

INGREDIENTS

1³/₈ cups water

3 tablespoons olive oil

1 teaspoon minced garlic

4 cups bread flour

3 tablespoons white sugar

2 teaspoons salt

¼ cup grated Parmesan cheese

1 teaspoon dried basil

1 teaspoon garlic powder

3 tablespoons chopped fresh chives

1 teaspoon coarsely ground black pepper

2½ teaspoons bread machine yeast

DIRECTIONS

1. Place ingredients in the bread machine pan in the order suggested by the manufacturer.

2. Select Basic or White Bread cycle, and press Start.

Cheese Herb Bread

Submitted by: **D. Reichel**

Makes: 1 -1½ pound loaf

Preparation: 10 minutes

Cooking: 40 minutes

Total: 3 hours

"Fantastic with any Italian dish! I use fresh herbs from my garden when they are available. When using fresh herbs, double the given amount. The smell will make it impossible to wait. ENJOY!"

INGREDIENTS

1¼ cups warm water (110°F / 45°C)

3 cups bread flour

2 tablespoons dry milk powder

2 tablespoons white sugar

1½ teaspoons salt

2 tablespoons butter, softened

3 tablespoons grated Parmesan cheese

1½ teaspoons dried marjoram

1½ teaspoons dried thyme

1 teaspoon dried basil

1 teaspoon dried oregano

1 tablespoon active dry yeast

DIRECTIONS

1. Place ingredients in bread machine pan in the order suggested by the manufacturer. Select the Basic or White Bread cycle, and press Start.

Jay's Signature Pizza Crust

Submitted by: **Jason Sharp**

Makes: 1 giant pizza crust
Preparation: 30 minutes
Cooking: 20 minutes
Total: 1 hour 50 minutes

"This recipe yields a crust that is soft and doughy on the inside and slightly crusty on the outside. Cover it with your favorite sauce and topping to make a delicious pizza."

INGREDIENTS

2¼ teaspoons active dry yeast

½ teaspoon brown sugar

1 teaspoon salt

2 tablespoons olive oil

1½ cups warm water (110°F / 45°C)

3⅓ cups all-purpose flour

DIRECTIONS

1. In a large bowl, dissolve the yeast and brown sugar in the water, and let sit for 10 minutes.

2. Stir the salt and oil into the yeast solution. Mix in 2½ cups of the flour.

3. Turn dough out onto a clean, well floured surface, and knead in more flour until the dough is no longer sticky. Place the dough into a well oiled bowl, and cover with a cloth. Let the dough rise until double; this should take about 1 hour. Punch down the dough, and form a tight ball. Allow the dough to relax for a minute before rolling out. Use for your favorite pizza recipe.

4. Preheat oven to 425°F (220°C). If you are baking the dough on a pizza stone, you may place your toppings on the dough, and bake immediately. If you are baking your pizza in a pan, lightly oil the pan, and let the dough rise for 15 or 20 minutes before topping and baking it.

5. Bake pizza in preheated oven, until the cheese and crust are golden brown, about 15 to 20 minutes.

Focaccia Bread

Submitted by: **Terri McCarrell**

Makes: 1 focaccia

Preparation: 20 minutes

Cooking: 15 minutes

Total: 1 hour

"A wonderful, quick alternative to garlic bread. Lots of herbs and lots of flavor!"

INGREDIENTS

2¾ cups all-purpose flour

1 teaspoon salt

1 teaspoon white sugar

1 tablespoon active dry yeast

1 teaspoon garlic powder

1 teaspoon dried oregano

1 teaspoon dried thyme

½ teaspoon dried basil

1 pinch ground black pepper

1 tablespoon vegetable oil

1 cup water

2 tablespoons olive oil

1 tablespoon grated Parmesan cheese

1 cup mozzarella

DIRECTIONS

1. In a large bowl, stir together the flour, salt, sugar, yeast, garlic powder, oregano, thyme, basil and black pepper. Mix in the vegetable oil and water.

2. When the dough has pulled together, turn it out onto a lightly floured surface, and knead until smooth and elastic. Lightly oil a large bowl, place the dough in the bowl, and turn to coat with oil. Cover with a damp cloth, and let rise in a warm place for 20 minutes.

3. Preheat oven to 450°F (230°C). Punch dough down; place on greased baking sheet. Pat into a ½ inch thick rectangle. Brush top with olive oil. Sprinkle with Parmesan cheese and mozzarella cheese.

4. Bake in preheated oven for 15 minutes, or until golden brown. Serve warm.

Bread Machine Bagels

Submitted by: **Cristy Chu**

Makes: 9 bagels

Preparation: 30 minutes

Cooking: 3 hours 25 minutes

Total: 3 hours 55 minutes

"Quick and easy bagels you can make with your bread machine! You can use whatever topping that you wish — many like poppy seeds."

INGREDIENTS

1 cup warm water (110°F / 45°C)

1½ teaspoons salt

2 tablespoons white sugar

3 cups bread flour

2¼ teaspoons active dry yeast

3 quarts boiling water

3 tablespoons white sugar

1 tablespoon cornmeal

1 egg white

3 tablespoons poppy seeds

DIRECTIONS

1. Place water, salt, sugar, flour and yeast in the bread machine pan in the order recommended by the manufacturer. Select Dough setting.

2. When cycle is complete, let dough rest on a lightly floured surface. Meanwhile, in a large pot bring 3 quarts of water to a boil. Stir in 3 tablespoons of sugar.

3. Cut dough into 9 equal pieces, and roll each piece into a small ball. Flatten balls. Poke a hole in the middle of each with your thumb. Twirl the dough on your finger or thumb to enlarge the hole, and to even out the dough around the hole. Cover bagels with a clean cloth, and let rest for 10 minutes.

4. Sprinkle an ungreased baking sheet with cornmeal. Carefully transfer bagels to boiling water. Boil for 1 minute, turning half way through. Drain briefly on clean towel. Arrange boiled bagels on baking sheet. Glaze tops with egg white, and sprinkle with your choice of toppings.

5. Bake in a preheated 375 degree F (190°C) oven for 20 to 25 minutes, until well browned.

Mall Pretzels

Submitted by: **Jeannie Yee**

Makes: 1 dozen pretzels

Preparation: 30 minutes

Cooking: 20 minutes

Total: 3 hours

"Big chewy pretzels like those sold in the mall! You may substitute garlic salt or cinnamon sugar for the coarse salt if you wish."

INGREDIENTS

1 (.25 ounce) package active dry yeast

2 tablespoons brown sugar

1⅛ teaspoons salt

1½ cups warm water (110°F / 45°C)

3 cups all-purpose flour

1 cup bread flour

2 cups warm water (110°F / 45°C)

2 tablespoons baking soda

2 tablespoons butter, melted

2 tablespoons coarse kosher salt

DIRECTIONS

1. In a large mixing bowl, dissolve the yeast, brown sugar and salt in 1½ cups warm water. Stir in flour, and knead dough on a floured surface until smooth and elastic, about 8 minutes. Place in a greased bowl, and turn to coat the surface. Cover, and let rise for one hour.

2. Combine 2 cups warm water and baking soda in an 8 inch square pan.

3. After dough has risen, cut into 12 pieces. Roll each piece into a 3 foot rope, pencil thin or thinner. Twist into a pretzel shape, and dip into the baking soda solution. Place on parchment covered cookie sheets, and let rise 15 to 20 minutes.

4. Bake at 450°F (230°C) for 8 to 10 minutes, or until golden brown. Brush with melted butter, and sprinkle with coarse salt, garlic salt or cinnamon sugar.

Irresistible Irish Soda Bread

Submitted by: **Karin Christian**

Makes: 1 - 9x5 inch loaf

Preparation: 15 minutes

Cooking: 1 hour 10 minutes

Total: 1 hour 25 minutes

"A very easy, very good tasting bread. Best if made the day before, or several hours before serving."

INGREDIENTS

3 cups all-purpose flour

1 tablespoon baking powder

1/3 cup white sugar

1 teaspoon salt

1 teaspoon baking soda

1 egg, lightly beaten

2 cups buttermilk

1/4 cup butter, melted

DIRECTIONS

1. Preheat oven to 325°F (165°C). Grease a 9x5 inch loaf pan.

2. Combine flour, baking powder, sugar, salt and baking soda. Blend eggs and buttermilk together, and add all at once to the flour mixture. Mix just until moistened. Stir in butter. Pour into prepared pan.

3. Bake for 65 to 70 minutes, or until a toothpick inserted in the bread comes out clean. Cool on a wire rack. Wrap in foil for several hours, or overnight, for best flavor.

Homesteader Cornbread

Submitted by: **Patricia Bergstrom**

Makes: 1 - 9x13 inch pan

Preparation: 15 minutes

Cooking: 30 minutes

Total: 50 minutes

"This recipe comes from my mother-in-law in Canada. It's the most moist corn bread that I have ever tasted. It's great with chili con carne or as stuffing for your holiday turkey."

INGREDIENTS

1½ cups cornmeal

2½ cups milk

2 cups all-purpose flour

1 tablespoon baking powder

1 teaspoon salt

²/3 cup white sugar

2 eggs

½ cup vegetable oil

DIRECTIONS

1. Preheat oven to 400°F (200°C). In a small bowl, combine corn meal and milk; let stand for 5 minutes.

2. In a large bowl, whisk together flour, baking powder, salt and sugar. Mix in the cornmeal mixture, eggs and oil until smooth. Pour batter into prepared pan.

3. Bake in preheated oven for 30 to 35 minutes, or until a knife inserted into the center of the cornbread comes out clean.

Golden Sweet Cornbread

Submitted by: **Lori White**

Makes: 1 - 9 inch round pan

Preparation: 10 minutes

Cooking: 25 minutes

Total: 35 minutes

"If you like sweet cornbread, this is the recipe for you! My mom made this for me as a child, and now it's my family's favorite."

INGREDIENTS

1 cup all-purpose flour

1 cup yellow cornmeal

2/3 cup white sugar

1 teaspoon salt

3 1/2 teaspoons baking powder

1 egg

1 cup milk

1/3 cup vegetable oil

DIRECTIONS

1. Preheat oven to 400°F (200°C). Spray or lightly grease a 9 inch round cake pan.

2. In a large bowl, combine flour, cornmeal, sugar, salt and baking powder. Stir in egg, milk and vegetable oil until well combined. Pour batter into prepared pan.

3. Bake in preheated oven for 20 to 25 minutes, or until a toothpick inserted into the center of the loaf comes out clean.

Apple Loaf

Submitted by: **Carol**

Makes: 1 loaf

Preparation: 15 minutes

Cooking: 1 hour

Total: 1 hour 25 minutes

"With a large abundance of apples on hand all year round, here is a recipe that is tender and has a delicate apple flavor."

INGREDIENTS

2 cups all-purpose flour

1 teaspoon baking powder

1/2 teaspoon baking soda

1/2 teaspoon salt

1/2 cup chopped walnuts

1/2 cup butter, softened

1 cup white sugar

2 eggs

1 teaspoon vanilla extract

1 cup apples - peeled, cored and shredded

DIRECTIONS

1. Preheat oven to 350°F (175°C). Grease one 9x5 inch loaf pan.

2. Mix together flour, baking powder, soda, salt and nuts.

3. In a large bowl, beat margarine, sugar and 1 egg until smooth. Beat in second egg, and stir in vanilla. Stir in shredded apples. Pour flour mixture into batter; stir just until moistened. Spread into prepared pan.

4. Bake for 50 to 60 minutes, or until an inserted toothpick comes out clean. Let stand 10 minutes, then remove from pan. Place on a rack to cool.

Banana Banana Bread

Submitted by: **Shelley Albeluhn**

Makes: 1 - 9x5 inch loaf

Preparation: 15 minutes

Cooking: 1 hour 5 minutes

Total: 1 hour 20 minutes

"Why compromise the banana flavor? This banana bread is moist and delicious with loads of banana flavor! Friends and family love my recipe and say it's by far the best! It's wonderful toasted!! Enjoy!"

INGREDIENTS

2 cups all-purpose flour

1 teaspoon baking soda

1/4 teaspoon salt

1/2 cup butter

3/4 cup brown sugar

2 eggs, beaten

2 1/3 cups mashed overripe bananas

DIRECTIONS

1. Preheat oven to 350°F (175°C). Lightly grease a 9x5 inch loaf pan.

2. In a large bowl, combine flour, baking soda and salt. In a separate bowl, cream together butter and brown sugar. Stir in eggs and mashed bananas until well blended. Stir banana mixture into flour mixture; stir just to moisten. Pour batter into prepared loaf pan.

3. Bake in preheated oven for 60 to 65 minutes, until a toothpick inserted into center of the loaf comes out clean. Let bread cool in pan for 10 minutes, then turn out onto a wire rack.

Banana Sour Cream Bread

Submitted by: **Esther Nelson**

Makes: 4 - 7x3 inch loaves

Preparation: 10 minutes

Cooking: 1 hour

Total: 1 hour 10 minutes

"I know, you're probably thinking, 'Oh no! Another banana bread recipe!' But this one is a little different: the sour cream makes this one so moist it melts in your mouth. The flavor is just wonderful! This one is great for gift giving and holidays. Loaves freeze well."

INGREDIENTS

¼ cup white sugar

1 teaspoon ground cinnamon

¾ cup butter

3 cups white sugar

3 eggs

6 very ripe bananas, mashed

1 (16 ounce) container sour cream

2 teaspoons vanilla extract

2 teaspoons ground cinnamon

½ teaspoon salt

3 teaspoons baking soda

4½ cups all-purpose flour

1 cup chopped walnuts (optional)

DIRECTIONS

1. Preheat oven to 300°F (150°C). Grease four 7x3 inch loaf pans. In a small bowl, stir together ¼ cup white sugar and 1 teaspoon cinnamon. Dust pans lightly with cinnamon and sugar mixture.

2. In a large bowl, cream butter and 3 cups sugar. Mix in eggs, mashed bananas, sour cream, vanilla and cinnamon. Mix in salt, baking soda and flour. Stir in nuts. Divide into prepared pans.

3. Bake for 1 hour, until a toothpick inserted in center comes out clean.

Chocolate Banana Bread

Submitted by: **Tracie P.**

Makes: 2 - 9x5 inch loaves

Preparation: 10 minutes

Cooking: 1 hour

Total: 1 hour 10 minutes

"This is a very different banana bread recipe; it has chocolate chips, cocoa, and a touch of sour cream. Delicious!"

INGREDIENTS

1 cup margarine, softened

2 cups white sugar

4 eggs

6 bananas, mashed

2 teaspoons vanilla extract

3 cups all-purpose flour

2 teaspoons baking soda

¼ cup unsweetened cocoa powder

1 cup lite sour cream

1 cup semisweet chocolate chips

DIRECTIONS

1. Preheat oven to 350°F (175°C). Lightly grease two 9x5 inch loaf pans.

2. In a large bowl, cream together margarine, sugar and eggs. Stir in bananas and vanilla. Sift in flour, baking soda and cocoa; mix well. Blend in sour cream and chocolate chips. Pour batter into prepared pans.

3. Bake in preheated oven for 60 minutes, or until a toothpick inserted into center of a loaf comes out clean.

Zucchini Bread IV

Submitted by: **Kristen**

Makes: 2 - 8x4 inch loaves

Preparation: 15 minutes

Cooking: 1 hour 10 minutes

Total: 1 hour 25 minutes

"This is the best zucchini bread I have made! I have other recipes, but this is the best! Thanks to my mother!"

INGREDIENTS

3 eggs

1 cup vegetable oil

2 cups white sugar

2 cups grated zucchini

2 teaspoons vanilla extract

1/2 cup chopped walnuts

1 teaspoon salt

1/4 teaspoon baking powder

3 cups all-purpose flour

3 teaspoons ground cinnamon

1 teaspoon baking soda

DIRECTIONS

1. Preheat oven to 325°F (165°C). Grease and flour two 8x4 inch loaf pans.

2. In a large bowl, beat eggs until light and frothy. Mix in oil and sugar. Stir in zucchini and vanilla. Combine flour, cinnamon, soda, baking powder, salt and nuts; stir into the egg mixture. Divide batter into prepared pans.

3. Bake for 60 to 70 minutes, or until done.

Downeast Maine Pumpkin Bread

Submitted by: **Laurie Bennett**

Makes: 3 - 7x3 inch loaf pans

Preparation: 15 minutes

Cooking: 50 minutes

Total: 1 hour 5 minutes

"This a great old Maine recipe, moist and spicy. The bread actually tastes even better the day after it is baked. Great for holiday gift giving!"

INGREDIENTS

1 (15 ounce) can pumpkin puree

4 eggs

1 cup vegetable oil

2/3 cup water

3 cups white sugar

3 1/2 cups all-purpose flour

2 teaspoons baking soda

1 1/2 teaspoons salt

1 teaspoon ground cinnamon

1 teaspoon ground nutmeg

1/2 teaspoon ground cloves

1/4 teaspoon ground ginger

DIRECTIONS

1. Preheat oven to 350°F (175°C). Grease and flour three 7x3 inch loaf pans.

2. In a large bowl, mix together pumpkin puree, eggs, oil, water and sugar until well blended. In a separate bowl, whisk together the flour, baking soda, salt, cinnamon, nutmeg, cloves and ginger. Stir the dry ingredients into the pumpkin mixture until just blended. Pour into the prepared pans.

3. Bake for about 50 minutes in the preheated oven. Loaves are done when toothpick inserted in center comes out clean.

Chocolate Chip Pumpkin Bread

Submitted by: **Star Pooley**

Makes: 3 - loaf pans

Preparation: 30 minutes

Cooking: 1 hour

Total: 1 hour 30 minutes

"I make this recipe during the holidays. It is moist, and freezes well! I bake them in coffee cans, and wrap them in colored cellophane to give as gifts."

INGREDIENTS

3 cups white sugar

1 (15 ounce) can pumpkin puree

1 cup vegetable oil

2/3 cup water

4 eggs

3 1/2 cups all-purpose flour

1 tablespoon ground cinnamon

1 tablespoon ground nutmeg

2 tablespoons baking soda

1 1/2 teaspoons salt

1 cup miniature semisweet chocolate chips

1/2 cup chopped walnuts (optional)

DIRECTIONS

1. Preheat oven to 350°F (175°C). Grease and flour three 1 pound size coffee cans, or three 9x5 inch loaf pans.

2. In a large bowl, combine sugar, pumpkin, oil, water and eggs. Beat until smooth. Blend in flour, cinnamon, nutmeg, baking soda and salt. Fold in chocolate chips and nuts. Fill cans ½ to ¾ full.

3. Bake for 1 hour, or until an inserted knife comes out clean. Cool on wire racks before removing from cans or pans.

cakes, pies & desserts

Looking for a sweet something that's deliciously decadent, but totally do-able? Wishing to create an elegant grand finale to a special dinner? Seeking a sweet shortcut when dinner is rushed? Yearning for that long-lost pie that Grandma baked? We've got an applause-winning cake, cheesecake, pie, cobbler, crisp, or pudding for every occasion.

Aunt Johnnie's Pound Cake

Submitted by: **Jean Higginbotham**

Makes: 1 - 10 inch Bundt cake

Preparation: 30 minutes

Cooking: 1 hour 30 minutes

Total: 2 hours

"This is a moist, very flavorful pound cake. Absolutely wonderful plain or served with strawberries and whipped cream."

INGREDIENTS

½ cup shortening

1 cup butter

2½ cups white sugar

5 eggs

2 teaspoons almond extract

1 cup milk

½ teaspoon baking powder

3 cups cake flour

DIRECTIONS

1. Preheat oven to 300°F (150°C). Lightly grease and flour a 10 inch Bundt pan.

2. Cream shortening, butter and sugar until light and fluffy (for best results use an electric mixer). This will take a while. Add eggs one at a time, beating well after each addition. Beat in almond extract.

3. Combine baking powder and flour. Stir into creamed mixture alternately with the milk, starting and ending with flour. Pour batter into prepared pan.

4. Bake in the preheated oven for 1 to 1½ hours, or until a toothpick inserted into the center of the cake comes out clean. Let cool in pan for 10 minutes, then turn out onto a wire rack and cool completely.

Pecan Sour Cream Pound Cake

Submitted by: **Carole Resnick**

Makes: 1 - 10-inch Bundt cake

Preparation: 30 minutes

Cooking: 1 hour 30 minutes

Total: 2 hours 20 minutes

"I won first place with this cake at the Cuyahoga County Fair (Cleveland, Ohio) in 1993. For a nuttier variation, you can substitute 1 cup of the flour with 1 cup of ground pecans."

INGREDIENTS

1/4 cup chopped pecans

3 cups cake flour

1/2 teaspoon salt

1/4 teaspoon baking soda

1 cup unsalted butter

3 cups white sugar

6 eggs

1 teaspoon vanilla extract

1 cup sour cream

1 cup confectioners' sugar

3 tablespoons orange juice

1 teaspoon vanilla extract

DIRECTIONS

1. Preheat oven to 300°F (150°C). Grease and flour a 10 inch Bundt or tube pan. Sprinkle pecans on bottom of pan; set aside. Sift together flour, salt, and baking soda into a medium bowl; set aside.

2. In a large bowl, cream butter and white sugar until light and fluffy. Beat in eggs one at a time, then stir in vanilla. Add flour mixture alternately with sour cream. Pour batter over pecans in prepared pan.

3. Bake in the preheated oven for 75 to 90 minutes, or until a toothpick inserted into the center of the cake comes out clean. Let cool in pan for 20 minutes, then turn out onto a wire rack and cool completely.

4. To prepare the glaze: In a small bowl, combine confectioners' sugar, orange juice and 1 teaspoon vanilla. Drizzle over cake while still warm.

Kentucky Butter Cake

Submitted by: **Suzanne Stull**

Makes: 1 - 10 inch Bundt cake

Preparation: 30 minutes

Cooking: 1 hour

Total: 2 hours

"Moist and buttery cake made from readily available ingredients with a luscious butter sauce."

INGREDIENTS

3 cups unbleached all-purpose flour

2 cups white sugar

1 teaspoon salt

1 teaspoon baking powder

½ teaspoon baking soda

1 cup buttermilk

1 cup butter

2 teaspoons vanilla extract

4 eggs

¾ cup white sugar

⅓ cup butter

3 tablespoons water

2 teaspoons vanilla extract

DIRECTIONS

1. Preheat oven to 325°F (165°C). Grease and flour a 10 inch Bundt pan.

2. In a large bowl, mix the flour, 2 cups sugar, salt, baking powder and baking soda. Blend in buttermilk, 1 cup of butter, 2 teaspoons of vanilla and 4 eggs. Beat for 3 minutes at medium speed. Pour batter into prepared pan.

3. Bake in preheated oven for 60 minutes, or until a wooden toothpick inserted into center of cake comes out clean. Prick holes in the still warm cake. Slowly pour sauce over cake. Let cake cool before removing from pan.

4. To Make Butter Sauce: In a saucepan combine the remaining ¾ cups sugar, ⅓ cup butter, 2 teaspoons vanilla, and the water. Cook over medium heat, until fully melted and combined, but do not boil.

Buttery Cinnamon Cake

Submitted by: **Leta Harris**

Makes: 1 - 10 inch Bundt cake

Preparation: 30 minutes

Cooking: 45 minutes

Total: 1 hour 35 minutes

"This cake is the best cinnamon cake I have ever made. Every time I serve it, the compliments never end. Serve it warm, about 45 minutes out of the oven, for an even greater pleasure."

INGREDIENTS

2 cups all-purpose flour

1 tablespoon baking powder

1 teaspoon ground cinnamon

3/4 teaspoon salt

2/3 cup shortening

1 1/3 cups white sugar

1 1/2 teaspoons vanilla extract

3 eggs

2/3 cup milk

1/2 cup white sugar

6 tablespoons butter

1/3 cup water

1 teaspoon vanilla extract

3/4 teaspoon ground cinnamon

DIRECTIONS

1. Preheat oven to 350°F (175°C). Grease and lightly flour a 10 inch Bundt pan. Stir together the flour, baking powder, 1 teaspoon ground cinnamon and salt; set aside.

2. In a large bowl, beat shortening, 1 1/3 cups white sugar and 1 1/2 teaspoon vanilla until light and fluffy. Add eggs one at a time, beating for at least 1 minute after each egg. Beat in the flour mixture alternately with the milk. Pour batter into prepared pan.

3. Bake in the preheated oven for 40 to 45 minutes, or until a toothpick inserted into the center of the cake comes out clean. Let cool in pan for 10 minutes, then turn out onto a wire rack. Remove cake from pan while it is still warm, and poke holes around the top of the cake with a fork. Pour the warm cinnamon syrup into the holes and onto the top and sides of the cake.

4. To Make Cinnamon Syrup: In a saucepan, combine 1/2 cup white sugar, butter, water, 1 teaspoon vanilla and 3/4 teaspoons ground cinnamon. Heat and stir until butter melts.

Incredibly Delicious Italian Cream Cake

Submitted by: **Rory**

Makes: 1 - 3 layer 9 inch cake

Preparation: 30 minutes

Cooking: 35 minutes

Total: 1 hour 35 minutes

"This is an old recipe from my aunt. It is both famous and infamous in our family. It is absolutely irresistible."

INGREDIENTS

1 cup buttermilk	2 cups all-purpose flour
1 teaspoon baking soda	8 ounces cream cheese
½ cup butter	½ cup butter
½ cup shortening	1 teaspoon vanilla extract
2 cups white sugar	4 cups confectioners' sugar
5 eggs	2 tablespoons light cream
1 teaspoon vanilla extract	½ cup chopped walnuts
1 cup flaked coconut	1 cup flaked coconut
1 teaspoon baking powder	

DIRECTIONS

1. Preheat oven to 350°F (175°F). Grease 3 - 9 inch round cake pans. In a small bowl, dissolve the baking soda in the buttermilk; set aside.

2. In a large bowl, cream together ½ cup butter, shortening and white sugar until light and fluffy. Mix in the eggs, buttermilk mixture, 1 teaspoon vanilla, 1 cup coconut, baking powder and flour. Stir until just combined. Pour batter into the prepared pans.

3. Bake in the preheated oven for 30 to 35 minutes, or until a toothpick inserted into the center of the cake comes out clean. Allow to cool.

4. To Make Frosting: In a medium bowl, combine cream cheese, ½ cup butter, 1 teaspoon vanilla and confectioners' sugar. Beat until light and fluffy. Mix in a small amount of cream to attain the desired consistency. Stir in chopped nuts and remaining flaked coconut. Spread between layers and on top and sides of cooled cake.

Awesome Carrot Cake with Cream Cheese Frosting

Submitted by: **Tracy Kirk**

Makes: 1 - 9x13 inch cake

Preparation: 30 minutes

Cooking: 40 minutes

Total: 1 hour 40 minutes

"A moist, dense and delicious cake."

INGREDIENTS

3 cups grated carrots

2 cups all-purpose flour

2 cups white sugar

2 teaspoons baking soda

1 teaspoon baking powder

1/2 teaspoon salt

1 teaspoon ground cinnamon

4 eggs

1 1/2 cups vegetable oil

1 1/4 teaspoons vanilla extract

1 (8 ounce) can crushed pineapple with juice

3/4 cup chopped pecans

3 1/2 cups confectioners' sugar

1 (8 ounce) package Neufchatel cheese

1/2 cup butter, softened

1 1/4 teaspoons vanilla extract

1 cup chopped pecans

DIRECTIONS

1. Preheat oven to 350°F (175°C). Grease and flour a 9x13 inch pan.

2. In a large bowl, combine grated carrots, flour, white sugar, baking soda, baking powder, salt and cinnamon. Stir in eggs, oil, 1¼ teaspoon vanilla, pineapple and ¾ cup chopped pecans. Spoon batter into prepared pan.

3. Bake in the preheated oven for 30 to 40 minutes, or until a toothpick inserted into the center of the cake comes out clean. Allow to cool.

4. To Make Frosting: In a medium bowl, combine confectioners' sugar, Neufchatel cheese, ½ cup butter or margarine and 1¼ teaspoons vanilla. Beat until smooth, then stir in 1 cup chopped pecans. Spread on cooled cake.

Carrot Cake III

Submitted by: **Tammy Elliott**

Makes: 1 - 9x13 inch cake

Preparation: 30 minutes

Cooking: 1 hour

Total: 2 hours

"I've tried many carrot cakes, and this is my favorite recipe. If you don't like pecans, feel free to leave them out."

INGREDIENTS

4 eggs

1¼ cups vegetable oil

2 cups white sugar

2 teaspoons vanilla extract

2 cups all-purpose flour

2 teaspoons baking soda

2 teaspoons baking powder

½ teaspoon salt

2 teaspoons ground cinnamon

3 cups grated carrots

1 cup chopped pecans

½ cup butter, softened

8 ounces cream cheese, softened

4 cups confectioners' sugar

1 teaspoon vanilla extract

1 cup chopped pecans

DIRECTIONS

1. Preheat oven to 350°F (175°C). Grease and flour a 9x13 inch pan.

2. In a large bowl, beat together eggs, oil, white sugar and 2 teaspoons vanilla. Mix in flour, baking soda, baking powder, salt and cinnamon. Stir in carrots. Fold in pecans. Pour into prepared pan.

3. Bake in the preheated oven for 40 to 50 minutes, or until a toothpick inserted into the center of the cake comes out clean. Let cool in pan for 10 minutes, then turn out onto a wire rack and cool completely.

4. To Make Frosting: In a medium bowl, combine butter, cream cheese, confectioners' sugar and 1 teaspoon vanilla. Beat until the mixture is smooth and creamy. Stir in chopped pecans. Frost the cooled cake.

Apple Bundt Cake

Submitted by: **Carol**

Makes: 1 - 10 inch Bundt cake

Preparation: 30 minutes

Cooking: 1 hour

Total: 2 hours

"This is a good wholesome cake, especially nice for the fall."

INGREDIENTS

2 cups apples - peeled, cored and diced

1 tablespoon white sugar

1 teaspoon ground cinnamon

3 cups all-purpose flour

3 teaspoons baking powder

1/2 teaspoon salt

2 cups white sugar

1 cup vegetable oil

1/4 cup orange juice

2 1/2 teaspoons vanilla extract

4 eggs

1 cup chopped walnuts

1/4 cup confectioners' sugar for dusting

DIRECTIONS

1. Preheat oven to 350°F (175°C). Grease and flour a 10 inch Bundt or tube pan. In a medium bowl, combine the diced apples, 1 tablespoon white sugar and 1 teaspoon cinnamon; set aside. Sift together the flour, baking powder and salt; set aside.

2. In a large bowl, combine 2 cups white sugar, oil, orange juice, vanilla and eggs. Beat at high speed until smooth. Stir in flour mixture. Fold in chopped walnuts.

3. Pour ⅓ of the batter into prepared pan. Sprinkle with ½ of the apple mixture. Alternate layers of batter and filling, ending with batter.

4. Bake in preheated oven for 55 to 60 minutes, or until the top springs back when lightly touched. Let cool in pan for 10 minutes, then turn out onto a wire rack and cool completely. Sprinkle with confectioners' sugar.

A-Number-1 Banana Cake

Submitted by: **Kevin Ryan**

Makes: 1 - 2 layer 8 inch cake

Preparation: 30 minutes

Cooking: 30 minutes

Total: 1 hour

"This is a very versatile and fast cake recipe. Not only is it moist and delicious, the same batter can be used to make banana bread and muffins. Delicious frosted with chocolate or cream cheese frosting."

INGREDIENTS

2½ cups all-purpose flour

1 tablespoon baking soda

1 pinch salt

½ cup unsalted butter

1 cup white sugar

¾ cup light brown sugar

2 eggs

4 ripe bananas, mashed

⅔ cup buttermilk

½ cup chopped walnuts

DIRECTIONS

1. Preheat oven to 350°F (175°C). Grease and flour 2 - 8 inch round pans. In a small bowl, whisk together flour, soda and salt; set aside.

2. In a large bowl, cream butter, white sugar and brown sugar until light and fluffy. Beat in eggs, one at a time. Mix in the bananas. Add flour mixture alternately with the buttermilk to the creamed mixture. Stir in chopped walnuts. Pour batter into the prepared pans.

3. Bake in the preheated oven for 30 minutes. Remove from oven, and place on a damp tea towel to cool.

Dark Chocolate Cake

Submitted by: **Carol**

Makes: 1 - 3 layer 9 inch cake

Preparation: 30 minutes

Cooking: 30 minutes

Total: 1 hour 20 minutes

"This is an elegant cake to make."

INGREDIENTS

2 cups boiling water

1 cup unsweetened cocoa powder

2³/₄ cups all-purpose flour

2 teaspoons baking soda

¹/₂ teaspoon baking powder

¹/₂ teaspoon salt

1 cup butter, softened

2¹/₄ cups white sugar

4 eggs

1¹/₂ teaspoons vanilla extract

DIRECTIONS

1. Preheat oven to 350°F (175°C). Grease 3 - 9 inch round cake pans. In medium bowl, pour boiling water over cocoa, and whisk until smooth. Let mixture cool. Sift together flour, baking soda, baking powder and salt; set aside.

2. In a large bowl, cream butter and sugar together until light and fluffy. Beat in eggs one at time, then stir in vanilla. Add the flour mixture alternately with the cocoa mixture. Spread batter evenly between the 3 prepared pans.

3. Bake in preheated oven for 25 to 30 minutes. Allow to cool.

Black Bottom Cupcakes

Submitted by: **Laura Duncan Allen**

Makes: 2 dozen cupcakes

Preparation: 30 minutes

Cooking: 30 minutes

Total: 1 hour

"Chocolate cream cheese cupcakes, rich and gooey. Serve these little gems with a tall glass of ice cold milk."

INGREDIENTS

1 (8 ounce) package cream cheese, softened

1 egg

1/3 cup white sugar

1/8 teaspoon salt

1 cup miniature semisweet chocolate chips

1½ cups all-purpose flour

1 cup white sugar

1/4 cup unsweetened cocoa powder

1 teaspoon baking soda

1/2 teaspoon salt

1 cup water

1/3 cup vegetable oil

1 tablespoon cider vinegar

1 teaspoon vanilla extract

DIRECTIONS

1. Preheat oven to 350°F (175°C). Line muffin tins with paper cups or lightly spray with non-stick cooking spray.

2. In a medium bowl, beat the cream cheese, egg, ⅓ cup sugar and 1/8 teaspoon salt until light and fluffy. Stir in the chocolate chips and set aside.

3. In a large bowl, mix together the flour, 1 cup sugar, cocoa, baking soda and ½ teaspoon salt. Make a well in the center and add the water, oil, vinegar and vanilla. Stir together until well blended. Fill muffin tins ⅓ full with the batter and top with a dollop of the cream cheese mixture.

4. Bake in preheated oven for 25 to 30 minutes.

Chocolate Lovers' Favorite Cake

Submitted by: **Susan Feiler**

Makes: 1 - 10 inch Bundt cake

Preparation: 30 minutes

Cooking: 1 hour

Total: 2 hours

"This easy recipe is a chocoholic's dream come true!"

INGREDIENTS

1 (18.25 ounce) package devil's food cake mix

1 (3 ounce) package instant chocolate pudding mix

2 cups sour cream

1 cup melted butter

5 eggs

1 teaspoon almond extract

2 cups semisweet chocolate chips

DIRECTIONS

1. Preheat oven to 350°F (175°C). Grease a 10 inch Bundt pan.

2. In a large bowl, stir together cake mix and pudding mix. Make a well in the center and pour in sour cream, melted butter, eggs and almond extract. Beat on low speed until blended. Scrape bowl, and beat 4 minutes on medium speed. Blend in chocolate chips. Pour batter into prepared pan.

3. Bake in preheated oven for 50 to 55 minutes. Let cool in pan for 10 minutes, then turn out onto a wire rack and cool completely.

Chocolate Cavity Maker Cake

Submitted by: **Caitlin Koch**

Makes: 1 - 10 inch Bundt cake

Preparation: 30 minutes

Cooking: 1 hour

Total: 2 hours

"Chocolate, chocolate, chocolate. This cake is so moist and rich there's absolutely no need for frosting. This cake made me an instant star with my clients. I quickly became known as 'that incredible chocolate cake lady!'"

INGREDIENTS

1 (18.25 ounce) package dark chocolate cake mix

1 (3 ounce) package instant chocolate pudding mix

1 (16 ounce) container sour cream

3 eggs

⅓ cup vegetable oil

½ cup coffee flavored liqueur

2 cups semisweet chocolate chips

DIRECTIONS

1. Preheat oven to 350°F (175°C). Grease and flour a 10 inch Bundt pan.

2. In a large bowl, combine cake mix, pudding mix, sour cream, eggs, oil and coffee liqueur. Beat until ingredients are well blended. Fold in chocolate chips. Batter will be thick. Spoon into prepared pan.

3. Bake in preheated oven for 1 hour, or until cake springs back when lightly tapped. Cool 10 minutes in pan, then turn out and cool completely on wire rack.

Honey Bun Cake

Submitted by: **Jennifer Walker**

Makes: 1 - 9x13 inch cake

Preparation: 30 minutes

Cooking: 1 hour

Total: 1 hour 45 minutes

"This cake tastes just like the name suggests - like a honey bun. It has been served to hundreds of people and everyone has said how much they liked it. It is a sweet cake and not for those that are watching their weight. Tastes wonderful if served with a small scoop of vanilla ice cream."

INGREDIENTS

1 (18.5 ounce) package yellow cake mix

¾ cup vegetable oil

4 eggs

1 (8 ounce) container sour cream

1 cup brown sugar

1 tablespoon ground cinnamon

2 cups confectioners' sugar

4 tablespoons milk

1 tablespoon vanilla extract

DIRECTIONS

1. Preheat oven to 325°F (165°C).

2. In a large mixing bowl, combine cake mix, oil, eggs and sour cream. Stir by hand approximately 50 strokes, or until most large lumps are gone. Pour half of the batter into an ungreased 9x13 inch glass baking dish. Combine the brown sugar and cinnamon, and sprinkle over the batter in the cake pan. Spoon the other half of the batter into the cake pan, covering the brown sugar and cinnamon. Twirl the cake with a butter knife or icing knife until it looks like a honey bun (or whatever design you want to make).

3. Bake in preheated oven for 40 minutes, or until a toothpick inserted into the center of the cake comes out clean. Frost cake while it is still fairly hot. Serve warm.

4. To Make the frosting: In a small bowl, whisk together the confectioner's sugar, milk and vanilla until smooth.

Orange Cream Cake

Submitted by: **Star Pooley and KC**

Makes: 1 - 9x13 inch cake

Preparation: 30 minutes

Cooking: 1 hour

Total: 4 hours 30 minutes

"Remember those yummy treats on a stick when you were a child? Frozen orange on the outside and creamy vanilla on the inside? Well, here's a cake that tastes just like those wonderful treats! Note: If you cannot find an orange cake mix, use a package of lemon cake mix and add 1 small envelope of orange drink mix powder."

INGREDIENTS

1 (18.25 ounce) package orange cake mix

2 (3 ounce) packages orange flavored gelatin mix

1 (3.5 ounce) package instant vanilla pudding mix

1 cup milk

1 teaspoon vanilla extract

1 (8 ounce) container frozen whipped topping, thawed

DIRECTIONS

1. Bake cake as directed in a 9x13 inch pan. When done, use a meat fork to poke holes across the top of the entire cake. Allow to cool.

2. In a medium bowl, mix together 1 box gelatin, 1 cup hot water and 1 cup cold water. Pour over top of cake. Refrigerate for 2 to 3 hours.

3. Mix remaining box of gelatin, pudding mix, milk and vanilla together. Beat well. Fold whipped topping into this mixture, and spread on top of cake. Chill in refrigerator until serving.

Orange Cake

Submitted by: **Angie LaSala**

Makes: 1 - 10 inch Bundt cake

Preparation: 30 minutes

Cooking: 1 hour

Total: 2 hours

"This is the best cake I have ever tasted. My mom gave me this recipe and I can't make it often because I would weigh 500 pounds. Hope it lasts more than a day at your house!"

INGREDIENTS

1 (18.5 ounce) package yellow cake mix

1 (3 ounce) package instant lemon pudding mix

¾ cup orange juice

½ cup vegetable oil

4 eggs

1 teaspoon lemon extract

⅓ cup orange juice

⅔ cup white sugar

¼ cup butter

DIRECTIONS

1. Grease a 10 inch Bundt pan. Preheat oven to 325°F (165°C).

2. In a large bowl, stir together cake mix and pudding mix. Make a well in the center and pour in ¾ cup orange juice, oil, eggs and lemon extract. Beat on low speed until blended. Scrape bowl, and beat 4 minutes on medium speed. Pour batter into prepared pan.

3. Bake in preheated oven for 50 to 60 minutes. Let cool in pan for 10 minutes, then turn out onto a wire rack and cool completely.

4. In a saucepan over medium heat, cook ⅓ cup orange juice, sugar and butter for two minutes. Drizzle over cake.

Mandarin Orange Cake

Submitted by: **Ellen**

"Quick and delicious!"

Makes: 1 - 9x13 inch cake

Preparation: 30 minutes

Cooking: 1 hour

Total: 2 hours

INGREDIENTS

1 (18.5 ounce) package yellow cake mix

4 eggs

1 cup vegetable oil

1 (11 ounce) can mandarin orange segments

1 (8 ounce) container frozen whipped topping, thawed

1 (20 ounce) can crushed pineapple with juice

1 (3.5 ounce) package instant vanilla pudding mix

DIRECTIONS

1. Preheat oven to 350°F (175°C). Grease and flour a 9x13 inch pan.

2. In a large bowl, combine cake mix, eggs, oil and mandarin oranges with juice. Beat until smooth. Pour batter into prepared pan.

3. Bake in the preheated oven for 35 to 40 minutes, or until a toothpick inserted into the center of the cake comes out clean. Allow to cool.

4. To make the topping: In a large bowl, beat together whipped topping, pineapple with juice and dry pudding mix until blended. Spread on cake.

Apple Cake III

Submitted by: **Mary Ann Benzon**

Makes: 1 - 9x13 inch cake

Preparation: 30 minutes

Cooking: 45 minutes

Total: 1 hour 30 minutes

"This is really an old recipe. It's quick and easy. Hope you enjoy it."

INGREDIENTS

1 (18.5 ounce) package yellow cake mix

3 eggs

1 (21 ounce) can apple pie filling

3/4 cup packed brown sugar

1 tablespoon all-purpose flour

1 tablespoon butter

1 teaspoon ground cinnamon

1 cup chopped walnuts

DIRECTIONS

1. Preheat oven to 350°F (175°C). Grease and flour a 9x13 inch baking pan.

2. In a large bowl, mix together the cake mix, eggs and apple pie filling. Pour into the prepared pan. Combine the brown sugar, flour, butter, cinnamon and walnuts. Sprinkle over the top of the batter.

3. Bake in the preheated oven for 35 to 40 minutes, or until a toothpick inserted into the center of the cake comes out clean. Allow to cool.

Coconut Poke Cake

Submitted by: **Leslie**

Makes: 1 - 9x13 inch cake

Preparation: 30 minutes

Cooking: 1 hour

Total: 2 hours

"White cake soaked in sweet creamy coconut milk and smothered in whipped topping and flaked coconut. A real treat for those with a sweet tooth."

INGREDIENTS

1 (18.25 ounce) package white cake mix

1 (14 ounce) can cream of coconut

1 (14 ounce) can sweetened condensed milk

1 (16 ounce) package frozen whipped topping, thawed

1 (8 ounce) package flaked coconut

DIRECTIONS

1. Prepare and bake white cake mix according to package directions. Remove cake from oven. While still hot, using a utility fork, poke holes all over the top of the cake.

2. Mix cream of coconut and sweetened condensed milk together. Pour over the top of the still hot cake. Let cake cool completely then frost with the whipped topping and top with the flaked coconut. Keep cake refrigerated.

Banana Pudding Cake

Submitted by: **Barbara**

Makes: 1 - 10 inch Bundt cake

Preparation: 30 minutes

Cooking: 1 hour

Total: 2 hours

"This cake is a very moist banana cake that travels well to pot lucks or picnics. It can also be baked in a 9x13 pan or an angel food cake pan. It is a family favorite."

INGREDIENTS

1 (18.5 ounce) package yellow cake mix

1 (3.5 ounce) package instant banana pudding mix

4 eggs

1 cup water

1/4 cup vegetable oil

3/4 cup mashed bananas

2 cups confectioners' sugar

2 tablespoons milk

1 dash vanilla extract

1/2 cup chopped walnuts (optional)

DIRECTIONS

1. Preheat oven to 350°F (175°C). Grease and flour a 10 inch Bundt pan.

2. In a large bowl, stir together cake mix and pudding mix. Make a well in the center and pour in eggs, water, oil and mashed banana. Beat on low speed until blended. Scrape bowl, and beat 4 minutes on medium speed. Pour batter into prepared pan.

3. Bake in a preheated oven for 50 to 55 minutes, or until cake tests done. Let cool in pan for 10 minutes, then turn out onto a wire rack and cool completely.

4. To make glaze: In a small bowl, combine confectioners' sugar, milk and vanilla. Whisk until smooth and of a drizzling consistency. When cake is cooled, drizzle icing over cake with a zigzag motion. Sprinkle chopped nuts over wet icing if desired.

Chantal's New York Cheesecake

Submitted by: **Chantal Rogers**

Makes: 1 - 9 inch cheesecake

Preparation: 30 minutes

Cooking: 1 hour

Total: 7 hours 30 minutes

"This cake is easy to make, and it's so delicious. Everyone that's tried it has said it tasted just like the ones in a deli! You'll love it!"

INGREDIENTS

15 graham crackers, crushed

2 tablespoons butter, melted

4 (8 ounce) packages cream cheese

1½ cups white sugar

¾ cup milk

4 eggs

1 cup sour cream

1 tablespoon vanilla extract

¼ cup all-purpose flour

DIRECTIONS

1. Preheat oven to 350°F (175°C). Grease a 9 inch springform pan.

2. In a medium bowl, mix graham cracker crumbs with melted butter. Press onto bottom of springform pan.

3. In a large bowl, mix cream cheese with sugar until smooth. Blend in milk, and then mix in the eggs one at a time, mixing just enough to incorporate. Mix in sour cream, vanilla and flour until smooth. Pour filling into prepared crust.

4. Bake in preheated oven for 1 hour. Turn the oven off, and let cake cool in oven with the door closed for 5 to 6 hours; this prevents cracking. Chill in refrigerator until serving.

Autumn Cheesecake

Submitted by: **Stephanie**

Makes: 1 - 9 inch cheesecake

Preparation: 30 minutes

Cooking: 1 hour 10 minutes

Total: 4 hours

"This is a delicious Apple Cheesecake that I usually make in the fall."

INGREDIENTS

1 cup graham cracker crumbs

1/2 cup finely chopped pecans

3 tablespoons white sugar

1/2 teaspoon ground cinnamon

1/4 cup unsalted butter, melted

2 (8 ounce) packages cream cheese, softened

1/2 cup white sugar

2 eggs

1/2 teaspoon vanilla extract

4 cups apples - peeled, cored and thinly sliced

1/3 cup white sugar

1/2 teaspoon ground cinnamon

1/4 cup chopped pecans

DIRECTIONS

1. Preheat oven to 350°F (175°C). In a large bowl, stir together the graham cracker crumbs, 1/2 cup finely chopped pecans, 3 tablespoons sugar, 1/2 teaspoon cinnamon and melted butter; press into the bottom of a 9 inch springform pan. Bake in preheated oven for 10 minutes.

2. In a large bowl, combine cream cheese and 1/2 cup sugar. Mix at medium speed until smooth. Beat in eggs one at a time, mixing well after each addition. Blend in vanilla; pour filling into the baked crust.

3. In a small bowl, stir together 1/3 cup sugar and 1/2 teaspoon cinnamon. Toss the cinnamon-sugar with the apples to coat. Spoon apple mixture over cream cheese layer and sprinkle with 1/4 cup chopped pecans.

4. Bake in preheated oven for 60 to 70 minutes. With a knife, loosen cake from rim of pan. Let cool, then remove the rim of pan. Chill cake before serving.

Irish Cream Chocolate Cheesecake

Submitted by: **Elaine**

Makes: 1 - 9 inch cheesecake

Preparation: 20 minutes

Cooking: 1 hour 20 minutes

Total: 9 hours 20 minutes

"If you like Irish cream and chocolate, you'll love this recipe. After numerous attempts with the ingredients this is the recipe I now use."

INGREDIENTS

1½ cups chocolate cookie crumbs

⅓ cup confectioners' sugar

⅓ cup unsweetened cocoa powder

¼ cup butter

3 (8 ounce) packages cream cheese, softened

1¼ cups white sugar

¼ cup unsweetened cocoa powder

3 tablespoons all-purpose flour

3 eggs

½ cup sour cream

¼ cup Irish cream liqueur

DIRECTIONS

1. Preheat oven to 350°F (175°C). In a large bowl, mix together the cookie crumbs, confectioners' sugar and ⅓ cup cocoa. Add melted butter and stir until well mixed. Pat into the bottom of a 9 inch springform pan. Bake in preheated oven for 10 minutes; set aside. Increase oven temperature to 450°F (230°C).

2. In a large bowl, combine cream cheese, white sugar, ¼ cup cocoa and flour. Beat at medium speed until well blended and smooth. Add eggs one at a time, mixing well after each addition. Blend in the sour cream and Irish cream liqueur; mixing on low speed. Pour filling over baked crust.

3. Bake at 450°F (230°C) for 10 minutes. Reduce oven temperature to 250°F (120°C), and continue baking for 60 minutes.

4. With a knife, loosen cake from rim of pan. Let cool, then remove the rim of pan. Chill before serving. If your cake cracks, a helpful tip is to dampen a spatula and smooth the top, then sprinkle with some chocolate wafer crumbs.

Chocolate Turtle Cheesecake

Submitted by: **Stephanie**

Makes: 1 - 9 inch cheesecake

Preparation: 30 minutes

Cooking: 1 hour

Total: 5 hours 30 minutes

"A cheesecake reminiscent of those turtle shaped chocolate and caramel nut bars. Garnish with whipped cream, chopped nuts, and maraschino cherries if desired."

INGREDIENTS

2 cups vanilla wafer crumbs

2 tablespoons unsalted butter, melted

1 (14 ounce) package individually wrapped caramels

1 (5 ounce) can evaporated milk

1 cup chopped pecans

2 (8 ounce) packages cream cheese, softened

1/2 cup white sugar

1 teaspoon vanilla extract

2 eggs

1/2 cup semisweet chocolate chips

DIRECTIONS

1. Preheat oven to 350°F (175°C). In a large bowl, mix together the cookie crumbs and melted butter. Press into the bottom of a 9 inch springform pan.

2. In a heavy saucepan over low heat, melt the caramels with the evaporated milk. Heat and stir frequently until smooth. Pour caramel sauce into crust, and top with pecans.

3. In a large bowl, combine cream cheese, sugar and vanilla; beat well until smooth. Add eggs one at a time, mixing well after each addition. Melt the chocolate, and blend into cream cheese mixture. Pour chocolate batter over pecans.

4. Bake in preheated oven for 40 to 50 minutes, or until filling is set. Loosen cake from the edges of pan, but do not remove rim until cooled to prevent the top from cracking. Chill in refrigerator for 4 hours, or overnight.

Brownie Caramel Cheesecake

Submitted by: **Jackie Meiborg**

Makes: 1 - 9 inch cheesecake

Preparation: 30 minutes

Cooking: 1 hour

Total: 4 hours 30 minutes

"This is a great recipe that gets compliments when ever I make it. It is very rich, and worth the time and calories."

INGREDIENTS

1 (9 ounce) package brownie mix

1 egg

1 tablespoon cold water

1 (14 ounce) package individually wrapped caramels, unwrapped

1 (5 ounce) can evaporated milk

2 (8 ounce) packages cream cheese, softened

1/2 cup white sugar

1 teaspoon vanilla extract

2 eggs

1 cup chocolate fudge topping

DIRECTIONS

1. Preheat oven to 350°F (175°C). Grease the bottom of a 9 inch springform pan.

2. In a small bowl, mix together brownie mix, 1 egg and water. Spread into the greased pan. Bake for 25 minutes.

3. Melt the caramels with the evaporated milk over low heat in a heavy saucepan. Stir often, and heat until mixture has a smooth consistency. Reserve 1/3 cup of this caramel mixture, and pour the remainder over the warm, baked brownie crust.

4. In a large bowl, beat the cream cheese, sugar and vanilla with an electric mixer until smooth. Add eggs one at a time, beating well after each addition. Pour cream cheese mixture over caramel mixture.

5. Bake cheesecake for 40 minutes. Chill in pan. When cake is thoroughly chilled, loosen by running a knife around the edge, and then remove the rim of the pan. Heat reserved caramel mixture, and spoon over cheesecake. Drizzle with the chocolate topping.

Double Layer Pumpkin Cheesecake

Submitted by: **Stephanie Phillips**

Makes: 1 - 9 inch pie

Preparation: 30 minutes

Cooking: 40 minutes

Total: 4 hours 10 minutes

"A great alternative to pumpkin pie, especially for those cheesecake fans out there."

INGREDIENTS

2 (8 ounce) packages cream cheese, softened

1/2 cup white sugar

1/2 teaspoon vanilla extract

2 eggs

1 (9 inch) prepared graham cracker crust

1/2 cup pumpkin puree

1/2 teaspoon ground cinnamon

1 pinch ground cloves

1 pinch ground nutmeg

1/2 cup frozen whipped topping, thawed

DIRECTIONS

1. Preheat oven to 325°F (165°C).

2. In a large bowl, combine cream cheese, sugar and vanilla. Beat until smooth. Blend in eggs one at a time. Remove 1 cup of batter and spread into bottom of crust; set aside.

3. Add pumpkin, cinnamon, cloves and nutmeg to the remaining batter and stir gently until well blended. Carefully spread over the batter in the crust.

4. Bake in preheated oven for 35 to 40 minutes, or until center is almost set. Allow to cool, then refrigerate for 3 hours or overnight. Cover with whipped topping before serving.

Apple Pie by Grandma Ople

Submitted by: **Rebecca Clyma**

Makes: 1 - 9 inch pie

Preparation: 30 minutes

Cooking: 1 hour

Total: 1 hour 30 minutes

"This was my grandmother's apple pie recipe. I have never seen another one quite like it. It will always be my favorite and has won me several first place prizes in local competitions. I hope it becomes one of your favorites as well!"

INGREDIENTS

1 recipe pastry for a 9 inch double crust pie

1/2 cup unsalted butter

3 tablespoons all-purpose flour

1/4 cup water

1/2 cup white sugar

1/2 cup packed brown sugar

8 Granny Smith apples - peeled, cored and sliced

DIRECTIONS

1. Preheat oven to 425°F (220°C). Melt the butter in a saucepan. Stir in flour to form a paste. Add water, white sugar and brown sugar, and bring to a boil. Reduce temperature and let simmer.

2. Place the bottom crust in your pan. Fill with apples, mounded slightly. Cover with a lattice work of crust. Gently pour the sugar and butter liquid over the crust. Pour slowly so that it does not run off.

3. Bake 15 minutes in the preheated oven. Reduce the temperature to 350°F (175°C). Continue baking for 35 to 45 minutes, until apples are soft.

Apple Crumble Pie

Submitted by: **Penny Lehoux**

Makes: 1 - 9 inch pie

Preparation: 30 minutes

Cooking: 1 hour

Total: 1 hour 30 minutes

"Yummy variety of apple pie that is quick and easy. I was a hit with my boyfriend's pals in university whenever I made this favorite!"

INGREDIENTS

1 recipe pastry for a 9 inch single crust pie

5 cups apples - peeled, cored and thinly sliced

½ cup white sugar

¾ teaspoon ground cinnamon

⅓ cup white sugar

¾ cup all-purpose flour

6 tablespoons butter

DIRECTIONS

1. Preheat oven to 400°F (200°C.) Arrange apple slices in unbaked pie shell. Mix ½ cup sugar and cinnamon; sprinkle over apples.

2. Mix ⅓ cup sugar with flour; cut in butter until crumbly. Spoon mixture over apples.

3. Bake in preheated oven for 35 to 40 minutes, or until apples are soft and top is lightly browned.

Award Winning Peaches and Cream Pie

Submitted by: **Debbi Borsick**

Makes: 1 - 10 inch pie

Preparation: 30 minutes

Cooking: 40 minutes

Total: 3 hours 30 minutes

"I am always asked for the recipe when I take this anywhere. Plus I won 5 blue ribbons and Best Pie of Show for this pie. It's a great pie."

INGREDIENTS

¾ cup all-purpose flour

½ teaspoon salt

1 teaspoon baking powder

1 (3.5 ounce) package instant vanilla pudding mix

3 tablespoons butter, softened

1 egg

½ cup milk

1 (29 ounce) can sliced peaches, drained and syrup reserved

1 (8 ounce) package cream cheese, softened

½ cup white sugar

1 tablespoon white sugar

1 teaspoon ground cinnamon

DIRECTIONS

1. Preheat oven to 350°F (175°C). Grease sides and bottom of a 10 inch deep-dish pie pan.

2. In a medium mixing bowl, mix together flour, salt, baking powder and pudding mix. Mix in butter, egg and milk. Beat for 2 minutes. Pour mixture into pie pan. Arrange the peach slices on top of the pudding mixture.

3. In a small mixing bowl, beat cream cheese until fluffy. Add ½ cup sugar and 3 tablespoons reserved peach syrup. Beat for 2 minutes. Spoon mixture over peaches to within 1 inch of pan edge. Mix together 1 tablespoon sugar and 1 teaspoon cinnamon, and sprinkle over top.

4. Bake in preheated oven for 30 to 35 minutes, until golden brown. Chill before serving.

Grandma's Lemon Meringue Pie

Submitted by: **Emilie S.**

Makes: 1 - 9 inch pie

Preparation: 30 minutes

Cooking: 10 minutes

Total: 40 minutes

"This is a very fun recipe to follow, because Grandma makes it sweet and simple. This pie is thickened with cornstarch and flour in addition to egg yolks, and contains no milk."

INGREDIENTS

1 cup white sugar

2 tablespoons all-purpose flour

3 tablespoons cornstarch

1/4 teaspoon salt

1 1/2 cups water

2 lemons, juiced and zested

2 tablespoons butter

4 egg yolks, beaten

1 (9 inch) pie crust, baked

4 egg whites

6 tablespoons white sugar

DIRECTIONS

1. Preheat oven to 350°F (175°C).

2. To Make Lemon Filling: In a medium saucepan, whisk together 1 cup sugar, flour, cornstarch, and salt. Stir in water, lemon juice and lemon zest. Cook over medium-high heat, stirring frequently, until mixture comes to a boil. Stir in butter. Place egg yolks in a small bowl and gradually whisk in 1/2 cup of hot sugar mixture. Whisk egg yolk mixture back into remaining sugar mixture. Bring to a boil and continue to cook while stirring constantly until thick. Remove from heat. Pour filling into baked pastry shell.

3. To Make Meringue: In a large glass or metal bowl, whip egg whites until foamy. Add sugar gradually, and continue to whip until stiff peaks form. Spread meringue over pie, sealing the edges at the crust.

4. Bake in preheated oven for 10 minutes, or until meringue is golden brown.

Big Guy Strawberry Pie

Submitted by: **Pat Collins**

Makes: 1 - 9 inch pie

Preparation: 30 minutes

Cooking: 30 minutes

Total: 4 hours

"This is a fresh berry pie, the fruit is not cooked. Serve with a dollop of whipped cream."

INGREDIENTS

1 cup water

¾ cup white sugar

¼ teaspoon salt

2 tablespoons cornstarch

¼ teaspoon red food coloring

1 cup all-purpose flour

½ cup margarine

3 tablespoons confectioners' sugar

1 teaspoon vanilla extract

1 quart fresh strawberries, hulled

DIRECTIONS

1. In a saucepan, combine water, white sugar, salt, cornstarch and food coloring. Bring to a boil, and cook for about 5 minutes or until thickened. Set aside to cool. Preheat oven to 350°F (175°C.)

2. In a large bowl, combine flour, margarine, confectioners' sugar and vanilla. Mix well and press into a 9 inch pie pan. Prick all over and bake in preheated oven for 8 to 10 minutes, or until lightly browned.

3. When crust is cool, place berries in the shell, and pour the thickened mixture over the top. Chill in refrigerator.

Old Fashioned Coconut Cream Pie

Submitted by: **Carol H.**

Makes: 1 - 9 inch pie

Preparation: 20 minutes

Cooking: 30 minutes

Total: 4 hours 50 minutes

"This is a tried and true, old fashioned coconut cream pie. Took many years of searching and baking to find the right one and this is it! Enjoy!"

INGREDIENTS

3 cups half-and-half cream

2 eggs

¾ cup white sugar

½ cup all-purpose flour

¼ teaspoon salt

1 cup flaked coconut, toasted

1 teaspoon vanilla extract

1 (9 inch) pie shell, baked

1 cup frozen whipped topping, thawed

DIRECTIONS

1. In a medium saucepan, combine half-and-half, eggs, sugar, flour and salt. Bring to a boil over low heat, stirring constantly. Remove from heat, and stir in ¾ cup of the coconut and the vanilla extract. Pour into pie shell and chill 2 to 4 hours, or until firm.

2. Top with whipped topping, and with remaining ¼ cup of coconut.

3. Note: To toast coconut, spread it in an ungreased pan and bake in a 350 degree F (175°C) oven for 5 to 7 minutes, or until golden brown, stirring occasionally.

Margarita Party Pie

Submitted by: **Beth**

Makes: 1 - 9 inch pie

Preparation: 30 minutes

Total: 4 hours 30 minutes

"This frozen pie is great for summer barbecues! Very tasty! Frozen strawberries may be used instead of fresh."

INGREDIENTS

1½ cups crushed pretzels

¼ cup white sugar

⅔ cup butter, melted

1 (14 ounce) can sweetened condensed milk

¼ cup fresh lime juice

¼ cup tequila

4 tablespoons orange liqueur

1 cup sliced fresh strawberries

2 drops red food coloring

2 drops yellow food coloring

2 cups whipped cream, divided

DIRECTIONS

1. In a large bowl, combine crushed pretzels, sugar and butter. Mix well and press onto the bottom and sides of a 9 inch pie pan.

2. In a large bowl, combine sweetened condensed milk, lime juice, tequila and orange liqueur. Pour half of the mixture into another bowl. Add strawberries and a few drops of red food coloring to one half. To other half, add only a drop or two of yellow food coloring. Fold one cup of whipped cream into each half.

3. Spoon into crust, alternating colors. Freeze for 4 hours or overnight.

Mom's Pumpkin Pie

Submitted by: **Jim Wright**

Makes: 1 - 9 inch pie

Preparation: 30 minutes

Cooking: 1 hour

Total: 1 hour 30 minutes

"This is the pumpkin pie that my mother has made for years. It is a rich pie with just the right amount of spices."

INGREDIENTS

1 recipe pastry for a 9 inch single crust pie

3 eggs

1 egg yolk

1/2 cup white sugar

1/2 cup packed brown sugar

1 teaspoon salt

1/2 teaspoon ground cinnamon

1/2 teaspoon ground nutmeg

1/2 teaspoon ground ginger

1/4 teaspoon ground cloves

1 1/2 cups milk

1/2 cup heavy whipping cream

2 cups pumpkin puree

DIRECTIONS

1. Preheat oven to 425°F (220°C.)

2. In a large bowl, combine eggs, egg yolk, white sugar and brown sugar. Add salt, cinnamon, nutmeg, ginger and cloves. Gradually stir in milk and cream. Stir in pumpkin. Pour filling into pie shell.

3. Bake for ten minutes in preheated oven. Reduce heat to 350°F (175°C), and bake for an additional 40 to 45 minutes, or until filling is set.

Sweet Potato Pie

Submitted by: **Joyce Waits**

"This recipe was shared with me by a special friend in Atlanta, Ga. It has long been a favorite, and everyone who tastes it says it is the best they have ever had."

INGREDIENTS

1 (1 pound) sweet potato

1/2 cup butter, softened

1 cup white sugar

1/2 cup milk

2 eggs

1/2 teaspoon ground nutmeg

1/2 teaspoon ground cinnamon

1 teaspoon vanilla extract

1 (9 inch) unbaked pie crust

DIRECTIONS

1. Boil sweet potato whole in skin for 40 to 50 minutes, or until done. Run cold water over the sweet potato, and remove the skin.

2. Break apart sweet potato in a bowl. Add butter, and mix well with mixer. Stir in sugar, milk, eggs, nutmeg, cinnamon and vanilla. Beat on medium speed until mixture is smooth. Pour filling into an unbaked pie crust.

3. Bake at 350°F (175°C) for 55 to 60 minutes, or until knife inserted in center comes out clean. Pie will puff up like a souffle, and then will sink down as it cools.

Best Apple Crisp Ever

Submitted by: **Olga**

Makes: 1 - 9 inch square pan

Preparation: 15 minutes

Cooking: 35 minutes

Total: 50 minutes

"Easy to make and delicious, with a thick, crunchy, cinnamony topping over brown sugar coated apple slices."

INGREDIENTS

4 apples - peeled, cored and sliced

½ cup brown sugar

1 cup all-purpose flour

¾ cup white sugar

1 teaspoon ground cinnamon

¼ teaspoon salt

1 egg, beaten

2 tablespoons butter, melted

DIRECTIONS

1. Preheat oven to 375 °F (190°C).

2. In a 9 inch square baking pan, mix sliced apples with brown sugar. In a large bowl, mix together flour, white sugar, cinnamon and salt. In a small bowl, beat together egg and melted butter. Stir into flour mixture. Spread evenly over apples.

3. Bake in preheated oven for 30 to 40 minutes, or until topping is golden and crisp.

Apple Crisp II

Submitted by: **Diane Kester**

Makes: 1 - 9x13 inch pan

Preparation: 30 minutes

Cooking: 45 minutes

Total: 1 hour 20 minutes

"A simple dessert that's great served with ice cream."

INGREDIENTS

10 cups thinly sliced apples

1 cup white sugar

1 tablespoon all-purpose flour

1 teaspoon ground cinnamon

1/2 cup water

1 cup quick-cooking oats

1 cup all-purpose flour

1 cup packed brown sugar

1/4 teaspoon baking powder

1/4 teaspoon baking soda

1/2 cup butter, melted

DIRECTIONS

1. Preheat oven to 350°F (175 degree C).

2. Place the sliced apples in a 9x13 inch pan. Mix the white sugar, 1 tablespoon flour and ground cinnamon together, and sprinkle over apples. Pour water evenly over all.

3. Combine the oats, 1 cup flour, brown sugar, baking powder, baking soda and melted butter together. Crumble evenly over the apple mixture.

4. Bake at 350°F (175°C) for about 45 minutes.

Best Peach Cobbler Ever

Submitted by: **Jill Saunders**

Makes: 1 - 9x13 inch cobbler

Preparation: 30 minutes

Cooking: 1 hour

Total: 1 hour 30 minutes

"This is a very moist cobbler - easy to make and delicious to eat!"

INGREDIENTS

1 (29 ounce) can sliced peaches

2 tablespoons butter, melted

1 pinch ground cinnamon

1 pinch ground nutmeg

1 tablespoon cornstarch

½ cup water

1 cup milk

1 cup white sugar

1 cup all-purpose flour

2 teaspoons baking powder

1 pinch salt

½ cup butter

1 teaspoon ground cinnamon

¼ teaspoon ground nutmeg

DIRECTIONS

1. Preheat oven to 350°F (175°C.) In a large bowl, combine sliced peaches with juice, 2 tablespoons melted butter, a pinch of cinnamon and a pinch of nutmeg. Dissolve cornstarch in water, then stir into peach mixture; set aside.

2. In another bowl, combine milk, sugar, flour, baking powder and salt. Beat until smooth - mixture will be thin.

3. Melt ½ cup butter in a 9x13 inch pan. Pour batter over melted butter. Spoon peaches over batter. Sprinkle top with additional cinnamon and nutmeg.

4. Bake in preheated oven for 1 hour, or until knife inserted comes out clean.

Fruit Pizza

Submitted by: **Anne**

Makes: 1 fruit pizza

Preparation: 25 minutes

Cooking: 10 minutes

Total: 1 hour 35 minutes

"A cookie dough crust, cream cheese filling, and fruit topping. Tip: For a quick crust, use one package of ready made sugar cookie dough rolled out to fit a pizza pan. Use an assortment of fresh fruit such as bananas, peaches, blueberries, kiwi, pineapple, and strawberries."

INGREDIENTS

1/2 cup butter, softened

3/4 cup white sugar

1 egg

1 1/4 cups all-purpose flour

1 teaspoon cream of tartar

1/2 teaspoon baking soda

1/4 teaspoon salt

1 (8 ounce) package cream cheese

1/2 cup white sugar

2 teaspoons vanilla extract

DIRECTIONS

1. Preheat oven to 350°F (175°C).

2. In a large bowl, cream together the butter and 3/4 cup sugar until smooth. Mix in egg. combine the flour, cream of tartar, baking soda and salt; stir into the creamed mixture until just blended. Press dough into an ungreased pizza pan.

3. Bake in preheated oven for 8 to 10 minutes, or until lightly browned. Cool.

4. In a large bowl, beat cream cheese with 1/2 cup sugar and vanilla until light. Spread on cooled crust.

5. Arrange desired fruit on top of filling, and chill.

Banana Pudding IV

Submitted by: **Patricia Osborne**

Makes: 1 - 9x13 inch dish
Preparation: 30 minutes
Total: 3 hours 30 minutes

"A quick and easy banana pudding recipe - enjoy!"

INGREDIENTS

1 (8 ounce) package cream cheese

1 (14 ounce) can sweetened condensed milk

1 (5 ounce) package instant vanilla pudding mix

3 cups cold milk

1 teaspoon vanilla extract

1 (8 ounce) container frozen whipped topping, thawed

4 bananas, sliced

½ (12 ounce) package vanilla wafers

DIRECTIONS

1. In a large bowl, beat cream cheese until fluffy. Beat in condensed milk, pudding mix, cold milk and vanilla until smooth. Fold in ½ of the whipped topping.

2. Line the bottom of a 9x13 inch dish with vanilla wafers. Arrange sliced bananas evenly over wafers. Spread with pudding mixture. Top with remaining whipped topping. Chill.

Bread Pudding II

Submitted by: **Ellen Warfield**

Makes: 1 - 8 inch square pan

Preparation: 30 minutes

Cooking: 45 minutes

Total: 1 hour 15 minutes

"My family LOVES bread pudding, and this recipe is one that I have fine tuned to their taste. I have to double this recipe, and bake it in a 9x13 inch pan for my family! It's great for breakfast or dessert and is delicious with milk poured on top! Enjoy!"

INGREDIENTS

6 slices day-old bread

2 tablespoons butter, melted

½ cup raisins (optional)

4 eggs, beaten

2 cups milk

¾ cup white sugar

1 teaspoon ground cinnamon

1 teaspoon vanilla extract

DIRECTIONS

1. Preheat oven to 350°F (175°C).

2. Break bread into small pieces into an 8 inch square baking pan. Drizzle melted butter or margarine over bread. If desired, sprinkle with raisins.

3. In a medium mixing bowl, combine eggs, milk, sugar, cinnamon, and vanilla. Beat until well mixed. Pour over bread, and lightly push down with a fork until bread is covered and soaking up the egg mixture.

4. Bake in the preheated oven for 45 minutes, or until the top springs back when lightly tapped.

Creamy Rice Pudding

Submitted by: **Erica G.**

Makes: 4 servings

Preparation: 25 minutes

Cooking: 20 minutes

Total: 45 minutes

"This is my mom's recipe for Rice Pudding. It's the best I've ever tasted and it gets rave reviews from everyone I serve it to. Sprinkle with nutmeg or cinnamon, if desired. For creamier pudding, use short or medium grain rice."

INGREDIENTS

¾ cup uncooked white rice

2 cups milk, divided

⅓ cup white sugar

¼ teaspoon salt

1 egg, beaten

⅔ cup golden raisins

1 tablespoon butter

½ teaspoon vanilla extract

DIRECTIONS

1. In a medium saucepan, bring 1½ cups water to a boil. Add rice and stir. Reduce heat, cover and simmer for 20 minutes.

2. In another saucepan, combine 1½ cups cooked rice, 1½ cups milk, sugar and salt. Cook over medium heat until thick and creamy, 15 to 20 minutes. Stir in remaining ½ cup milk, beaten egg and raisins. Cook 2 minutes more, stirring constantly. Remove from heat, and stir in butter and vanilla. Serve warm.

Cream Puffs

Submitted by: **Shellie Wendel**

Makes: 20 to 25 cream puffs
Preparation: 30 minutes
Cooking: 25 minutes
Total: 55 minutes

"An easy and impressive way to make a great dessert. Whip them up and watch them disappear!"

INGREDIENTS

2 (3.5 ounce) packages instant vanilla pudding mix

2 cups heavy cream

1 cup milk

1/2 cup butter

1 cup water

1/4 teaspoon salt

1 cup all-purpose flour

4 eggs

DIRECTIONS

1. Mix together vanilla instant pudding mix, cream and milk. Cover and refrigerate to set.

2. Preheat oven to 425°F (220°C).

3. In a large pot, bring water and butter to a rolling boil. Stir in flour and salt until the mixture forms a ball. Transfer the dough to a large mixing bowl. Using a wooden spoon or stand mixer, beat in the eggs one at a time, mixing well after each. Drop by tablespoonfuls onto an ungreased baking sheet.

4. Bake for 20 to 25 minutes in the preheated oven, until golden brown. Centers should be dry.

5. When the shells are cool, either split and fill them with the pudding mixture, or use a pastry bag to pipe the pudding into the shells.

Chocolate Trifle

Submitted by: **Wayne**

Makes: 12 servings

Preparation: 30 minutes

Cooking: 25 minutes

Total: 8 hours 55 minutes

"At church functions, folks line up for this trifle. And it is so easy to make!"

INGREDIENTS

1 (19.8 ounce) package brownie mix

1 (3.4 ounce) package instant chocolate pudding mix

½ cup water

1 (14 ounce) can sweetened condensed milk

1 (8 ounce) container frozen whipped topping, thawed

1 (12 ounce) container frozen whipped topping, thawed

1 (1.5 ounce) bar chocolate candy

DIRECTIONS

1. Prepare brownie mix according to package directions and cool completely. Cut into 1 inch squares.

2. In a large bowl, combine pudding mix, water and sweetened condensed milk. Mix until smooth, then fold in 8 ounces whipped topping until no streaks remain.

3. In a trifle bowl or glass serving dish, place half of the brownies, half of the pudding mixture and half of the 12 ounce container of whipped topping. Repeat layers. Shave chocolate onto top layer for garnish. Refrigerate 8 hours before serving.

cookies & candies

More than just handy bite-sized morsels to stave off a sweet tooth, cookies, brownies and candies are dear to our hearts. They're the ultimate way to say 'I love you' — the world's most perfect, portable dessert. Choose crispy ones, chewy ones, hearty down-home snacks, or delicate little dunkers — your cookie jar will never be lonely again.

Aunt Cora's World's Greatest Cookies

Submitted by: **Mary Hays**

Makes: 4 dozen

Preparation: 15 minutes

Cooking: 15 minutes

Total: 1 hour 15 minutes

"Aunt Cora's recipe. WORLD'S BEST CHOCOLATE CHIP PEANUT BUTTER COOKIES!"

INGREDIENTS

1 cup margarine, softened

1 cup peanut butter

1 cup white sugar

1 cup packed brown sugar

2 eggs

2 cups unbleached all-purpose flour

1 teaspoon baking soda

2 cups semisweet chocolate chips

DIRECTIONS

1. Preheat oven to 325°F (165°C).

2. In a large bowl, cream together the margarine, peanut butter, white sugar and brown sugar until smooth. Beat in the eggs one at a time, mixing well after each. Combine the flour and baking soda; stir into the peanut butter mixture. Mix in chocolate chips. Drop by heaping spoonfuls onto ungreased cookie sheets.

3. Bake for 12 to 15 minutes in the preheated oven, until lightly browned at the edges. Allow cookies to cool for a minute before removing to wire racks to cool completely.

Award Winning
Soft Chocolate Chip Cookies

Makes: 6 dozen

Preparation: 15 minutes

Cooking: 12 minutes

Total: 1 hour 40 minutes

Submitted by: **Debbi Borsick**

"Everybody wants this recipe when I take them in for a carry-in. To make them award winning, my daughter, Tegan, made them for a cookie baking contest and won a red ribbon! You can use any flavor pudding you like for this recipe."

INGREDIENTS

4½ cups all-purpose flour

2 teaspoons baking soda

2 cups butter, softened

1½ cups packed brown sugar

½ cup white sugar

2 (3.4 ounce) packages instant vanilla pudding mix

4 eggs

2 teaspoons vanilla extract

4 cups semisweet chocolate chips

2 cups chopped walnuts (optional)

DIRECTIONS

1. Preheat oven to 350°F (175°C). Sift together the flour and baking soda, set aside.

2. In a large bowl, cream together the butter, brown sugar and white sugar. Beat in the instant pudding mix until blended. Stir in the eggs and vanilla. Blend in the flour mixture. Finally, stir in the chocolate chips and nuts. Drop cookies by rounded spoonfuls onto ungreased cookie sheets.

3. Bake for 10 to 12 minutes in the preheated oven. Edges should be golden brown.

Best Chocolate Chip Cookies

Submitted by: **Dora**

"Crisp edges, chewy middles."

Makes: 4 dozen

Preparation: 20 minutes

Cooking: 10 minutes

Total: 1 hour

INGREDIENTS

1 cup butter, softened

1 cup white sugar

1 cup packed brown sugar

2 eggs

2 teaspoons vanilla extract

3 cups all-purpose flour

1 teaspoon baking soda

2 teaspoons hot water

½ teaspoon salt

2 cups semisweet chocolate chips

1 cup chopped walnuts

DIRECTIONS

1. Preheat oven to 350°F (175°C).

2. Cream together the butter, white sugar and brown sugar until smooth. Beat in the eggs one at a time, then stir in the vanilla. Dissolve baking soda in hot water. Add to batter along with salt. Stir in flour, chocolate chips and nuts. Drop by large spoonfuls onto ungreased pans.

3. Bake for about 10 minutes in the preheated oven, or until edges are nicely browned.

Urban Legend Chocolate Chip Cookies

Submitted by: **Rene Kratz**

Makes: 5 dozen

Preparation: 15 minutes

Cooking: 8 minutes

Total: 1 hour

"You may have heard this story…a woman asks to buy a cookie recipe and is told it will cost 'two-fifty.' She thinks this means $2.50, but then she gets her credit card bill back and finds out it is $250.00. Outraged, she spreads the recipe far and wide to try and get her money's worth. I first heard this story 6 years ago and was given a recipe on a sheet of paper which bore the date '1986.' The supposed originator of the recipe was a well-known cookie company. I have since heard this tale again several times, with the recipe originating from different upscale department stores. True story? Who knows, but it's a darn good cookie. Here's my version."

INGREDIENTS

1 cup butter, softened

1 cup white sugar

1 cup packed brown sugar

2 eggs

1 teaspoon vanilla extract

2 cups all-purpose flour

2 1/2 cups rolled oats

1/2 teaspoon salt

1 teaspoon baking powder

1 teaspoon baking soda

2 cups semisweet chocolate chips

4 ounces milk chocolate, grated

1 1/2 cups chopped walnuts

DIRECTIONS

1. Preheat oven to 375°F (190°C). Measure oats into a blender or food processor, and then blend to a fine powder. Set aside.

2. In a large bowl, cream together butter and sugars. Beat in the eggs one at a time, then stir in the vanilla. In a separate bowl, mix together flour, oats, salt, baking powder and baking soda. Stir dry ingredients into creamed butter and sugar. Add chocolate chips, grated chocolate and nuts.

3. Drop by rounded teaspoons onto ungreased cookie sheets. Bake for 6 to 8 minutes in the preheated oven.

Chewy Chocolate Cookies

Submitted by: **Linda Whittaker**

Makes: 4 dozen

Preparation: 15 minutes

Cooking: 10 minutes

Total: 55 minutes

"These are GREAT chocolate chocolate chip cookies. Always a request at Christmas from friends and family!"

INGREDIENTS

1¼ cups butter, softened

2 cups white sugar

2 eggs

2 teaspoons vanilla extract

2 cups all-purpose flour

¾ cup unsweetened cocoa powder

1 teaspoon baking soda

½ teaspoon salt

2 cups semisweet chocolate chips

DIRECTIONS

1. Preheat oven to 350°F (175°C).

2. In a large bowl, cream together the butter and sugar until light and fluffy. Beat in the eggs one at a time, then stir in the vanilla. Sift together the flour, cocoa, baking soda and salt; stir into the creamed mixture. Mix in the chocolate chips. Drop dough by teaspoonfuls onto ungreased cookie sheets.

3. Bake 8 to 9 minutes in the preheated oven. Cookies will be soft. Cool slightly on cookie sheet; remove from sheet onto wire rack to cool completely.

Chewy Peanut Butter Chocolate Chip Cookies

Makes: 2 dozen

Preparation: 15 minutes

Cooking: 15 minutes

Total: 45 minutes

Submitted by: **Kathy Bliesner**

"These cookies are really chewy and addictive."

INGREDIENTS

½ cup butter, softened

½ cup peanut butter

1 cup packed brown sugar

½ cup white sugar

2 eggs

2 tablespoons light corn syrup

2 tablespoons water

2 teaspoons vanilla extract

2½ cups all-purpose flour

1 teaspoon baking soda

½ teaspoon salt

2 cups chopped semisweet chocolate

DIRECTIONS

1. Preheat oven to 375°F (190°C).

2. In a large bowl, cream together the butter, peanut butter, brown sugar and white sugar until smooth. Beat in the eggs one at a time, then stir in the corn syrup, water and vanilla. Combine the flour, baking soda and salt; stir into the peanut butter mixture. Fold in chocolate chunks. Drop by ¼ cupfuls 3 inches apart onto ungreased baking sheets.

3. Bake for 12 to 14 minutes in the preheated oven, or until edges are golden. Allow cookies to cool for 1 minute on the cookie sheet before removing to wire racks to cool completely.

Banana Chocolate Chip Cookies

Submitted by: **Evelyn Brown**

Makes: 3 dozen

Preparation: 15 minutes

Cooking: 15 minutes

Total: 1 hour

"This recipe uses very ripe bananas, the ones which you would not want to eat. The riper the bananas are, the more flavor they have."

INGREDIENTS

2½ cups all-purpose flour

2 teaspoons baking powder

½ teaspoon salt

¼ teaspoon baking soda

1 cup white sugar

⅔ cup butter, softened

2 eggs

1 teaspoon vanilla extract

1 cup mashed bananas

2 cups semi-sweet chocolate chips

DIRECTIONS

1. Preheat oven to 400°F (205°C). Sift the flour, baking powder, salt and baking soda together and set aside.

2. Cream the butter with the sugar until light and fluffy. Beat in the eggs and vanilla. Mix in the mashed bananas. Add the flour mixture and stir until just combined. Stir in the chocolate chips. Drop by spoonfuls onto greased cookie sheets.

3. Bake in preheated oven for 12 to 15 minutes.

Elaine's Peanut Butter Cookies

Submitted by: **Janet Kay**

Makes: 3 dozen

Preparation: 10 minutes

Cooking: 12 minutes

Total: 45 minutes

"This is a quick recipe for cookies when you are in a crunch for time and need to have something for the dessert platter now! These are very soft and taste great. I have yet to have anyone toss these cookies back on my platter."

INGREDIENTS

1 (18.5 ounce) package yellow cake mix

1 cup creamy peanut butter

½ cup vegetable oil

2 eggs

2 tablespoons water

DIRECTIONS

1. Preheat oven to 350°F (175°C).

2. Pour the cake mix into a large bowl. Make a well in the center, and add peanut butter, oil, eggs and water. Mix until well blended. Drop by teaspoonfuls onto ungreased cookie sheets. Flatten them slightly using a fork dipped in water.

3. Bake for 10 to 12 minutes in the preheated oven. Let cookies set on cookie sheet for 2 to 3 minutes before carefully removing from cookie sheet to cool on wire racks.

Joey's Peanut Butter Cookies

Submitted by: **P.L. Weiss**

Makes: 3 dozen

Preparation: 15 minutes

Cooking: 10 minutes

Total: 45 minutes

"My boyfriend's special recipe makes the peanut butteriest tasting cookie I have ever tasted. These soft and chewy peanut buttery cookies are the best!"

INGREDIENTS

1 cup peanut butter

½ cup butter, softened

½ cup white sugar

½ cup packed brown sugar

1 egg

3 tablespoons milk

1 teaspoon vanilla extract

1¼ cups all-purpose flour

¾ teaspoon baking powder

¼ teaspoon salt

DIRECTIONS

1. Preheat oven to 375 °F (190°C).

2. In a large bowl, cream together the peanut butter, butter, white sugar and brown sugar until well blended. Beat in the egg, milk and vanilla one at a time. Combine the flour, baking powder and salt; stir into creamed mixture. Roll tablespoonfuls of dough into balls. Place cookies 2 inches apart onto ungreased cookie sheets. Press each ball once with fork tines.

3. Bake for 8 to 10 minutes in the preheated oven, or until edges are lightly browned.

Chocolate Peanut Butter Cup Cookies

Submitted by: **Joanna Knudsen**

Makes: 3 dozen

Preparation: 15 minutes

Cooking: 10 minutes

Total: 45 minutes

"These are THE BEST cookies I have ever eaten. They are a definite hit. If you like peanut butter and chocolate - these cookies are for you!"

INGREDIENTS

1 cup butter, softened

3/4 cup creamy peanut butter

3/4 cup white sugar

3/4 cup packed brown sugar

2 eggs

1 teaspoon vanilla extract

2 1/3 cups all-purpose flour

1/3 cup cocoa powder

1 teaspoon baking soda

1 cup semisweet chocolate chips

1 cup peanut butter chips

10 chocolate covered peanut butter cups, cut into eighths

DIRECTIONS

1. Preheat oven to 350°F (180°C).

2. In a large bowl, cream together the butter, peanut butter, white sugar and brown sugar until smooth. Beat in the eggs one at a time, then stir in the vanilla. Combine the flour, cocoa and baking soda; stir into the peanut butter mixture. Fold in the chocolate chips, peanut butter chips and peanut butter cups. Drop by spoonfuls onto ungreased cookie sheets.

3. Bake for 8 to 10 minutes in the preheated oven. Let cool for 1 or 2 minutes on sheet before removing or they will fall apart.

Oatmeal Peanut Butter Cookies

Submitted by: **Michele**

Makes: 4 dozen

Preparation: 15 minutes

Cooking: 15 minutes

Total: 1 hour 15 minutes

"A nice change of pace from the usual peanut butter cookie. My husband never liked peanut butter cookies until I made him this recipe."

INGREDIENTS

½ cup shortening

½ cup margarine, softened

1 cup packed brown sugar

¾ cup white sugar

1 cup peanut butter

2 eggs

1½ cups all-purpose flour

2 teaspoons baking soda

1 teaspoon salt

1 cup quick-cooking oats

DIRECTIONS

1. Preheat oven to 350°F (180°C).

2. In a large bowl, cream together shortening, margarine, brown sugar, white sugar and peanut butter until smooth. Beat in the eggs one at a time until well blended. Combine the flour, baking soda and salt; stir into the creamed mixture. Mix in the oats until just combined. Drop by teaspoonfuls onto ungreased cookie sheets.

3. Bake for 15 minutes in the preheated oven, or until just light brown. Don't over-bake. Cool and store in an airtight container.

No Bake Cookies

Submitted by: **Denise**

Makes: 3 dozen

Preparation: 10 minutes

Total: 45 minutes

"Tasty no-bake cookies made with oatmeal, peanut butter and cocoa. Start timing when mixture reaches a full rolling boil; this is the trick to successful cookies. If you boil too long the cookies will be dry and crumbly. If you don't boil long enough, the cookies won't form properly."

INGREDIENTS

1¾ cups white sugar

½ cup milk

½ cup butter

4 tablespoons unsweetened cocoa powder

½ cup crunchy peanut butter

3 cups quick-cooking oats

1 teaspoon vanilla extract

DIRECTIONS

1. In a medium saucepan, combine sugar, milk, butter and cocoa. Bring to a boil, and cook for 1½ minutes. Remove from heat and stir in peanut butter, oats and vanilla. Drop by teaspoonfuls onto wax paper. Let cool until hardened.

The Best Rolled Sugar Cookies

Submitted by: **Jill Saunders**

Makes: 5 dozen

Preparation: 45 minutes

Cooking: 8 minutes

Total: 3 hours

"Whenever you make these cookies for someone, be sure to bring along several copies of the recipe! You will be asked for it, I promise!!! NOTE: I make icing with confectioners' sugar and milk. I make it fairly thin, as I 'paint' the icing on the cookies with a pastry brush. Thin enough to spread easily but not so thin that it just makes your cookies wet and runs off."

INGREDIENTS

1½ cups butter, softened

2 cups white sugar

4 eggs

1 teaspoon vanilla extract

5 cups all-purpose flour

2 teaspoons baking powder

1 teaspoon salt

DIRECTIONS

1. In a large bowl, cream together butter and sugar until smooth. Beat in eggs and vanilla. Stir in the flour, baking powder and salt. Cover and chill dough for at least one hour (or overnight).

2. Preheat oven to 400°F (200°C). Roll out dough on floured surface ¼ to ½ inch thick. Cut into shapes with any cookie cutter. Place cookies 1 inch apart onto an ungreased cookie sheet.

3. Bake 6 to 8 minutes in the preheated oven. Cool completely.

Cream Cheese Sugar Cookies

Submitted by: **Karin Christian**

Makes: 6 dozen

Preparation: 15 minutes

Cooking: 10 minutes

Total: 9 hours 25 minutes

"A soft, chewy and flavorful sugar cookie. It is very important to chill the dough, as it is too sticky to roll unless well chilled."

INGREDIENTS

1 cup white sugar

1 cup butter, softened

1 (3 ounce) package cream cheese, softened

1/2 teaspoon salt

1/2 teaspoon almond extract

1/2 teaspoon vanilla extract

1 egg yolk

2 1/4 cups all-purpose flour

DIRECTIONS

1. In a large bowl, combine the sugar, butter, cream cheese, salt, almond extract, vanilla and egg yolk. Beat until smooth. Stir in the flour until well blended. Chill the dough for 8 hours, or overnight.

2. Preheat oven to 375°F (190°C).

3. On a lightly floured surface, roll out the dough 1/3 at a time to 1/8 inch thickness, refrigerating remaining dough until ready to use. Cut into desired shapes with lightly floured cookie cutters. Place 1 inch apart on ungreased cookie sheets. Leave cookies plain for frosting, or brush with slightly beaten egg white and sprinkle with candy sprinkles or colored sugar.

4. Bake for 7 to 10 minutes in the preheated oven, or until light and golden brown. Cool cookies completely before frosting.

Amish Cookies

Submitted by: **Alice Hoff**

Makes: 5 dozen

Preparation: 10 minutes

Cooking: 10 minutes

Total: 1 hour

"This recipe is used by the Amish in the Midwest...around Wisconsin and Iowa."

INGREDIENTS

1 cup butter, softened

1 cup vegetable oil

1 cup white sugar

1 cup confectioners' sugar

2 eggs

$^1/_2$ teaspoon vanilla extract

$4^1/_2$ cups all-purpose flour

1 teaspoon baking soda

$^3/_4$ teaspoon cream of tartar

DIRECTIONS

1. Preheat the oven to 375°F (190°C). Grease cookie sheets.

2. In a large bowl, cream together the butter, oil, white sugar and confectioners' sugar until smooth. Beat in the eggs one at a time, then stir in the vanilla. Combine the flour, baking soda and cream of tartar. Stir into the sugar mixture until just combined. Drop dough by teaspoonfuls onto the prepared cookie sheets.

3. Bake for 8 to 10 minutes in the preheated oven, or until bottoms are lightly browned. Remove from baking sheets to cool on wire racks.

Mrs. Sigg's Snickerdoodles

Submitted by: Beth Sigworth

Makes: 4 dozen

Preparation: 20 minutes

Cooking: 10 minutes

Total: 1 hour

"These wonderful cinnamon-sugar cookies became very popular with my friends at church. My pastor loves them! You will too! Crispy edges, and chewy centers; these cookies are a crowd pleaser for sure!"

INGREDIENTS

½ cup butter, softened

½ cup shortening

1½ cups white sugar

2 eggs

2 teaspoons vanilla extract

2¾ cups all-purpose flour

2 teaspoons cream of tartar

1 teaspoon baking soda

¼ teaspoon salt

2 tablespoons white sugar

2 teaspoons ground cinnamon

DIRECTIONS

1. Preheat oven to 400°F (205°C).

2. Cream together butter, shortening, 1½ cups sugar, the eggs and the vanilla. Blend in the flour, cream of tartar, soda and salt. Shape dough by rounded spoonfuls into balls.

3. Mix the 2 tablespoons sugar and the cinnamon. Roll balls of dough in mixture. Place 2 inches apart on ungreased baking sheets.

4. Bake 8 to 10 minutes, or until set but not too hard. Remove immediately from baking sheets.

Cookie in a Jar

Submitted by: **Linda**

Makes: 2½ dozen

Preparation: 20 minutes

Total: 20 minutes

"This cookie in a jar mix has a little bit of everything in it. A great gift idea!"

INGREDIENTS

½ cup white chocolate chips

½ cup crispy rice cereal

1½ cups all-purpose flour

¾ teaspoon baking soda

¼ teaspoon baking powder

½ cup packed brown sugar

½ cup semisweet chocolate chips

½ cup rolled oats

½ cup white sugar

DIRECTIONS

1. In a 1 quart jar, layer the ingredients in the order listed. Pack down firmly after each addition.

2. Attach a tag with the following instructions:

COOKIE IN A JAR

1. Preheat the oven to 350°F (175°C).

2. In a large bowl, cream together 2 tablespoons of water, ½ cup of margarine and 1 egg until light and fluffy. Add the entire contents of the jar, and stir until well blended. Drop by rounded spoonfuls onto an ungreased cookie sheet.

3. Bake for 10 to 12 minutes in the preheated oven. Remove from baking sheets to cool on wire racks.

Cowboy Cookie Mix in a Jar

Submitted by: **Phyllis**

Makes: 3 dozen

Preparation: 25 minutes

Total: 25 minutes

"Cookie mix layered in a jar. They are great for gift-giving or bake sales."

INGREDIENTS

1 1/3 cups rolled oats

1/2 cup packed brown sugar

1/2 cup white sugar

1/2 cup chopped pecans

1 cup semisweet chocolate chips

1 1/3 cups all-purpose flour

1 teaspoon baking powder

1 teaspoon baking soda

1/4 teaspoon salt

DIRECTIONS

1. Layer the ingredients in a 1 quart jar in the order given. Press each layer firmly in place before adding the next one.

2. Include a card with the following instructions:

   COWBOY COOKIE MIX IN A JAR

   1. Preheat oven to 350°F (175°C). Grease cookie sheets.

   2. In a medium bowl, cream together 1/2 cup of butter or margarine, 1 egg and 1 teaspoon of vanilla. Stir in the entire contents of the jar. You may need to use your hands to finish mixing. Shape into walnut sized balls. Place 2 inches apart on the prepared cookie sheets.

   3. Bake for 11 to 13 minutes in the preheated oven. Remove from cookie sheets to cool on wire racks.

Cranberry Hootycreeks

Submitted by: **Susan O'Dell**

"A beautifully festive cookie in a jar recipe. These make great gifts."

INGREDIENTS

5/8 cup all-purpose flour

1/2 cup rolled oats

1/2 cup all-purpose flour

1/2 teaspoon baking soda

1/2 teaspoon salt

1/3 cup brown sugar

1/3 cup white sugar

1/2 cup dried cranberries

1/2 cup white chocolate chips

1/2 cup chopped pecans

DIRECTIONS

1. Layer the ingredients in a 1 quart or 1 liter jar, in the order listed.

2. Attach a tag with the following instructions:

   CRANBERRY HOOTYCREEKS

   1. Preheat oven to 350°F (175°C). Grease a cookie sheet or line with parchment paper.

   2. In a medium bowl, cream together 1/2 cup butter, 1 egg and 1 teaspoon of vanilla until fluffy. Add the entire jar of ingredients, and mix together by hand until well blended. Drop by heaping spoonfuls onto the prepared baking sheets.

   3. Bake for 8 to 10 minutes, until edges start to brown. Cool on baking sheets, or remove to cool on wire racks.

Sand Art Brownies

Submitted by: **Janet**

Makes: 1 - 9x9 inch pan

Preparation: 15 minutes

Total: 15 minutes

"Mix ingredients in a wide mouth quart size jar, just like sand art that kids make today."

INGREDIENTS

5/8 cup all-purpose flour

3/4 teaspoon salt

1/3 cup unsweetened cocoa powder

1/2 cup all-purpose flour

2/3 cup packed brown sugar

2/3 cup white sugar

1/2 cup semisweet chocolate chips

1/2 cup vanilla baking chips

1/2 cup walnuts

DIRECTIONS

1. Mix the 5/8 cup of flour with salt. In a clean wide-mouth 1 quart, or 1 liter jar, layer the ingredients in the order given. Starting with the flour and salt mixture and ending with the walnuts.

2. Attach a decorative tag to the out side of the jar with the following directions:

   SAND ART BROWNIES

   1. Preheat oven to 350°F (175°C). Grease one 9x9 inch square baking pan

   2. Pour the contents of the jar into a large bowl, and mix well. Stir in 1 teaspoon vanilla, 2/3 cup vegetable oil and 3 eggs. Beat until just combined. Pour the batter into the prepared pan.

   3. Bake in the preheated oven for 25 to 30 minutes.

Beth's Spicy Oatmeal Raisin Cookies

Submitted by: **Beth Sigworth**

Makes: 3 dozen

Preparation: 15 minutes

Cooking: 12 minutes

Total: 50 minutes

"With a little experimenting, I came up with these chewy, spicy, oatmeal raisin cookies. They make your kitchen smell wonderful while they are baking. They almost remind me of Christmas because the spices smell so good."

INGREDIENTS

½ cup butter, softened

½ cup butter flavored shortening

1 cup packed light brown sugar

½ cup white sugar

2 eggs

1 teaspoon vanilla extract

1½ cups all-purpose flour

1 teaspoon baking soda

1 teaspoon ground cinnamon

½ teaspoon ground cloves

½ teaspoon salt

3 cups rolled oats

1 cup raisins

DIRECTIONS

1. Preheat oven to 350°F (175°C).

2. In a large bowl, cream together the butter, butter flavored shortening, brown sugar, white sugar, eggs and vanilla until smooth. Combine the flour, baking soda, cinnamon, cloves and salt; stir into the sugar mixture. Stir in the oats and raisins. Drop by rounded teaspoonfuls onto ungreased cookie sheets.

3. Bake 10 to 12 minutes until light and golden. Do not over-bake. Let them cool for 2 minutes before removing from cookie sheets to cool completely. Store in airtight container. Make sure you get some, because they don't last long!

Oatmeal Raisin Cookies

Submitted by: **Darlene**

Makes: 4 dozen

Preparation: 15 minutes

Cooking: 10 minutes

Total: 1 hour

"An old stand-by that the whole family loves."

INGREDIENTS

3/4 cup butter, softened

3/4 cup white sugar

3/4 cup light brown sugar

2 eggs

1 teaspoon vanilla extract

11/4 cups all-purpose flour

1 teaspoon baking soda

3/4 teaspoon ground cinnamon

1/2 teaspoon salt

23/4 cups rolled oats

1 cup raisins

DIRECTIONS

1. Preheat oven to 375°F (190°C).

2. In large bowl, beat butter, white sugar and brown sugar with electric mixer until well mixed. Beat in the eggs and vanilla until creamy.

3. Stir together flour, baking soda, cinnamon and salt. Gradually beat into butter mixture. Stir in oats and raisins. Drop by teaspoon onto ungreased cookie sheet.

4. Bake 8 to 10 minutes, or until golden brown. Cool slightly, remove from sheet to wire rack. Cool completely.

Big Soft Ginger Cookies

Submitted by: **Amy Sacha**

Makes: 2 dozen

Preparation: 15 minutes

Cooking: 10 minutes

Total: 40 minutes

"These are just what they say: big, soft, gingerbread cookies. They stay soft, too. My oldest son's favorite."

INGREDIENTS

2¼ cups all-purpose flour

2 teaspoons ground ginger

1 teaspoon baking soda

¾ teaspoon ground cinnamon

½ teaspoon ground cloves

¼ teaspoon salt

¾ cup margarine, softened

1 cup white sugar

1 egg

1 tablespoon water

¼ cup molasses

2 tablespoons white sugar

DIRECTIONS

1. Preheat oven to 350°F (175°C). Sift together the flour, ginger, baking soda, cinnamon, cloves and salt. Set aside.

2. In a large bowl, cream together the margarine and 1 cup sugar until light and fluffy. Beat in the egg, then stir in the water and molasses. Gradually stir the sifted ingredients into the molasses mixture. Shape dough into walnut sized balls and roll them in the remaining 2 tablespoons of sugar. Place the cookies 2 inches apart onto an ungreased cookie sheet and flatten slightly.

3. Bake for 8 to 10 minutes in the preheated oven. Allow cookies to cool on baking sheet for 5 minutes before removing to a wire rack to cool completely. Store in an airtight container.

Caramel Filled Chocolate Cookies

Submitted by: **Lisa**

Makes: 4 dozen

Preparation: 20 minutes

Cooking: 10 minutes

Total: 3 hours

"Chocolate cookie dough is wrapped around caramel filled chocolate candies. We have these at Christmas time each year. They are delicious! Hope you enjoy them too."

INGREDIENTS

1 cup butter, softened

1 cup white sugar

1 cup packed brown sugar

2 eggs

2 teaspoons vanilla extract

2¼ cups all-purpose flour

1 teaspoon baking soda

¾ cup unsweetened cocoa powder

1 cup chopped walnuts

1 tablespoon white sugar

48 chocolate-covered caramel candies

DIRECTIONS

1. Beat butter or margarine until creamy. Gradually beat in white sugar and brown sugar. Beat in eggs and vanilla. Combine flour, baking soda and cocoa. Gradually add to butter mixture, beating well. Stir in ½ cup walnuts. Cover and chill at least 2 hours.

2. Preheat oven to 375°F (190°C).

3. Combine remaining ½ cup nuts with the 1 tablespoon sugar. Divide the dough into 4 parts. Work with one part at a time, leaving the remainder in the refrigerator until needed. Divide each part into 12 pieces. Quickly press each piece of dough around a chocolate covered caramel. Roll into a ball. Dip the tops into the sugar mixture. Place sugar side up, 2 inches apart on greased baking sheets.

4. Bake for 8 minutes in the preheated oven. Let cool for 3 to 4 minutes on the baking sheets before removing to wire racks to cool completely.

Adam's Dirt Cookies

Submitted by: **Adam Mitchell**

Makes: 4 dozen

Preparation: 10 minutes

Cooking: 10 minutes

Total: 1 hour 20 minutes

"Why smash perfectly good cookies just to make another batch of cookies? 'Cause they're YUMMY! Made with crushed sandwich cookies, the small pieces of broken cookie dust make the dough speckled - I've been told they look like they're made with dirt!"

INGREDIENTS

2¼ cups all-purpose flour

1 teaspoon baking soda

1 teaspoon salt

1 cup white sugar

½ cup packed brown sugar

1 cup butter, softened

2 eggs

1 teaspoon vanilla extract

1½ cups chocolate sandwich cookie crumbs

DIRECTIONS

1. Sift together the flour, baking soda and salt. Set aside. In a medium bowl, cream the white sugar, brown sugar, and the butter together until smooth. Stir in the eggs and vanilla. Add the flour mixture, and stir until just combined. Stir the crushed cookies into the dough. Cover and chill the dough for ½ hour.

2. Preheat the oven to 375°F (190°C). Grease cookie sheets.

3. Drop dough by rounded spoonfuls onto the prepared cookie sheet. Bake for 10 to 11 minutes in the preheated oven. Remove to cool on wire racks.

White Chocolate and Cranberry Cookies

Submitted by: **Diane Abed**

Makes: 2 dozen

Preparation: 15 minutes

Cooking: 10 minutes

Total: 40 minutes

"I make a basic chocolate chip cookie dough, but use white chocolate chips, dried cranberries, and brandy (instead of vanilla). Great for Christmas time!"

INGREDIENTS

1/2 cup butter, softened

1/2 cup packed brown sugar

1/2 cup white sugar

1 egg

1 tablespoon brandy

1 1/2 cups all-purpose flour

1/2 teaspoon baking soda

3/4 cup white chocolate chips

1 cup dried cranberries

DIRECTIONS

1. Preheat oven to 375 °F (190°C). Grease cookie sheets.

2. In a large bowl, cream together the butter, brown sugar and white sugar until smooth. Beat in the egg and brandy. Combine the flour and baking soda; stir into the sugar mixture. Mix in the white chocolate chips and cranberries. Drop by heaping spoonfuls onto the prepared cookie sheets.

3. Bake for 8 to 10 minutes in the preheated oven. For best results, take them out while they are still doughy. Allow cookies to cool for 1 minute on the cookie sheets before removing to wire racks to cool completely.

Apricot Cream Cheese Thumbprints

Submitted by: **Mellan**

Makes: 7 dozen

Preparation: 15 minutes

Cooking: 15 minutes

Total: 2 hours 30 minutes

"These always look so pretty on the cookie plates I give for Christmas."

INGREDIENTS

1½ cups butter, softened

1½ cups white sugar

1 (8 ounce) package cream cheese, softened

2 eggs

2 tablespoons lemon juice

1½ teaspoons lemon zest

4½ cups all-purpose flour

1½ teaspoons baking powder

1 cup apricot preserves

⅓ cup confectioners' sugar for decoration

DIRECTIONS

1. In a large bowl, cream together the butter, sugar and cream cheese until smooth. Beat in the eggs one at a time, then stir in the lemon juice and lemon zest. Combine the flour and baking powder; stir into the cream cheese mixture until just combined. Cover and chill until firm, about 1 hour.

2. Preheat oven to 350°F (175°C). Roll tablespoonfuls of dough into balls, and place them 2 inches apart onto ungreased cookie sheets. Using your finger, make an indention in the center of each ball and fill with ½ teaspoon of apricot preserves.

3. Bake for 15 minutes in the preheated oven, or until edges are golden. Allow cookies to cool on the baking sheets for 2 minutes before removing to wire racks to cool completely. Sprinkle with confectioner's sugar.

Brownie Biscotti

Submitted by: **Linda Foster**

Makes: 30 cookies

Preparation: 30 minutes

Cooking: 45 minutes

Total: 1 hour 55 minutes

"A chocolate version of an Italian favorite. You can substitute milk for the water in the egg wash, if you wish."

INGREDIENTS

⅓ cup butter, softened

⅔ cup white sugar

2 eggs

1 teaspoon vanilla extract

1¾ cups all-purpose flour

⅓ cup unsweetened cocoa powder

2 teaspoons baking powder

½ cup miniature semisweet chocolate chips

¼ cup chopped walnuts

1 egg yolk, beaten

1 tablespoon water

DIRECTIONS

1. Preheat oven to 375 °F (190°C). Grease baking sheets, or line with parchment paper.

2. In a large bowl, cream together the butter and sugar until smooth. Beat in the eggs one at a time, then stir in the vanilla. Combine the flour, cocoa and baking powder; stir into the creamed mixture until well blended. Dough will be stiff, so mix in the last bit by hand. Mix in the chocolate chips and walnuts.

3. Divide dough into two equal parts. Shape into 9x2x1 inch loaves. Place onto baking sheet 4 inches apart. Brush with mixture of water and yolk.

4. Bake for 20 to 25 minutes in the preheated oven, or until firm. Cool on baking sheet for 30 minutes.

5. Using a serrated knife, slice the loaves diagonally into 1 inch slices. Return the slices to the baking sheet, placing them on their sides. Bake for 10 to 15 minutes on each side, or until dry. Cool completely and store in an airtight container.

Iced Pumpkin Cookies

Submitted by: **Gina**

Makes: 3 dozen

Preparation: 20 minutes

Cooking: 20 minutes

Total: 1 hour 20 minutes

"Wonderful spicy iced pumpkin cookies that both kids and adults love!"

INGREDIENTS

2½ cups all-purpose flour

1 teaspoon baking powder

1 teaspoon baking soda

2 teaspoons ground cinnamon

½ teaspoon ground nutmeg

½ teaspoon ground cloves

½ teaspoon salt

½ cup butter, softened

1½ cups white sugar

1 cup canned pumpkin puree

1 egg

1 teaspoon vanilla extract

2 cups confectioners' sugar

3 tablespoons milk

1 tablespoon melted butter

1 teaspoon vanilla extract

DIRECTIONS

1. Preheat oven to 350°F (175°C). Combine flour, baking powder, baking soda, cinnamon, nutmeg, ground cloves and salt; set aside.

2. In a medium bowl, cream together the ½ cup of butter and white sugar. Add pumpkin, egg and 1 teaspoon vanilla to butter mixture and beat until creamy. Mix in dry ingredients. Drop on cookie sheet by tablespoonfuls; flatten slightly.

3. Bake for 15 to 20 minutes in the preheated oven. Cool cookies, then drizzle glaze with fork.

4. To Make Glaze: Combine confectioners' sugar, milk, 1 tablespoon melted butter and 1 teaspoon vanilla. Add milk as needed, to achieve drizzling consistency.

Cream Cheese Cookies

Submitted by: **Robin**

Makes: 6 dozen

Preparation: 10 minutes

Cooking: 15 minutes

Total: 25 minutes

"These cookies are delicate when made with a press, or hardy when dropped by spoonfuls. I fill centers of press cookies with preserves or a chocolate chip for added variety."

INGREDIENTS

1 cup butter, softened

1 (3 ounce) package cream cheese, softened

1 cup white sugar

1 egg yolk

1/2 teaspoon vanilla extract

2 1/2 cups all-purpose flour

DIRECTIONS

1. Preheat oven to 325°F (170°C). Lightly grease cookie sheets.

2. In a large bowl, cream together the butter, cream cheese and sugar until light and fluffy. Beat in the egg yolk and vanilla. Stir in the flour until well blended. Drop dough by spoonfuls or use a cookie press to place onto prepared cookie sheets.

3. Bake for 15 minutes in the preheated oven. Cookies should be pale. If using floral cookie press design, make an indentation in the center with a thimble, fill with preserves, or press candy into center.

Best Brownies

Submitted by: **Angie**

"These brownies always turn out!"

Makes: 16 brownies

Preparation: 25 minutes

Cooking: 35 minutes

Total: 1 hour

INGREDIENTS

½ cup butter

1 cup white sugar

2 eggs

1 teaspoon vanilla extract

⅓ cup unsweetened cocoa powder

½ cup all-purpose flour

¼ teaspoon salt

¼ teaspoon baking powder

3 tablespoons butter, softened

3 tablespoons unsweetened cocoa powder

1 tablespoon honey

1 teaspoon vanilla extract

1 cup confectioners' sugar

DIRECTIONS

1. Preheat oven to 350°F (175°C). Grease and flour an 8 inch square pan.

2. In a large saucepan, melt ½ cup butter. Remove from heat and stir in sugar, eggs and 1 teaspoon vanilla. Beat in ⅓ cup cocoa, ½ cup flour, salt and baking powder. Spread batter into prepared pan.

3. Bake in preheated oven for 25 to 30 minutes. Do not overcook.

4. To Make Frosting: Combine 3 tablespoons butter, 3 tablespoons cocoa, 1 tablespoon honey, 1 teaspoon vanilla and 1 cup confectioners' sugar. Frost brownies while they are still warm.

Cheesecake Topped Brownies

Submitted by: **Nancy Gervasi**

Makes: 1 - 9x13 inch pan

Preparation: 20 minutes

Cooking: 45 minutes

Total: 1 hour 5 minutes

"This recipe came about purely by luck. A few years back, I had to make a last minute dessert for a party. I had wanted to make cheesecake but I did not have graham cracker crumbs. I did have a package of brownie mix and frosting. They were a hit at the party and I have made them ever since."

INGREDIENTS

1 (21.5 ounce) package brownie mix

1 (8 ounce) package cream cheese, softened

2 tablespoons butter, softened

1 tablespoon cornstarch

1 (14 ounce) can sweetened condensed milk

1 egg

1 teaspoon vanilla extract

1 (16 ounce) container prepared chocolate frosting

DIRECTIONS

1. Preheat oven 350°F (175°C). Grease a 9x13 inch baking pan.

2. Prepare brownie mix according to the directions on the package. Spread into prepared baking pan.

3. In a medium bowl, beat cream cheese, butter and cornstarch until fluffy. Gradually beat in sweetened condensed milk, egg and vanilla until smooth. Pour cream cheese mixture evenly over brownie batter.

4. Bake in preheated oven for 45 minutes, or until top is lightly browned. Allow to cool, spread with frosting, and cut into bars. Store covered in refrigerator, or freeze in a single layer for up to 2 weeks.

Bake Sale Lemon Bars

Submitted by: **Elaine**

Makes: 1 - 9x13 inch pan

Preparation: 15 minutes

Cooking: 45 minutes

Total: 1 hour

"They are very, very easy to make, and really fabulously delicious."

INGREDIENTS

1 1/2 cups all-purpose flour

2/3 cup confectioners' sugar

3/4 cup butter, softened

3 eggs

1 1/2 cups white sugar

3 tablespoons all-purpose flour

1/4 cup lemon juice

1/3 cup confectioners' sugar for decoration

DIRECTIONS

1. Preheat the oven to 375°F (190°C). Grease a 9x13 inch baking pan.

2. Combine the flour, 2/3 cup confectioners' sugar and butter. Pat dough into the prepared pan.

3. Bake for 20 minutes in the preheated oven, until slightly golden. While the crust is baking, whisk together eggs, white sugar, flour and lemon juice until frothy. Pour this lemon mixture over the hot crust.

4. Return to the preheated oven for an additional 20 to 25 minutes, or until light golden brown. Cool on a wire rack. Dust the top with confectioners' sugar. Cut into squares.

Paul's Pumpkin Bars

Submitted by: **Deb Martin**

Makes: 2 dozen

Preparation: 15 minutes

Cooking: 30 minutes

Total: 45 minutes

"These are very moist, and so far I haven't found anyone who doesn't love them!"

INGREDIENTS

4 eggs

1²/₃ cups white sugar

1 cup vegetable oil

1 (15 ounce) can pumpkin puree

2 cups all-purpose flour

2 teaspoons baking powder

1 teaspoon baking soda

2 teaspoons ground cinnamon

1 teaspoon salt

4 ounces cream cheese, softened

½ cup butter, softened

1 teaspoon vanilla extract

2 cups sifted confectioners' sugar

DIRECTIONS

1. Preheat oven to 350°F (175°C).

2. In a medium bowl, mix the eggs, sugar, oil and pumpkin with an electric mixer until light and fluffy. Sift together the flour, baking powder, baking soda, cinnamon and salt. Stir into the pumpkin mixture until thoroughly combined.

3. Spread the batter evenly into an ungreased 10x15 inch jellyroll pan. Bake for 25 to 30 minutes in the preheated oven. Cool before frosting.

4. To make the frosting, cream together the cream cheese and butter. Stir in vanilla. Add confectioners' sugar a little at a time, beating until mixture is smooth. Spread evenly on top of the cooled bars. Cut into squares.

Aunt Teen's Creamy Chocolate Fudge

Submitted by: **Kelly Phillips**

Makes: 1 - 8x8 inch pan

Preparation: 10 minutes

Cooking: 20 minutes

Total: 30 minutes

"This was my aunt's recipe for fudge, passed down through the family. It's better than any fudge I've ever had at the Jersey shore, and easy enough to whip up in 15 minutes or so."

INGREDIENTS

1 (7 ounce) jar marshmallow creme

1½ cups white sugar

⅔ cup evaporated milk

¼ cup butter

¼ teaspoon salt

2 cups milk chocolate chips

1 cup semisweet chocolate chips

½ cup chopped nuts

1 teaspoon vanilla extract

DIRECTIONS

1. Line an 8x8 inch pan with aluminum foil. Set aside.

2. In a large saucepan over medium heat, combine marshmallow cream, sugar, evaporated milk, butter and salt. Bring to a full boil, and cook for 5 minutes, stirring constantly.

3. Remove from heat and pour in semisweet chocolate chips and milk chocolate chips. Stir until chocolate is melted and mixture is smooth. Stir in nuts and vanilla. Pour into prepared pan. Chill in refrigerator for 2 hours, or until firm.

Microwave Oven Peanut Brittle

Submitted by: **Linda C.**

Makes: 16 servings

Preparation: 10 minutes

Cooking: 20 minutes

Total: 30 minutes

"I have used this for years and it is very good; much easier than the traditional method and tastes just as good."

INGREDIENTS

1¹⁄₂ cups peanuts

1 cup white sugar

¹⁄₂ cup light corn syrup

1 pinch salt (optional)

1 tablespoon butter

1 teaspoon vanilla extract

1 teaspoon baking soda

DIRECTIONS

1. Grease a baking sheet and set aside. In a glass bowl, combine peanuts, sugar, corn syrup, and salt. Cook in microwave for 6 to 7 minutes on High (700 W); mixture should be bubbly and peanuts browned. Stir in butter and vanilla; cook 2 to 3 minutes longer.

2. Quickly stir in baking soda, just until mixture is foamy. Pour immediately onto greased baking sheet. Let cool 15 minutes, or until set. Break into pieces and store in an airtight container.

recipe contributors

Adam Mitchell 328
Alan Harasimowicz 172
Alice Hoff 318
Alicia Navarro 147
Amy Eckert 117
Amy Miazga 144
Amy Sacha 326
Amy The 178
Andrea McInnis 38
Angie 334
Angie LaSala 273
Angie Zayac 18, 89
Anne 296
Arnie Williams 173
Bailey 193
Barbara (I) 93
Barbara (II) 277
Barbara (III) 156
Barrie Tapp 163
Behr Kleine 136
Beth (I) 290
Beth (II) 132
Beth Sigworth 319, 324
Bob 78
Bob Cody 199
Bobbie 91
Bonnie 224
Bonnie A. Deger 36
Brandy 106
Brenda Arnold 105
Bruticus 202
Caitlin Koch 270
Caity-O 134
Carol 219, 249, 265, 267
Carol H. 289
Carole Resnick 259
Cassandra Kennedy 41
Cathy (I) 184
Cathy (II) 95
Cathy Martin 200
Cathy T 59
Chantal Rogers 278
Charlene Kaunert 228
Charlie 102
Christine Johnson 104, 176
Colleen 223

Colleen B. Smith 80
Corwynn Darkholme 47, 107
'Cotton' Couch 158
Courtney 203
Cristy Chu 244
Cyndi Smith 164
D. L. Mooney 35
D. Reichel 241
Darlene 325
Dawn 124
Dawn Edberg 111
Dayna 43
Deb Martin 337
Debbi Borsick 286, 305
Debbie Donham 166
Debbie Pleau 231
Deborah Corda 181
Deborah Westbrook 177
Denise 315
Denise Goodman 28
Diane Abed 329
Diane Kester 294
Dianne McKenzie 16
Dierdre Dee 62
Donna Lasater 198
Dora 306
Duane Glende 174
Elaine (I) 336
Elaine (II) 280
Eleanor Johnson 40
Ellen (I) 274
Ellen (II) 75
Ellen Rainey 42
Ellen Warfield 298
Emilie S. 287
Emily 98
Erica G. 299
Ericka Ettinger 206
Erin 201
Esther Nelson 251
Evelyn Brown 310
Gail Laulette 182
Gail Wagner 45
Gina (I) 140
Gina (II) 332
Gina Williams 209

Hillary Roberts 162
Holly 76
Holly Murphy 180
Jackie 53
Jackie Meiborg 282
Jamie Hensley 37
Jan Taylor 110
Janeen 55
Janet 323
Janet Kay 311
Janet M. 161
Janet Shannon 139
Jason Sharp 242
Jean Higginbotham 258
Jeannie Yee 245
Jenn Hall 235
Jennifer (I) 83
Jennifer (II) 150
Jennifer (III) 126
Jennifer Walker 271
Jenny English 159
Jenny Kernan 240
Jessica 109
Jill 92
Jill B. Mittelstadt 190
Jill Saunders 295, 316
Jim Wright 291
Joanna Knudsen 313
John Pickett 230
Joyce Waits 292
Judi Johnston 149
Judy McNamara 44
Judy Taubert 236
Karen Weir 34
Karen Bush 148
Karen C. Greenlee 192
Karen K. 115, 189, 234
Karen Marshall 52
Karen Pitschneider 64
Karen Toellner 119
Karena H. Denton 56, 112, 188
Karin Christian 60, 246, 317
Kat Wood 24
Kathi J. McClaren 99
Kathleen White 121
Kathy Bliesner 309

allrecipes tried & true favorites │ recipe contributors

Kathy Jenkins 19
Kathy Statham 113, 114
Kathy Walstrom 26
Katy B. Minchew 183
Kelli 20
Kelly Berenger 94
Kelly Grimes 22
Kelly Phillips 338
Kevin Ryan 266
Kevin S. Weiss 191
Kiersten 146
Kim Fischer 145
Klara Yudovich 194
Kristen 253
Kristin Zaharias 237
LaDonna 79
Lalena 71
Larry Lampert 207
Laura 225
Laura Duncan Allen 268
Laura Ramanjooloo 160
Laurie Bennett 254
Laurie O'Grady 27
Leah Shaw 63
Leslie (I) 276
Leslie (II) 100
Leslye Miyashiro 157
Lessalee 142
Leta Harris 261
Linda (I) 320
Linda (II) 169
Linda C. 339
Linda Foster 331
Linda Vergura 179
Linda Whittaker 308
Lisa (I) 327
Lisa (II) 232
Lisa (III) 133
Lisa Kreft 221
Lloyd Rushing 120
Loll 118
Loretta Buffa 72
Lori 220
Lori White 248
LuAnn Connolly 218
M.K. Meredith 128

Marian Collins 68, 152
Marie Kenney 205
Martha Dibblee 90
Mary (I) 39
Mary (II) 58
Mary Ann Benzon 275
Mary Hays 304
Meghan Brand 17
Melanie Burton 165
Melinda Halvorson 238
Mellan 330
Merrilee 239
Michele 314
Michelle Chapman 123
Michelle Chen 51
Mike Kennon 204
Misty 135
Morgan 175
Nancy 137
Nancy Gervasi 335
Nora Donovan 222
Normala 86
Olga 293
P.L. Weiss 312
Pam Vienneau 226
Pat Collins 288
Pat Lowe 73
Patricia Bergstrom 247
Patricia Osborne 297
Peg 233
Penelope Holmes 87
Penny Lehoux 285
Phyllis 321
Rebecca 151, 208
Rebecca Clyma 284
Rebecca Miller 49
Rene 127
Rene Kratz 307
Rhoda McIntosh 30
Robert J. Arsenault 61
Robin 333
Robin C. 167
Robyn Bloomquist 108
Rory 262
Rosalie Carter 212
Rosemary Stoker 77

Ruthie Crickmer 211
Sally 229
Sandir 81
Sandy 155
Sara Blanchard 153
Shannon R. 82
Sharon Johnson 185
Shelley Albeluhn 250
Shellie Wendel 300
Sher Garfield 103
Sherlie Magaret 195, 227
Sherrie D. 25
Sherry Haupt 57
SmKat 141
Solana 88
Stacy B. 96
Stacy M. Polcyn 210
Star Pooley 50, 54, 168, 255
Star Pooley and KC 272
Stefanie Sierk 97
Stephanie 279, 281
Stephanie Knewasser 217
Stephanie Phillips 283
Susan Feiler 269
Susan Navarrete 29
Susan O'Dell 322
Suzanne M. Munson 101
Suzanne Stull 260
Tammy Elliott 264
Tammy Schill 70
Tania 216
Teresa C. Rouzer 122, 143
Terri Martin 125
Terri McCarrell 243
Thomas 48
Tina 74
Tom Quinlin 46
Tony Cortez 23
Tracie P. 252
Tracy Kirk 263
Valerie Serao 138
Vicki Frew 154
Vivian Chu 21
Wayne 301
Wendy 116
Wendy Mercadante 69

index

credits

the staff at allrecipes

Jennifer Anderson
Kala Anderson
Karen Anderson
Barbara Antonio
Emily Brune
Scotty Carreiro
Sydney Carter
Jeffrey Cummings
Michael DeLashmutt
Steven Hamilton
Michael Henderlight
Christie Howard
Tim Hunt

Richard Kozel
William Marken
Wendy McKay
Bill Moore
Todd Moore
Yann Oehl
Alicia Power
Elizabeth Rogers
Judy St. John
Britt Swearingen
Jean Webber
Esmee Williams

thanks

The staff would like to thank the following people whose comments, feedback, and support have made this a much better book: Brenda Hunt, David Quinn, Hillary Quinn, Dan Shepherd, Rebecca Staffel, and Jana Stone.

very special thanks

Finally, the staff would like to acknowledge the extraordinary contributions of Tim Hunt. His creativity, tireless dedication, and high standards have served as an inspiration to us all. Our site, and this book, are the realization of his vision.

the allrecipes tried & true series

Our *Tried & True* cookbooks feature the very best recipes from the world's greatest home cooks! Allrecipes.com, the #1 recipe website, brings you the "Best of the Best" dishes and treats, selected from over 20,000 recipes! We hand-picked only those recipes that have been awarded 5-star ratings time and time again by our worldwide community of home cooks to fill these books, so you know every dish is a winner.

Current titles include:

Allrecipes Tried & True Favorites; Top 300 Recipes

Treat yourself to America's Favorite Recipes! Filled with the best-loved recipes from Allrecipes.com - these have all won repeated standing ovations from millions of home cooks and their families, intrepid eaters and picky kids alike. *Tried & True Favorites* is a welcome addition to any home cook's kitchen!

Allrecipes Tried & True Cookies; Top 200 Recipes

Cookie lovers rejoice! Enjoy the world's best cookie recipes and invaluable baking tips and tricks that will turn anyone into an expert on preparing, decorating and sharing cookies. With over 230 cookie recipes, you'll find tried and true recipes for all your old favorites, and lots of new favorites you just haven't discovered yet!

Allrecipes Tried & True Quick & Easy; Top 200 Recipes

Great-tasting meals in minutes! This cookbook features delicious dishes that can be prepared in an hour or less, and are even organized by total cooking time for your convenience. Discover the joys of cooking without spending hours in the kitchen!

Allrecipes *Tried & True* cookbooks are available at select bookstores, by visiting our website at http://www.allrecipes.com, or by calling 206-292-3990 ext. #239. Watch for more *Tried & True* cookbooks to come!

For more information on Allrecipes and our *Tried & True* cookbooks, visit http://www.allrecipes.com today!

Allrecipes.com
524 Dexter Avenue North
Seattle, WA 98109 USA
Phone: (206) 292-3990, Ext. 239
Web: www.allrecipes.com